Minnesota's Literary Visitors

MINNESOTA'S LITERARY VISITORS

John T. Flanagan

ISBN 1-880654-01-6.

Library of Congress Catalogue Card No. 92-050850.

The essays which constitute this book were previously published in
various issues of *Minnesota History* (March 1935, March and December,
1936, June and December 1937, December 1938, June and December
1939 and June 1941). The essay entitled "The Minnesota Backgrounds
of Sinclair Lewis' Fiction" was reprinted from *Minnesota History,* Vol. 37
(March 1960), copyright 1960 by the Minnesota Historical Society; used
with permission; and "A French Humorist Visits Minnesota" was
reprinted from *Minnesota History,* Vol. 40 (Spring 1966), copyright 1966
by the Minnesota Historical Society;
used with permission.

Illustration credits on page 234.

**Cover adapted from the watercolor "Laughing Waters" by
Seth Eastman, used by permission of the James J. Hill Reference
Library, St. Paul, Minnesota.**

CONTENTS

AN EXPLANATORY NOTE

At the end of January, 1867, Ralph Waldo Emerson, having traveled to the Mississippi River by railroad, was driven in an open sleigh from La Crosse, Wisconsin to Winona. He entered the state of Minnesota at Winona on January 28th when the temperature dropped to twenty degrees below zero. Emerson was scheduled to give six lectures at Faribault, St. Paul, and Minneapolis. His subject bore the title of "The Man of the World," which was never published as a group although fragments of it appeared in other essays. From 1852 when Emerson spoke in St. Louis he traveled west almost annually but he never lectured again in Minnesota. Possibly the exigencies of winter transportation explain this decision, but he was well received and was invited to return later. A full account of Emerson's reception during his single Minnesota visit was written by Hubert Hoeltje and published in *Minnesota History* (June, 1930, XI: 145–159).

Hoeltje's article suggested to me that an examination of the visits of other celebrities might be both interesting and profitable. The magnitude of such a list might well be insuperable but personal prejudice and a few basic criteria could limit it somewhat. After all, the period between the visit in 1835 at Fort Snelling of George Catlin, the extraordinary painter of Indian life, and the brief residence of the Swedish novelist Vilhelm Moberg in Chisago County, Minnesota, in 1948, when he worked on his fictional trilogy of pioneer settlement, *The Emigrants, Unto a Good Land,* and *The Last Letter Home,* provides ample latitude. Many writers, both professional journalists and less well known novelists, wrote of their journeys to Minnesota. Their work appeared in now obscure volumes and in the pages of magazines such as *Putnam's, Blackwood's, Harper's,* and *Scribner's.* More than thirty newspaper editors, for example, joined the Great Railway Excursion of 1854

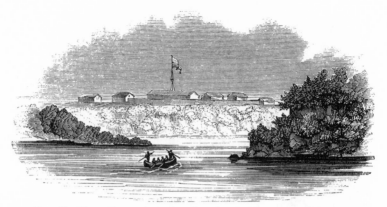

Fort Snelling. Engraving after drawing by Laurence Oliphant.

from Rock Island, Illinois to St. Paul, and many of them filed reports of their adventures. (See William J. Petersen, "The Rock Island Railroad Excursion of 1854," *Minnesota History,* 15: 405–420.) However, the eleven writers I selected shared certain characteristics. First of all, they were well known writers. With the exception of Sinclair Lewis, none of the figures here profiled were Minnesota-born. All of them traveled extensively, gave speeches or interviews, and published correspondence or books confirming their experience.

The reasons for travel expressed by the visitors vary considerably. Henry Thoreau, subject of the first article, expressed his hope for somewhat better health in the west. But he also showed considerable interest in attending a scheduled annuity payment meeting with the Sioux Indians at the Redwood Agency on the Minnesota River. Thoreau also wanted to see a prairie gopher and a wild crabapple plant. He was disappointed that he failed to find a buffalo. Edward Eggleston, who also came to Minnesota in frail health, sought to improve his physical condition and ended up by becoming both a Methodist minister and St. Paul's first librarian. Fredrika Bremer, a prominent Swedish journalist, was greatly interested in the role of women in the New World and also wished to examine the impact of slavery, especially in the southern states. Mark Twain was eager to explore the Upper Mississippi and wished to compare it with the flow of the great river as he knew it south of St. Louis. Hamlin Garland lived in both Iowa and Wisconsin and frequently traversed Minnesota in search of employment. His fiction generally dealt with middle western farmers and reflected the populism of the prairies.

Bayard Taylor, widely known for his world travels and ability to please his audiences with personal recollections of distant places, visited Minnesota on three different occasions. For many years he was a popular professional lecturer. In similar fashion Oscar Wilde satisfied public curiosity about his appearance and celebrity and probably was well compensated for his lecture tours. Captain Marryat came to the United States at the end of his career in the British navy and after he had published several novels about his naval experiences. He was obviously interested in seeing something of Canada as well as getting glimpses of a frontier state which still had Indian residents. Knut Hamsun chose to visit America for reasons unlike those of the other figures listed here, but came simply as a possible emigrant who saw no future in Norway. After working in the North Dakota wheatfields and living in both Chicago and Minneapolis he returned to his homeland. Max O'Rell, a successful French journalist, fluent in two languages and a clever humorist and satirist, enjoyed a brief career in the United States.

Many of the literary travelers in the Middle West before the Civil War were overly ambitious in their efforts to observe different developments of social life or perhaps found the Mississippi River a barrier. Mrs. Frances Trollope's *Domestic Manners of the Americans* (1832) became a familiar document of life in Cincinnati and along the Ohio River, although some readers resented it. Her son Anthony Trollope wrote an excellent account of his experiences in a huge tome entitled *North America* which was published in 1862 in two volumes of over six hundred pages each. He devoted little space to Minnesota but

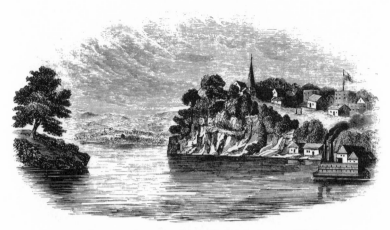

St. Paul. Engraving after drawing by Laurence Oliphant.

was generally flattering in his brief account. He was especially enthusiastic about the Upper Mississippi above Lake Pepin and thought that the river scenery exceeded in beauty that of the Rhine. St. Paul then had about 14,000 people and a large hotel and Minneapolis was little more than a village. Trollope was disinclined to marvel at the Falls of Minnehaha which he termed "a pretty little cascade" which might do for a picnic in fair weather. In sum he devoted about eight pages to Minnesota and to my knowledge made no speeches about his reception.

Trollope's trip was made during the early months of the Civil War. He was surprised to find a hotel capable of housing three hundred guests in St. Paul as he doubted future travelers would ever visit the city except for those who wished to take up residence or intended to try hunting farther north. Yet, even before Trollope's visit, tourists were discovering Minnesota. The earliest visitors came by steamboat, up the Mississippi River from Galena to St. Paul during the navigable months from April to November. Before the construction of local hotels they stayed, as did Fredrika Bremer and Captain Marryat, with prominent, hospitable citizens.

St. Anthony. Engraving after drawing by Laurence Oliphant.

According to Theodore Blegen it was George Catlin who first suggested that travelers should take a "fashionable tour" by steamboat from Illinois to the head of navigation at the Falls of St. Anthony. After arriving in St. Paul tourists could go by stagecoach to see the Falls of St. Anthony, Minnehaha Falls, and Fort Snelling, the triumvirate of significant local attractions. The era of the Fashionable Tour by steamboat passed when railroads were completed linking Minnesota with the east, making it possible for vacationers to linger longer in Minnesota's lake regions. (See Blegen's "The 'Fashionable Tour' on the Upper Mississippi," in *Minnesota History,* December, 1939, XX: 4, 377–396.)

The railroads, of course, made it easier for professional lecturers to include Minnesota on their circuit of appearances. One such lecturer, Julia Ward Howe, made several visits to Minnesota between 1870 and 1900. She delivered speeches on ethics ("Is a Polite Society Polite"), woman suffrage ("The benefit that women may hope to derive from suffrage"), and literary figures whom she had known ("Reminiscences of [old neighbors] Holmes, Emerson, Longfellow and Whittier").

Julia Ward Howe.

This last lecture, presented in 1900 when Mrs. Howe was 81, was described almost as the farewell tour of a famous personality. It ended, as her appearances often did, with the recital of her poem "The Battle Hymn of the Republic." Unfortunately, while Julia Ward Howe did publish accounts of her other travels, her journeys to Minnesota were only recorded in letters and in her diary.

At the end of this discussion of literary visitors to Minnesota it seems appropriate to include a tribute to Sinclair Lewis, the first American writer to win a Nobel Prize in Literature. During a long career Lewis was a frequent commentator on his native state. He wrote journalistic articles into which he sometimes introduced his own characters, taught university classes, and occasionally appeared on the stage. In addition he used his knowledge of Minnesota to supply backgrounds for his fiction.

Other Minnesota writers have also depended on their own lives to supply themes and settings. One thinks of F. Scott Fitzgerald immediately. His novel *The Great Gatsby* indirectly includes memories of Minnesota although it is localized in Long Island. Stories like "The Ice Palace" with its recollection of the St. Paul Winter Carnival or "Winter Dreams" with its romanticized suggestion of the White Bear Lake Yacht Club activities depend heavily on the writer's personal life. James Farl Powers in novels like *Morte d'Urban* and in his subsequent fiction put to good use his knowledge of Stearns County and Catholic ecclesiastical life near St. John's University at Collegeville. More recently Garrison Keillor in his books, short stories and radio monologues (on his program "A Prairie Home Companion"), utilized in many ways his boyhood in Anoka with its tangle of ethnic elements and religious affinities. He was clearly aided by long exposure to small town habits and ways. His Lake Wobegon is certainly not one of Minnesota's eleven thousand lakes and is appropriately located in Mist County. Michael Fedo suggested in his biography of Keillor, *The Man from Lake Wobegon* (1987), that both Freeport (a town near St. Cloud) and Marine-on-St. Croix had served as source material for Keillor's invented town.

In 1950 I surveyed three decades of Minnesota fiction and was able to list one hundred novels with Minnesota settings published in that period of time ("Thirty Years of Minnesota

Fiction," *Minnesota History,* September, 1950, XXXI: 3, 129–147). This list included only fiction written for an adult audience. By that date Maud Hart Lovelace had published a series of Betsy-Tacy books for children dealing with her childhood in Mankato, and Laura Ingalls Wilder's Little Prairie books, partly set in Walnut Grove, had also appeared. Since 1950 many writers have used Minnesota settings for their fiction. While in the past their viewpoint might have been colored by a Scandinavian or Slavic heritage, some of Minnesota's newer novelists reflect Native American, Asian, and African American sensibilities in their work.

Once it was outsiders who visited Minnesota to report on its scenic wonders and development. Minnesotans now write about their own environment, their own "loci literati." A concluding chapter of this book presents an overview of the state's Community of the Book: the journals, presses, booksellers and friends of literature who encourage and support its writers. No attempt will be made to list the state's many authors, past or present. But without great difficulty visitors to the state can create their own "Fashionable Literary Tour" with stops at Sauk Centre, St. Paul, Walnut Grove, Mankato and Lindstrom. While the Moberg Trail in Chisago County is marked, the path to Lake Wobegon is not as yet indicated. So, the literary pilgrim will have to find his or her own way to the heart of Keillor country looking for the little town that time forgot with its population of Norwegian bachelor farmers, strong women, good looking men, and above-average children.

John T. Flanagan
Chisago City, Minnesota
August 15, 1992.

Minnesota's Literary Visitors

Captain Frederick Marryat.

CAPTAIN MARRYAT AT OLD
ST. PETER'S

The obscurity that now shrouds the name of Captain Frederick Marryat is a good illustration of the rapidity with which literary prestige can evaporate. In the middle of the last century Marryat's reputation was wide and seemed secure. Hailed as a master of ocean narrative in the bold manner of Smollett and bringing to his work as rich and as varied an experience on the high seas as even Joseph Conrad could claim, the captain produced book after book which satisfied a large audience. But there was something lacking. At the height of his fame the old sea dog discovered that he was losing his command over material which for a number of years had proved a very bonanza to him. Perhaps, as Poe remarked unkindly, it was only Marryat's essential mediocrity asserting itself. At any rate the captain found his audience vanishing, and abandoning his forte with the facility of a veteran skipper tacking before the wind, he turned to the production of juveniles. Today his name is associated less with the honest attempts to recreate the sea atmosphere which were baptized *Peter Simple* and *Mr. Midshipman Easy* than with such exemplary children's stories as the *Settlers in Canada*. And the literary historian is only too willing to relegate Marryat's name to a footnote.

But in 1837–38, when the captain was emboldened by curiosity and an empty purse to pay a visit to North America, he was a great literary lion who expected a favorable reception. The United States had not proved especially amenable to the strictures of his predecessors. The books of Mrs. Trollope and Harriet Martineau, to mention no others, had provoked a storm of hostility and derision, until it came to pass that every literary foreigner who set

foot on the soil of the New World was suspect. Thus
Marryat discovered that the Americans, though they might
read his books, were under no compunction to esteem his
person, and his resultant pique may well account for the fact
that he was remembered by various observers as a surly, ill-
tempered Briton. At any rate, as the captain remarked in
his *Diary*:

They [*the Americans*] had no right to insult and annoy me in the
manner they did, from nearly one end of the Union to the other,
either because my predecessors had expressed an unfavourable opinion
of them before my arrival, or because they expected that I would do
the same upon my return to my own country.[1]

Nevertheless, Marryat was quite correct in observing the
feeling of distrust and antagonism which greeted him when
he disembarked at a New York pier on May 4, 1837 — a
feeling which was in no way helped by the great panic which
followed Jackson's second administration.[2]

Ostensibly the captain had been drawn to America to see
how democracy was functioning among the insurgent off-
spring of the country whose sword he bore. But wherever
he went he took notes, observed as widely as he could, and
if possible refused what hospitalities were tendered him so
that he would not be obligated to his hosts and thereby pre-
vented from speaking his mind. His tour of the continent
embraced a large part of the United States and included sojourns in several sections of Canada. He visited all the
large cities of the East and Middle West, making speeches
in a good many and being introduced to such celebrities as
Charlotte Cushman, the actress, Governor Mason of Michi-

[1] Frederick Marryat, *A Diary in America*, 1:14 (London, 1839).
Marryat wrote two series of American diaries; all citations in the present article are to the first series. The actual diary of Marryat's trip
ends at page 214 of volume 2, the rest of the work being devoted to long,
rambling essays about American institutions. The portion of the diary
that deals with Minnesota has been reprinted, with a brief introduction,
in MINNESOTA HISTORY, 6:168–184 (June, 1925).

[2] Florence Marryat, *Life and Letters of Captain Marryat*, 2:3 (London, 1872).

gan, Henry Clay, and many others.[3]   But the journey which
is of special interest to residents of the Northwest did not
begin until the spring of 1838.

Having chosen the Great Lakes route to the West, Captain Marryat boarded the "Michigan" at Windsor, On-
tario, and traveled by water as far as Green Bay.   It had
been his intention to take the usual route thence via Chicago
and Galena to St. Louis, but at the Wisconsin post he
chanced to meet a detachment of troops bound for Fort
Winnebago and decided to avail himself of the opportunity
to go overland.   The route led along the Fox River to the
famous portage.   At Fort Winnebago Marryat took a
keelboat and descended the Wisconsin River as far as Prairie du Chien, where it meets the Mississippi.   There once
more luck favored him, and he was enabled to join General
Henry Atkinson, then on an inspection tour of frontier
posts, and to continue his journey up the Mississippi by
steamboat.   On June 13, 1838, the "Burlington" under
Captain Throckmorton reached the wharf at St. Peter's, as
Mendota was then called, and as Major Lawrence Taliaferro noted in his journal, among the passengers was the
famous novelist, Captain Marryat.[4]

Despite his extensive traveling on the North American
continent, the Briton was not unimpressed by the beauties
of the great river.   At Prairie du Chien he had noticed the
"beautiful clear blue stream, intersected with verdant
islands, and very different in appearance from the Lower
Mississippi, after it has been joined by the Missouri."   He
had also appreciated the bold bluffs of the valley and the
majesty of Lake Pepin, while to the Wisconsin territory in
general he had ascribed the finest soil and the most salubri-

[3] Arno L. Bader, "Captain Marryat in Michigan," in *Michigan History Magazine*, 20:169 (Spring and Summer, 1936). An article in
which the same author traces Marryat's American tour, "The Gallant
Captain and Brother Jonathan," appears in the *Colophon*, 2:114–129
(New Series — Autumn, 1936).

[4] Marryat, *Diary*, 2:42, 54, 78. The Taliaferro Journals are in the
possession of the Minnesota Historical Society.

ous climate in America.   Indeed, Marryat's comments on
the weather have considerable interest.   The most unusual
factor which he observed about the American climate was
its changeability, not only the obvious seasonal alterations
but rapid shifts of heat and cold within the twenty-four
hour span.   He writes:

> When I was on Lake Superior the thermometer stood between 90°
> and 100° during the day, and at night was nearly down to the freez-
> ing point.   When at St. Peter's, which is nearly as far north, and
> farther west, the thermometer stood generally at 100° to 106° during
> the day, and I found it to be the case in all the northern States when
> the winter is most severe, as well as in the more southern.

Furthermore, he declared that the winters in Missouri,
Iowa, and Wisconsin " are dry and healthy, enabling the inhabitants to take any quantity of exercise, and I found that
the people looked forward to their winters with pleasure,
longing for the heat of the summer to abate."   Marryat's
final estimate of the American climate was unfavorable,
since he held that it enervated the body and demoralized the
mind.   But he was inclined to make an exception of the
Northwest despite its meteorological extremes.   The only
insurmountable obstacles he found to his enjoyment of the
upper Mississippi Valley were mosquitoes and snakes.[5]

At St. Peter's Marryat was the guest of Henry H. Sibley, then the resident agent of the American Fur Company,
who later became the first governor of the state of Minnesota.   A mutual friend at Green Bay had given the captain
a letter of introduction to Sibley, thus assuring the visitor
a hospitable reception.   It reads as follows:

GREEN BAY May 21st 1838

DEAR HEN

I take great pleasure in introducing to you Capt Marryatt, who is
now on a visit to your place.   Any attention you can pay him will be
both pleasant to yourself & gratifying to me

Yours truly
CHAS. R. BRUSH [6]

[5] *Diary*, 2:69, 72, 75, 79, 125; 3:255, 263, 270.   There are numerous
references to both insect and reptile pests scattered throughout the *Diary*.
[6] Sibley Papers, in the possession of the Minnesota Historical Society.

To Sibley, of course, distinguished guests were nothing new. Among others, he had entertained George Catlin, the painter, John C. Frémont, and Joseph N. Nicollet, all of whom were sincerely grateful to their host. Marryat, too, expressed his appreciation of Sibley's courtesies, but there is reason to suppose that Sibley found him a rather arrogant and uncongenial visitor.

Almost the first thing that impressed the captain was Fort Snelling itself and its formidable site. The fort, he wrote in his *Diary*, " is about a mile from the factory [*Mendota*], and is situated on a steep promontory, in a commanding position; it is built of stone, and may be considered as impregnable to any attempt which the Indians might make, provided that it has a sufficient garrison." He also remarked the great sweep of prairie almost immediately behind the post. On the day following the arrival, General Atkinson's party visited the Falls of St. Anthony and the neighboring lakes, and it seems likely that Marryat was a member of the expedition. At any rate, he early expressed his disappointment upon seeing the famous cataract: " The Falls of St. Anthony are not very imposing, although not devoid of beauty." He estimated the fall at thirty-five feet, and declared that with the rapids below, the river descended probably a hundred feet, certainly not a grand spectacle to one in whose memory Niagara was still fresh. On the other hand, he thought that the large masses of rock piled indiscriminately lent a certain picturesque charm to the scene.[7]

But the captain was a good deal more interested in the inhabitants than he was in the scenery. As a naval officer he had sailed most of the seven seas and had come in contact with a majority of the races of man, but the Indian was still relatively unfamiliar to him and proportionately fascinating. Thus he noted almost at once that the Sioux were

[7] *Diary,* 2:80, 81; Taliaferro Journal, June 14, 1838.

the first red men he had seen in the primitive state (which may be interpreted to mean the first red men he had seen sober!). He recorded in his *Diary* that the Sioux were divided into six or seven tribes and numbered about thirty thousand individuals. Soon after his arrival at St. Peter's he made an excursion to Lake Calhoun to visit Cloudman's village. There he was surprised to learn that the Sioux had "fixed habitations as well as tents; their tents are large and commodious, made of buffalo skins dressed without the hair, and very often handsomely painted on the outside." Even more amazing to the captain was the relative cleanliness of the interior of the lodges. He also remarked with great interest that a missionary residing at the village — the Reverend Jedediah D. Stevens — had begun to teach the braves agriculture with some success.[8]

Indeed the whole attempt of the whites to civilize the red men evoked Marryat's wrapt attention. During his stay at St. Peter's Joseph Renville came to the agency with a large band of Indians, some of whom, Marryat claimed, fraternized with him. "These warriors of Mr. Rainville's [*sic*] were constantly with me, for they knew that I was an *English* warrior, as they called me, and they are very partial to the English." Furthermore, these Indians from Lac qui Parle had been partially civilized, said the captain, and "they are all converted to Christianity." Partly through Renville's assistance and partly through the labors of two missionaries, this band of Sioux had achieved a certain level of literacy and their language had been roughly confined within the limits of the English alphabet. Marryat himself possessed an elementary spelling book and a catechism in the vernacular. Certainly one of the most vivid pictures the captain limns has for its subject a Sioux warrior with a copy book:

It was really a pleasing sight, and a subject for meditation, to see one of these fine fellows, dressed in all his wild magnificence, with his

[8] *Diary*, 2:81–84.

buffalo robe on his shoulders, and his tomahawk by his side, seated at a table, and writing out for me a Sioux translation of the Psalms of David.[9]

During Marryat's stay at St. Peter's, Renville's Indians performed a dance close to the factory, donning for the occasion all their tribal regalia. The captain was particularly interested in the elaborate costumes of the dancers and could not rest content until he himself owned one. His desire was all the more eager in that he had seen Catlin's collection of Indian curios only to discover that the painter lacked one of these ceremonial outfits. The dress in question included a kilt of fine skins, beautifully ornamented with quills and feathers, garters made from the tails of animals, and a headdress to which both the eagle and the ermine had contributed. The Indians, understandably, did not wish to part with such a costume and even Renville's intervention did not produce the desired gift. Finally, according to Marryat, a presentation was made at which Renville served as interpreter. Speeches were made in which the Sioux declared that their only reason for conferring so unusual an honor on a visitor was the nationality of that visitor, that they remembered the English and the good quality of their rifles and blankets, and that they wished to prove their respect for an English warrior. Marryat, never notable for his tact, replied that he appreciated the gift deeply, the more so that it had been refused Americans who had previously solicited it. Furthermore, he said:

I am very glad that you do not forget the English, and that you say they kept their word, and that their rifles and blankets were good. I know that the blankets of the Americans are thin and cold. (I did not think it worth while to say that they were all made in England.) We have buried the hatchet now; but should the tomahawk be raised

---

[9] *Diary,* 2: 89–92. Taliaferro noted in his journal for Sunday, June 17, that the Reverend Stephen R. Riggs preached at Fort Snelling and " we were entertained with divine songs by the Indians of Lac qui parle. These wild savages sung correctly & in good time to the astonishment of the audience of whites." It may well be that Marryat was in the audience that Sabbath.

again between the Americans and the English, you must not take part with the Americans.[10]

Fortunately there were no serious repercussions to so ill-advised a speech. The chronic restlessness of the tribes in the fur area was not greatly increased by Marryat's inflammatory eloquence, and he himself proved to be the chief sufferer. For, although Marryat had undoubtedly intended to see more of the Northwest than the military post and the fur agency, the Indian agent was quickly informed of the seditious speech " and it was delicately intimated to the captain that his exploration of the country closed at Fort Snelling." [11]

During the course of his stay Marryat was entertained socially by the officers of the post and was well initiated into the amenities of garrison life. For Major Joseph Plympton, then the commanding officer, he had special esteem, but he also met during his sojourn such transient celebrities as Jack Fraser, the half-breed, and the well-known nimrod, Captain Martin Scott, of whose exploits he has left a long account in his diary. Indeed his picture of Fort Snelling in 1838 is rather a pleasant one:

Fort Snelling is well built, and beautifully situated: as usual, I found the officers gentlemanlike, intelligent, and hospitable; and, together with their wives and families, the society was the most agreeable that I became acquainted with in America. They are better supplied here than either at Fort Crawford or Fort Winnebago, having a fine stock of cattle on the prairie, and an extensive garden cultivated for the use of the garrison.[12]

Marryat found that the principal amusement of the fort was the chase; game, of course, was plentiful and within easy reach and the officers were well supplied with good dogs.

The captain concluded his account of his Minnesota visit

[10] *Diary*, 2:113–115, 117.
[11] Lawrence Taliaferro, "Auto-biography," in *Minnesota Historical Collections*, 6:240.
[12] *Diary*, 2:92–94, 101–112.

with a discussion of the arms and appearance of the Sioux brave and of the strange division of labor which entailed upon the woman all the duties of cleaning and preparing game, cutting fuel, and moving the lodge.   He commented on the great accuracy and power of the Indian archers and claimed that one celebrated chief had actually killed two buffalo with one arrow.   The physical perfection of the red men also impressed him, although he thought that in proportion to their bodies their arms were small and slight. Finally, on leaving St. Peter's, he again remarked on the fine qualities of the Sioux and declared that, considering humanity as a mass, the Indians were "the most perfect gentlemen in America." [13]

Exactly when Marryat left Minnesota is uncertain.   By early July, however, he was in St. Louis, as in a speech which he made later at Cincinnati he referred to his presence in the Missouri metropolis on July 4 and to a demonstration in which he saw himself paraded in effigy with a halter around his neck.   Obviously he departed before he had originally planned to leave, since in a letter to Sibley, written from Lac qui Parle several weeks after the captain reached St. Louis, John C. Frémont refers to Marryat and alludes to a contemplated excursion into the Sioux country in which Marryat was to have been accompanied among others by Sibley and Captain Scott.   The letter has an interesting sidelight, too, in that Frémont intimates that Marryat may have had the desire to emulate Cooper and to write a narrative of the West based on his own experiences. [14]

As the recipient of many kindnesses during his stay of about a fortnight, however, Marryat was not ungrateful and he spoke sincerely of "my kind host, Mr. Sibley" and of his pleasant stay at the factor's house.   There are, more-

[13] *Diary*, 2:122, 123, 125.
[14] Marryat, *Life and Letters*, 2:47; Marryat to Sibley, July 6, 1838; Frémont to Sibley, July 16, 1838, Sibley Papers.

over, at least two letters extant in which he sent his regards
to Sibley and discussed the fulfillment of one or two com-
missions with which he had been burdened.   The first, written apparently shortly after his arrival in St. Louis, reads
as follows:

Sт. Louis July 6th/38

My dear Sibley
    I have procured you the *Kreosote* [*whisky*] in this town   I send
it to you by mail through Dousman that you may not be without it.
No news here, except that they hanged me on the 4th of July, but
that appears to be my fate as I go along   I am waiting here for a
day or two to see if the Antelope will return — after which I go on
to Philadelphia.   I will write again by then — of course you know
that the treaty is ratified & the Palmyra has the goods.   Commend
me to Major Plympton, Smith [*ms. illegible*]

Ever yours in haste
F Marryat

What an Awful pen! [15]

Almost four months later Marryat again wrote to Sibley,
probably the last time that he corresponded with any resident of Minnesota.   The letter, dated at Philadelphia on
November 4, 1838, informed his erstwhile host that his own
plans had been disrupted because of the pertinacity with
which the Southerners had attacked him.   He wrote that
he had been corresponding with the American Fur Company at St. Louis and that the agent there had promised
him to get "some skins & other things worth having that
might arrive by the Antelope."   He instructed Sibley to

[15] *Diary*, 2:125.   The letter is in the Sibley Papers.   The reference to
being hanged in effigy suggests that Marryat had not yet lived down the
unpopularity which was his portion after he participated in the suppres-
sion of the Canadian insurrection late in 1837.   As a result of public
utterances in which he praised the English attack on and burning of the
American vessel "Caroline," he was condemned throughout the land and
his books were publicly burned in several places, including Detroit.   See
Bader, in *Michigan History Magazine*, 20:170–175.   The treaties nego-
tiated with the Sioux and the Chippewa in 1837, by which the large delta
between the St. Croix and the Mississippi became white man's country,
were ratified by the Senate on June 15, 1838, and are referred to by
Marryat as "the treaty."   See William W. Folwell, *A History of Minnesota*, 1:160 (St. Paul, 1921).   The "Antelope" and the "Palmyra"
were river steamboats, the first owned by the American Fur Company.

keep whatever curios he had picked up for Marryat until a good opportunity of remitting them came along.[16] Furthermore, the captain commented on the rancor borne him by the natives of the Ohio Valley and "how anxious they were to *lynch me.*" Perhaps it was for this reason that he told Sibley that he had made a small collection of bowie knives! Alluding to his friends at Fort Snelling, Marryat asserted that he had written to Captain Scott but had received no answer, and then informed Sibley that he had procured a set of De Tocqueville which he was sending back to St. Peter's. The letter concludes: "Remember me to Major Plympton & family Capt Scott Smith & all the rest. I am very sorry that I stand no better chance of seeing you again — but who knows?"[17] Before his signature Marryat gave his London address. There is no record that any of his Minnesota acquaintances ever used it. For although Marryat left St. Peter's feeling apparently that he had had a pleasant sojourn and that he carried away with him the sincere good wishes of his hosts, there is no doubt at all of the opinion entertained of him by the men who had associated with the captain. In fact their unanimity of impression is striking.

Henry Rowe Schoolcraft, who had been Marryat's host at Mackinac in the summer of 1837, described the Englishman as one of Smollett's sea captains, "a perfect sea urchin, ugly, rough, ill-mannered, and conceited beyond all bounds." Schoolcraft had gone to considerable trouble to show his guest the beauties of the island and as a result had seen a great deal of Marryat. To the famous scientist and explorer Marryat's "manners and style of conversation ap-

[16] Marryat took back to London with him various curiosities, some of which caused a mild sensation. As his biographer remarked, "the bowie-knives were harmless enough, but the skins with which his rooms were literally hung, the chairs covered, and the floors carpeted, were very much the contrary. They had never been properly dressed, and, in plain English, they were *tenanted,* and strongly required a visit to the furrier." Marryat, *Life and Letters,* 2:79.

[17] Sibley Papers.

peared to be those of a sailor, and such as we should look
for in his own Peter Simple." The captain seemed obtuse,
ill-informed, and uncommonly disputatious.[18] Somewhat the
same view was expressed by Major Taliaferro who, as we
have seen, was infuriated by Marryat's disregard for convention and common decency in his intercourse with the
Sioux. To the distinguished Indian agent at St. Peter's,
Marryat was "a rough, self-conceited John Bull," and the
implication in the portrait is that the territory was far better off with the departure of "Snarleygow or the Dog
Fiend" or, rather, its author.[19] Finally, there is the ver-
dict of Sibley, who had perhaps the best opportunity,
through constant association with his English visitor, to
judge the man. Marryat, he said, was his guest at Mendota for several weeks.

He had little of the gentleman either in his manners or appearance,
nor can reliance be placed upon his statements of facts in his printed
works. Like Featherstonhaugh, he was a thorough aristocrat in
feeling, and like him, he manifested anything but friendship for the
United States and its institutions.[20]

It is obvious that Marryat made a distinctly unfavorable
impression during his visit to the Northwest. Not only was
he a literary celebrity who had not been lionized in the way
he had expected, but the limitations of his own temperament
were such as to irritate almost everyone with whom he came
in contact. Marryat had entered the navy as a lad des-
perately in need of discipline. He found the school of experience a hard one and one not calculated to refine what
was by nature rough and coarse. Furthermore, the navy
in his day was the navy depicted by Melville and Dana, with
flogging and hard drinking alike rampant. Marryat worked
his way up through the ranks to the position of captain, no

[18] Henry R. Schoolcraft, *Personal Memoirs*, 562–564 (Philadelphia,
1851).
[19] Taliaferro, in *Minnesota Historical Collections*, 6:240.
[20] Henry H. Sibley, "Reminiscences, Historical and Personal," in *Minnesota Historical Collections*, 1:482.

mean achievement for one with his antecedents.   But, like his own Midshipman Easy, he remained essentially what he was at the beginning, truculent, opinionated, invariably convinced of his own knowledge and position.

Hardest of all for his associates to stomach, perhaps, was his calm assumption that aristocracy was *ipso facto* superior to democracy and that Americans were little more than prodigal children who had deserted the maternal home. For although Marryat professed himself to be impartially interested in the workings of the democratic system, he was constantly comparing and contrasting institutions to the inevitable disadvantage of the United States.   Thus, after careful analysis he found that American schools and American legislative bodies, American police and American architecture, were definitely inferior to their English counterparts.   The surprising thing is that in his famous *Diary* he repressed any great display of hostility or resentment for the undoubted slights he had suffered, but instead maintained throughout a tone of remarkable good nature.

Minnesota has had many foreign visitors, from Groseilliers to Hugh Walpole, but it is doubtful if any one of them had so rough and vigorous a personality as that of Captain Frederick Marryat.   The mere fact that he rubbed such honest and blunt men as Taliaferro and Sibley the wrong way adds an element of interest to his reminiscences.   It is a pity that he was not allowed to penetrate farther than Fort Snelling.   A novel about the Sioux in the style of Marryat's sea narrative embroidered with his cherished puns would indeed be something to add to the literature of the Northwest.

Fredrika Bremer.

FREDRIKA BREMER: TRAVELER AND PROPHET

THE RECENT VISITS to Minnesota of various members of the Scandinavian royal houses remind one that the Old World has long been interested in the colonies and settlements across the Atlantic and that a whole procession of travelers has come to view the success of the emigrants. One of the most distinguished of these visitors early predicted a magnificent future for the Scandinavians of the Mississippi Valley, that " future home of more than two hundred and seventy-five millions of people." Indeed, she exclaimed, "What a glorious new Scandinavia might not Minnesota become! Here would the Swede find again his clear, romantic lakes, the plains of Scania rich in corn, and the valleys of Norrland; here would the Norwegian find his rapid rivers. . . . The Danes might here pasture their flocks and herds, and lay out their farms on richer and less misty coasts than those of Denmark." The very mythology of the homeland she transplanted to the great river, where the joys of Valhalla would not be wanting "in the New Vineland of the vine-crowned islands of the Mississippi, and the great divine hog Schrimmer has nowhere such multitudes of descendants as in the New World." Many parts of America evoked enthusiastic responses from this Swedish lady, but nowhere else did she envisage such prosperity for the Scandinavian emigrants; to her none of the American states had "a greater or a more beautiful future before them than Minnesota." [1]

Three years before she actually arrived in the United States Fredrika Bremer wrote to an anonymous American thanking him for a book which she had recently received

[1] Fredrika Bremer, *The Homes of the New World; Impressions of America,* 2:56, 57, 120 (New York, 1853).

and acknowledging his friendly invitation to visit the New World.[2] The letter, hitherto unpublished, is worth quoting in part.

> To your gift you have also joyned a most friendly invitation. I sincerily hope to be so happy once to say you personally my thanks for it. It has long been a wish of my heart to visit America and to see with my own eyes that new, rising world. Indeed there is no foreign land in the world that I wish to know out of North America and that especially for the peculiar turn of mind of its people and its management of life in public as in private life, in the state, the home, in society and in Nature.

Here are revealed both Miss Bremer's fumbling command of English idiom and her early desire to cross the Atlantic. Obviously she had long turned her thoughts westward.

Early in October, 1849, Fredrika Bremer landed in New York City, but she did not immediately travel toward the Scandinavian settlements. The fame of a new country and the welcome of its citizens claimed her attention, and before she finally boarded a lake steamer for Chicago she had spent the good part of a year along the Atlantic seaboard and in the South. Even then it was difficult to evade the hospitality of such intimate friends as Andrew Downing and James Russell Lowell and his brilliant young wife Maria.[3] The Lowells accompanied her westward to Niagara Falls; from there she proceeded alone.

Miss Bremer reached Chicago early in September, 1850, and found a miserable and ugly city which in her estimation resembled a huckstress rather than a queen. But the prairies, which she saw at the very periphery of the city, were

[2] Letter written from Årsta, October 23, 1846, in the possession of the Minnesota Historical Society. It probably was written to Andrew J. Downing.

[3] Downing, now recognized as the father of American landscaping, was Miss Bremer's first host in the United States. " Fredrika Bremer stayed three weeks with us," Lowell wrote to a friend, " and I do not *like* her, I *love* her. She is one of the most beautiful persons I have ever known — so clear, so simple, so right-minded and -hearted, and so full of judgment." C. E. Norton, ed., *Letters of James Russell Lowell,* 1:174 (New York, 1894).

quite something else.   Rapturously she described the great
sea of grass with its birds and flowers and undulating horizon.   The occasional log cabin marking a settler's pre-
emption was a bird's nest floating on a sea.   Sunflowers
reached skyward four yards and more.   To the astonished
visitor the prairie was a sight less common and more magnificent than Niagara itself.[4]

After a brief pause in Milwaukee, where she was lionized
in the fashion which she had come to anticipate in American
cities, she spent a day at Pine Lake, Wisconsin, which, although one of the first Swedish settlements in the West, had
even then shrunk to a mere half dozen families.   Nevertheless, she was given a royal welcome, and the thrill of hearing
her own tongue spoken freely and of once more seeing
familiar customs was ample compensation for all the rigors
of travel.   When she and the blacksmith danced the " Nigar
Polka " together, electrifying the small gathering, her cup
of joy was complete.[5]   It is not hard to picture in this setting the amiable lady whom Hawthorne deemed worthy to
be the maiden aunt of the whole human race.

Before Miss Bremer could board a Mississippi steamboat
for the journey to St. Paul a long arduous stage ride to
Galena was necessary.   On its completion she was thank-
ful that she was still sound in body and limbs and felt positive
that the worst feature of her western trip was over: "no
one could possibly perform that uneasy journey through
Wisconsin without having something to remember as long
as he lived."   After a short stopover at Galena occasioned
by steamboat schedules, she boarded the "Nominee" on
October 12, 1850.   Among the passengers were Henry
Hastings Sibley and Mrs. Sibley on a return journey from
Washington, where he served in Congress as territorial dele-
gate from Minnesota.

The voyage up the Mississippi in October gave as much

[4] *Homes of the New World*, 1:601–603.
[5] *Homes of the New World*, 1:617–626.

pleasure to Miss Bremer as it has given to countless other travelers. Particularly was she delighted with the purity of the water, for she had come to consider the river as a giant like the titans of old, strong but somewhat defiled. "Here its waters were clear, of a fresh, light-green color, and within their beautiful frame of distant violet-blue mountains, they lay like a heavenly mirror, bearing on their bosom verdant, vine-covered islands, like islands of the blest." As the boat crept northward she alternately praised the rocky hills which hemmed in the valley and the vegetation which covered their slopes, particularly the tangled network of vines everywhere fruitful. Indeed the steamboat trip was too short for her eager eyes; she wished that it might last eight days.[6]

The "Nominee" reached St. Paul late in the afternoon of October 17. To Miss Bremer the trip had been extremely pleasant; she not only thought six dollars an unusually low price for the comforts of her passage but she appreciated the courtesy of Captain Orrin Smith and the novelty of the scenery. She felt especially obligated to Sibley, "a clever, kind man, and extremely interesting to me from his knowledge of the people of this region, and their circumstances." He explained to her many of the peculiarities of the Sioux and often when passing an Indian village he would utter a wild cry, which invariably drew an exulting response from the shore. At the wharf the visitor was met by Governor and Mrs. Alexander Ramsey, who immediately extended to her their hospitality. Thus the Ramsey home became Miss Bremer's headquarters during her week's stay in Minnesota, and Ramsey himself acted as a kind of cicerone.[7]

[6] *Homes of the New World,* 1:651; 2:3, 4, 16, 17, 21.
[7] *Homes of the New World,* 2:19, 22, 25; *Minnesota Pioneer* (St. Paul), October 17, 1850; Ramsey Diary, October 17, 1850. The Minnesota Historical Society has a copy of the Ramsey Diary.

She religiously saw all the places of interest. The day following her arrival she accompanied her host to the Falls of St. Anthony, but found them like the cascade of a great milldam. "River, falls, country, views, every thing here has more breadth than grandeur," she records. The visitors then called upon Mrs. John W. North, who lived on Nicollet Island, and to reach whose house it was necessary to cross a jam of pine logs lying in the water above the milldam. Miss Bremer was at first terrified by the prospect, but eventually made the crossing and was rewarded by finding a cultural oasis above the rapids, a home filled with music and books and pictures. Mrs. North entertained her guests with vocal and instrumental music, but when Fredrika Bremer was asked to sing she declined, saying, "I only sing for God in the church, and for little children." Ramsey wrote in his diary that evening that Miss Bremer had remarked gentleness of manner as a characteristic of the Americans, but observed also in them a great energy of purpose and will which made them less pleasing than the English.[8]

Other places to which the Swedish author was introduced included Fort Snelling, Fountain Cave, and the Little Falls — more familiar to a later generation as Minnehaha Falls — which she found elusively lovely and worthy of their own song. "The whitest of foam, the blackest of crags, the most graceful, and, at the same time, wild and gentle fall! Small things may become great through their perfection." Sunday morning, October 20, she and Mrs. Ramsey attended services in the Presbyterian church at St. Paul and heard the Reverend Edward D. Neill preach, and later in the day Miss Bremer accompanied the governor on a stroll along the bluffs back of St. Paul, appreciating the warmth of

[8] *Homes of the New World*, 2:27, 32; Ramsey Diary, October 18, 1850; Mrs. Rebecca Marshall Cathcart, "A Sheaf of Reminiscences," in *Minnesota Historical Collections*, 15:532.

Indian summer and the glorious colors of autumn. She apparently also visited the dalles of the St. Croix River, for an eyewitness recorded later that on looking into the great gorge of the stream she exclaimed, "One of God's beauteous spots of earth." Another interesting incident of her stay in Minnesota is her meeting with a Danish merchant, Dr. Charles W. W. Borup, who had made a small fortune out of furs and had married a woman with Indian blood.[9]

But whatever the original object of Fredrika Bremer's visit to the Northwest may have been, there is little doubt that her chief interest was the Indians. She observed the savages, their physique, bearing, dress, their dwellings and manner of life, their sports and ceremonies, the condition of their women. And through the intervention of Ramsey she got more than one Indian to pose for her so that she could carry away with her sketches to complement her verbal pictures.

This interest in the red man she manifested almost as soon as she commenced her river trip. On board the "Nominee" were several Indians, a Winnebago family of three and two young Sioux warriors. The latter especially caught her attention, as they reminded her of parading roosters. "They strut about now and then, and look proud, and then they squat themselves down on their hams, like apes, and chatter away as volubly as any two old gossips ever did." She observed also their hawk's bill noses and the hard, inhuman glance of the eyes, like that of a bird of prey scenting its quarry from afar. Three miles below

[9] Ramsey Diary, October 20, 1850; *Homes of the New World*, 2:54, 55, 58; William H. C. Folsom, "History of Lumbering in the St. Croix Valley," in *Minnesota Historical Collections*, 9:315. Folsom, incidentally, misdates Miss Bremer's visit by a year. Borup settled in St. Paul in 1848; he died, one of its wealthiest citizens, in 1859. John H. Stevens remembered Miss Bremer's enthusiasm for the picturesque scenery along the Mississippi and for the radiance of the autumn coloring. See his *Personal Recollections of Minnesota and Its People*, 90 (Minneapolis, 1890).

St. Paul she noticed the Sioux village of Kaposia, with its twenty wigwams and the log house of the missionary, Dr. Thomas S. Williamson.   And the streets of the infant city, she declared, swarmed with Indians fantastically painted and ornamented with an utter lack of taste.   " Here comes an Indian who has painted a great red spot in the middle of his nose; here another who has painted the whole of his forehead in small lines of yellow and black; there a third with coal-black rings round his eyes.   All have eagles' or cocks' feathers in their hair, for the most part colored, or with scarlet tassels of worsted at the ends."   In general, she thought, the women wore less paint and showed better taste than the men; also they seemed less rigid and more humane.   But the women were obviously the beasts of burden for their husbands.

Fredrika Bremer was interested almost as much in sketching as she was in writing, and she took back with her to Sweden portraits of Longfellow, Emerson, and other celebrities whom she had induced to pose.   She was extremely eager to draw some of the Indians from life, and with this purpose in mind she visited several tepees, "four very respectable Indian huts" close to Fort Snelling.   Governor Ramsey and an interpreter accompanied her, and the group spent a full day at the St. Peter's Indian agency.   Miss Bremer was rather surprised to find, not the dirt and poverty which she had anticipated, but a rude oriental splendor, blankets in profusion, showy cushions, pipes, and of course the implements of hunting.   She sampled the thin soup which was simmering in a huge kettle, a flavorless broth without salt, and she ate a cake which the squaw had just baked and pronounced it excellent.[10]

Shortly after, she persuaded an old chief to become her

[10] *Homes of the New World,* 2: 20, 24, 26, 34; Ramsey Diary, October 22, 1850.

model, although he grumbled at being painted without his ceremonial regalia; and when she had finished this sketch she drew a young Indian woman who appeared attired in her wedding finery. Feather Cloudwoman, the name of Miss Bremer's subject, was apparently of unusual beauty, and her remarkably light coloring, magnificent eyes, and modest carriage made a deep impression on the artist. But her general difficulty in getting models she attributed to the Indian belief that a likeness on paper subtracts from the life span of the person delineated.[11]

Miss Bremer's experiences with the Indians naturally led her to reflect on their condition, especially that of the women. An ardent feminist herself, she thought often of the subjection of the Indian squaw and the degradation of a life from which the only escape was suicide. Winona and Ampato Sapa, both of whom killed themselves rather than submit to domestic ignominy, exemplified most clearly to her the deeply tragic life of the savage women. The only advantage which she perceived in the Indian's existence was freedom from the artificial bonds and prohibitions of society, a liberty which her own experiences had taught her to value highly.

One of the last events of Miss Bremer's stay in Minnesota was a medicine dance in which about a hundred Indians participated, dancing to the unmelodious music of drums and gourds and shaking silver bells violently as they performed their saltations. Such an experience led her to reflect on the religious life of the red man, and for the edification of her invalid sister at Årsta she put together what she had seen and learned of Indian theology. Always a conscientious traveler, Miss Bremer made every attempt to learn the history and ideology of the people among whom she traveled, but one suspects that in regard to the Indians

[11] *Homes of the New World,* 2: 38–40.

her attention was chiefly that of the artist, focused on the picturesque and the novel. At any rate when her stay had drawn to a close she confessed her unwillingness to depart. "I wish to see more of the Indians," she wrote home, "and their way of life, and feel something like a hungry person who is obliged to leave a meal which he had just commenced." [12]

Contemporary accounts of her visit reveal the pleasure which she gave as well as received during her residence as Governor Ramsey's guest. The *Minnesota Pioneer* of October 24 expressed its gratification that so distinguished a person as the Swedish author had come to Minnesota to see this "Stockholm of America."

Though far away from her native land, she is not a stranger to us, for she is one of those individuals whom all lands love to claim, and whose birth place is soon forgotten, because her presence is felt everywhere. Her manners are natural and her expressions candid. Unlike those literary women, whom Byron hated, and called "Blue Stockings," she makes no display, and loves not to talk about her own productions, but desires to place herself, in the attitude of a learner.

The *Pioneer* then proceeded to compare her literary work, invariably revealing a sound and pure mind, with the productions of Eugene Sue and that brazen amazon, George Sand; and closed its editorial account by expressing regret that Miss Bremer felt obliged to leave Minnesota for the dark pine forests and tranquil lakes of Sweden. Similarly, the *Minnesota Chronicle and Register* of October 21 declared its appreciation of the visitor.

We only regret that she should have delayed her visit until the frost has seriously marred the beauty of our landscapes. But we are assured that she, nor any other true lover of the beautiful, will ever regret a visit to Minnesota, at any season of the year, always excepting the last of March and first week of April.

When the "Nominee" departed for Galena on October 25, 1850, the paper praised her fulsomely. "Miss Bremer, by

[12] *Homes of the New World,* 2:36, 44, 58.

her kind cordiality and simplicity of manner, made many friends while here, and she has the best wishes of our community for health, happiness and prosperity." [13]

As the steamboat forged down the Mississippi Fredrika Bremer must often have thought of the land which she envisaged as a new home for her emigrant countrymen, and many allusions in her later writings bespeak the deep impression which Minnesota made upon her. Writing from near St. Louis to her friend Andrew Downing on November 11, 1850, she said:

Well, I have been among the Savages since last I wrote to you, have seen them by their fires, in their "Tipis," seen their graves and strange life, and when we meet I shall show you sketches of and speak more about them. I have also seen the scenery on the upper Mississippi, its high bluffs crowned with autumn-golden oaks, and rocks like ruined walls and towers, ruins from the times when the Megatherium and mastodons walked the earth, — and how I did enjoy it!

And she repeated her prophecy that the valley of the Mississippi would some day provide a livelihood for millions of people, asking questions of heaven and earth about futurity. [14]

Fredrika Bremer was neither the first nor the last of the Swedish visitors to the United States. [15] But in a rare degree she combined literary grace and skill with the power to observe and the energy to see. Extremely fortunate in her translator Mary Howitt, she saw her book on America published in London and New York almost as soon as it appeared in Sweden; and her already large audience in the

[13] *Minnesota Chronicle and Register* (St. Paul), October 28, 1850; Ramsey Diary, October 25, 1850. The *Chronicle and Register* for November 4 contains a long appreciation of Jenny Lind written by Miss Bremer; the *Pioneer* for October 24 reprints an obituary notice of President Taylor which Miss Bremer had written for the eastern papers.

[14] Adolph B. Benson, ed., "Fredrika Bremer's Unpublished Letters to the Downings," in *Scandinavian Studies*, 11:192 (May, 1931).

[15] See for example Roy W. Swanson, "Fredrika Bremer's Predecessors," in *Swedish-American Historical Bulletin*, 1:53–62 (March, 1928).

United States was multiplied by the general interest in her volumes of travel.   Judged by the candid and forthright accounts of more recent travelers, Miss Bremer's *Homes of the New World* — her chief claim to immortality — may seem somewhat prolix and dull; but her observations will always retain a historical value and her prediction of a new Scandinavia in Minnesota will not soon be forgotten.   An astute and careful traveler who was preoccupied with social and economic conditions, she chronicled whatever she saw, and interest in her work has not lagged despite the fact that it is almost a century ago that the America fever was raging high.

Edward Eggleston.

THE HOOSIER SCHOOLMASTER
IN MINNESOTA[1]

On July 4, 1857, a boating expedition near Cannon City, Minnesota, ended catastrophically with the capsizing of the craft and the drowning of four people. When the time for the funeral arrived, it was discovered that the regularly officiating minister was unavoidably engaged elsewhere. At this juncture a stripling but recently arrived from Indiana announced himself a Methodist minister and volunteered his services. Thus it was that a lad of twenty who had journeyed to Minnesota chiefly afoot performed the memorial ceremonies. That stripling was Edward Eggleston, later nationally famous as the first of the Hoosier realists and everywhere known as the "Hoosier Schoolmaster," and that boating accident became one of the central incidents in Eggleston's only Minnesota novel, *The Mystery of Metropolisville*.[2]

But Eggleston's first visit to the territory had come over twelve months earlier. In the spring of 1856 the boy's health had broken down completely; lung hemorrhages had developed and he was apparently destined to an early death from consumption. Hoping to ameliorate his condition somewhat his mother took him on a river voyage to St. Louis. There the boy fell in with a group of similarly af-

[1] A paper read on June 18, 1937, at the Little Falls session of the fifteenth state historical convention held under the auspices of the Minnesota Historical Society. *Ed.*

[2] William McKinley, *A Story of Minnesota Methodism,* 64 (Cincinnati, 1911).

flicted people who were en route for Minnesota, which had been represented to them as having an ideal climate for those suffering from tuberculosis. Eggleston, although obliged to leave his mother and having cash enough to defray only the cost of his passage, agreed to join the rest. So it was that he arrived in Minnesota in May, penniless and alone.[3]

But whatever the lad lacked in strength and endurance he made up in spirit. Undeterred by his physical condition, he threw himself wholeheartedly into the life of the frontier community. Jobs were plentiful if hardly remunerative, and Eggleston, demanding little but a chance to work in the open air, had no trouble in keeping himself busy. He was chain bearer for a surveying party, amateur surveyor himself, driver of a three-yoke ox team engaged in breaking the prairie loam, peddler of a recipe for making soap. In after years he was twitted for the unministerial character of some of his occupations, particularly the last. But his reply was firm: "I am prouder of my soap recipe selling than I am of my preaching there; for the soap was above criticism, while the sermons certainly were not." As his brother George, his only biographer, wrote, Edward's labors may have lacked dignity, but they were indubitably honest.[4]

By the end of the summer of 1856 the lad found his health marvelously improved, so much so that he determined for awhile to contribute whatever he could to the free state cause in Kansas. Securing a dirk pocketknife and equipping himself with a plentiful supply of cheese and crackers (they made up in economy for their lack of nutrition!), he wandered west and south as far as Cedar Falls, Iowa. There he decided that his zeal for the Kansans was hardly equal to the task of transporting himself on foot to the scene of action, and reluctantly he turned eastward. At

[3] George Cary Eggleston, *The First of the Hoosiers*, 261, 264 (Philadelphia, 1903).
[4] Eggleston, *First of the Hoosiers*, 265.

Muscatine he crossed the Mississippi, and at Galesburg he spent what little money he still had for railroad transportation back to his home at Vevay, Indiana. Although his months in Minnesota had not supplied enough energy to enable him to reach Kansas, they had done wonders for a naturally frail constitution, so much so that he walked between three hundred and four hundred miles before he finally deemed it wiser to journey by rail.[5]

Home once more, Eggleston decided to renew his studies for the ministry, and he succeeded so well, without the benefit of much formal education, that that very autumn he was ordained and was assigned a circuit containing ten different preaching stations in southeastern Indiana. Plunging into his work with characteristic abandon, he was a welcome addition, despite his youth and inexperience, to the ministry of the state. But he soon overtaxed himself and after a period of severe clerical labor he became convinced that he could not live longer in his native climate. "At the end of six months of zealous preaching," he wrote long afterward, "I was again a candidate for the grave." At that time the tide of immigration westward was at a crest, and Eggleston had no difficulty in turning his thoughts and aspirations toward the frontier. But his motive was not that which impelled the land-hungry mobs in the direction of the setting sun. "The only fortune he sought," declared his brother George, "was the privilege of living, the ability to go on breathing in spite of the condition of his lungs. Beyond that he had no hope or expectation, no desire, even, except to do well and faithfully the work in the world to which he believed that God had called him."[6] Obviously it was the quest for health which led Eggleston back to Minnesota, just as it was the search for a more suitable climate that induced Thoreau to penetrate the trans-Mississippi country at

[5] Edward Eggleston, " Formative Influences," in *The Forum,* 10: 288 (November, 1890).
[6] Eggleston, *First of the Hoosiers,* 305.

the tag end of his life.   Nine years were to elapse before
Eggleston again left the frontier.

At the session of the Minnesota Methodist conference
held in Winona in August, 1857, the ministerial status of
Edward Eggleston was discussed.   His papers had not yet
arrived from Indiana, but on motion of Bishop Edward R.
Ames the conference waived the formality and examined the
candidate regarding his orthodoxy and ability.   According
to one of his later colleagues, the Reverend William McKinley, members of the examining board were amazed by the
contrast between the aspirant's youth and his mental maturity; they accorded him a hearty and unanimous recom-
mendation.   As McKinley asserted, "There was something
about him that attracted people at once.   His powers of
observation, description, and conversation were phenomenal.
He could talk more and talk better than any man I ever
knew.   His geniality, natural eloquence, and magnetic personality made him a favorite everywhere." [7]

Eggleston's first charge was at Traverse des Sioux, where
he preached in one of the earliest churches built in southwestern Minnesota.   His congregation was hardly numerous, consisting of fifteen members and twenty probationers.
They included a few white settlers, hunters, trappers, half-
breeds, and Indians.   His duties involved an immense
amount of travel, usually on foot, both in summer and winter.   He lived in the open air almost as much as if he had
been a *voyageur* — naturally the best possible existence for
him.   Sometimes he chose to walk only because he was too
poor to buy or rent a horse, for salaries were meager and
hardships common in the Methodist ministry of the day.
Annual stipends ranged from nine to forty dollars, such pitiful returns in a sparsely settled land that the men were frequently obliged to resort to hunting in order to obtain food.
One preacher was in the habit of shooting red squirrels for
his dinner as he rode to visit his scattered parishioners.

[7] McKinley, *Minnesota Methodism,* 64.

Eggleston himself pastured sheep part of the day.   In some manner, however, the young clergyman must have managed to scrape together a pittance, for on March 18, 1858, he took himself a wife, Lizzie Snider of St. Peter.[8]

One incident of his first year's pastorate attests eloquently to Eggleston's energy and determination. Frail as he was, he once enlisted in a volunteer troop raised for a punitive expedition against Indian marauders. For some time all went well.   But after a particularly long march his commander said to him, "Parson, you're a good fellow, but you're not strong enough for a soldier. Now, I've got more men than horses here, and I want you to quit as a man and let me have your horse for a strong young fellow to ride."   Humiliated, but perforce consenting, Eggleston dismounted and returned to the settlements on foot. The state later paid him for his horse.[9]

Eggleston's probationary period on the frontier was short. Despite the fact that the annual roll of the church indicated a drop in membership in the Traverse and St. Peter parish, the young preacher was promoted in 1859 to the Market Street Church in St. Paul. In the *Minutes* of the Minnesota conference of the Methodist Episcopal church for 1859 Eggleston is listed as a full-fledged member — he had previously been included as "on trial" — and he was ordained in the same year. His services, moreover, were recognized in a different field, for the record contains this comment on his part in the dissemination of the Bible in the young community: "The American Bible Society has not abated its activity. Its auxiliary in this State, under the efficient agency of REV. E. EGGLESTON, has now sixty branch societies, five hundred local agents, and has raised $1,000 during the year, and purchased $1,500 worth of Bibles and

[8] Eggleston, *First of the Hoosiers*, 314; Minnesota Annual Conference of the Methodist Episcopal Church, *Minutes*, 1858; Chauncey Hobart, *History of Methodism in Minnesota*, 166 (Red Wing, 1887); *Dictionary of American Biography*, 6:54 (New York, 1931).
[9] Eggleston, *First of the Hoosiers*, 315.

Testaments from the American Bible Society." [10]   Thus his
record was so remarkable that at the age of twenty-one, in
October, 1859, Eggleston found himself pastor, in the capital city, of one of the largest Methodist churches in Minnesota.

He remained in his St. Paul pastorate for a little over a
year before the itinerant system of the Methodist church
compelled his removal to Stillwater.   During that period
he became well known in the religious life of the city.   At
an anniversary of the Minnesota Sabbath School Society
held in St. Paul on June 12, 1860, he gave the chief address
of welcome to the delegates, and on the same evening at
the meeting of the Minnesota Bible Society he opened the
session with a few remarks about the distribution of books
and with some pointed criticism of the sermon delivered by
Bishop Thomas L. Grace on the previous St. Patrick's
Day.[11]   Of the second address the St. Paul *Daily Pioneer
and Democrat* for June 14 remarked acidly, "Mr. E. is a
fluent speaker, and made a good address, barring a little
uncharitableness."

But the most interesting incident of Eggleston's earliest
St. Paul residence has no connection with his ecclesiastical
career.   In the early summer of 1860 a group of scientists
from Cambridge, Massachusetts, passed through Minnesota
en route to Cumberland House on the Saskatchewan River,
where they hoped to view a total eclipse of the sun on July
18.   This party, led by Simon Newcomb, the distinguished
astronomer, also included William Ferrel, the mathematician, and Samuel Scudder, the entomologist.   During an en-
forced delay in St. Paul because of transportation difficulties
the scientists extended an invitation to the young minister
to join them, at least on part of their journey, and Eggles-

[10] Minnesota Annual Conference of the Methodist Episcopal Church,
Minutes, 1869, p. 7.
[11] *Daily Pioneer and Democrat* (St. Paul), June 13, 14, 1860.   The
criticism of Bishop Grace evoked certain epistolary comments in which
Eggleston's name figured.   See *Pioneer and Democrat,* June 16, 17, 1860.

ton eagerly consented.   So it was that the latter part of
June and almost all of July found him absent on an expedition which was hardly consonant with his clerical duties.
But Eggleston's health was always unreliable and there is
little doubt that he accompanied the expedition chiefly for
the opportunity it gave him to live in the open air.[12]

The party left St. Paul on June 16, 1860, and reached
the Willis House at St. Cloud the same night, their convey-
ance being one of the stagecoaches which Burbank and Company had recently inaugurated between St. Paul and the Red
River.   From St. Cloud westward the progress of the party
was recorded by Eggleston himself, who at intervals sent
longish letters back to the *Daily Minnesotian* of St. Paul.
These missives, signed "E. E.," are not only excellent first-
hand accounts of the country and the almost insuperable
obstacles met by the travelers; they are also remarkable for
their graphic accuracy and they suggest Eggleston's later
mastery of provincial scenes and characters.   Certainly it is
not difficult to see the mature realist in such a picture of a
stage companion as the following.   At one of the stops,
according to the writer, a very amusing native entered the
coach and at once began to denounce temperance houses.
Whence ensued this colloquy:

"Do you sell whiskey?"

"Yes, I keep a leetle for a case of immergency, it's mighty good for
colicky horses.   You can tell one of these 'ere temperance houses by
the great number of dead horses layin' about them."

"Ah, then you only keep liquor for horses?"

"I keep it for the public, sir, it's mighty good for sickness."

"Well," we rejoined, "then you don't sell to any but sick people."

"I don't axe 'em whether they're sick or not, there's a heap o' sick
people passes along this road."

-----

[12] Scudder, using the pseudonym of "A. Rochester Fellow," wrote an
account of the trip, which was published under the title *The Winnipeg
Country, or Roughing It with an Eclipse Party* (Boston, 1886).   Curiously enough, he makes no mention whatever of Eggleston.   Scudder's
pictures of the party's experiences en route to Fort Garry harmonize
perfectly with the accounts sent by Eggleston to the *Daily Minnesotian*
of St. Paul, but are considerably less vivid.

Eggleston's second letter, dated June 18, was written from Kandota, in Todd County.   He reported first his departure, against his will, on Sunday, but, he added philosophically, "it is a stern fact that eclipses wait for no one. There was no alternative but that of traveling or of being too late."   So he solaced himself by reading the Episcopal service out of doors.   His attention was almost immediately attracted by the terrain he was traversing.

I have never seen a more handsome or more fertile valley than that of the Sauk.   We have not seen a foot of poor ground in the last sixty miles.   The prairie is rolling, but not broken, and popple and tamarack are almost the only kinds of timber.   I saw a house built of tamarack with the bark peeled off, so as to leave it spotted by the pieces of underbark.   At a short distance it appeared almost as beautiful as rosewood.

Kandota, a townsite platted in 1856, he found consisting of one house and five people.   And yet he approved.   "The town is like Eden before the creation of Eve." [13]

In his next letter, written from Breckenridge on June 20, Eggleston devoted much of his space to objurgations on the roads and the impediments confronting the traveler.

We have sometimes sunk into the hubs where there were no fence rails and then we would fall to work unloading and afterwards reloading our thousand pounds of baggage.   We have waded, on an average, one slough per hour, in order to lighten the stage.   Sometimes we have had to wade the worst sloughs with boxes or trunks on our shoulders.   We reached here at 11½ o'clock last night in lumber wagons, having abandoned the coach on account of the roads. Our boots were full of water and our nether garments completely saturated.

In addition to the roads, the insect pests drew Eggleston's attention, and he professed himself unable to find words to depict the voracity of Red River mosquitoes.   "We threw our netting over our faces but they worked their way through every opening.   For hour after hour they found their way to face, hands, eyes and nose but with stoical fortitude we 'grinned and bore it.'"   Despite these drawbacks,

[13] *Minnesotian,* June 22, 1860.

however, Eggleston still viewed the country with enthusiasm.

The finest country I have ever seen is on the ridges that separate the waters of the Mississippi from those of Red River. The country is beautifully undulating, and completely dotted over with the most beautiful poplar groves. Among these little hills and groves, are lakes of the most enchanting beauty. . . . The left hand of the Sauk is tolerably well timbered, but the right has hardly a tree on it. I am satisfied from the inquiries I have made, that the soil both on the Sauk river and on the "divide" is not surpassed by any in the world. And yet not one claim in ten is yet taken in all this magnificent section of our State.

The correspondent ended his letter with the remark that, although Alexandria and Evansville were listed as towns, the former had only two families resident and the latter one. At Breckenridge, where a new two-story hotel was building, the party stopped at a sod tavern. Eggleston also commented on the fare which obtained at the various houses en route: salt pork, raw bread, and potatoes, and coffee which invariably grew weaker the farther west they advanced.[14]

At the next stage of the journey, Georgetown on the Red River, the traveler noticed especially the conformation of the valley, its flatness and wetness, and the marked topographical change away from the water.

The whole country there is beautifully undulating and very fertile. The soil in the Valley of the Red River is, as far as I can learn, very much like that of Indiana and Ohio, — not so quick as that of Minnesota generally, but very fertile. It is on this account that it is not profitable to raise Indian corn here, though it is a fine wheat and potatoe country. The water has not that transparent appearance here that it has through other parts of the State.

He observed also that the greatest obstacle to settlement of the Red River Valley was the absence of timber and yet, predicting on the basis of what had happened in the treeless prairies of Illinois, he foresaw a future population for the area.

[14] *Minnesotian,* July 6, 1860.

At Georgetown the party was welcomed by the howls of dogs and the shouts of the *bois brulés*. More formally the travelers were received by Alexander Murray, the manager of the Hudson's Bay Company trading post, and by Isaac Atwater, the United States government surveyor. Eggleston was unquestionably glad to be met so hospitably and to be once more in reputable lodgings, but he did not speak well of the dish with which the group was regaled the first night — "rub-a-boo" or pemmican cooked with potatoes!

Chief among the sights at Georgetown was the "Anson Northup," the tiny river steamer which was to convey the scientific party to Fort Garry. Eggleston described vividly how the entire population of the hamlet, twenty-five in all, awaited eagerly the whistle and smoke puff of "the little forerunner of civilization." Nor has anyone better depicted the vessel itself as it rounded the bend:

One chimney — rough looking hull — and a steering oar fixed on in front to aid the pilot in making the sudden turns necessary in order to navigate the bends. I could not imagine that this non-descript, but neat looking little affair, had any features of resemblance — any traits in common with the steamboats below — until I saw the colored chambermaid looking out one of the port holes intended to represent windows. Diminutive as is the Anson Northrup [*sic*], she is a model of neatness within.

It was not always, however, that the traveler superseded the clergyman in Eggleston, and he proudly recorded for the gratification of the readers of his letter that, to the best of his knowledge, he had preached the first Protestant sermon ever heard in the upper Red River country.[15]

Eggleston's last letter was written when he was still

[15] *Minnesotian,* July 11, 1860. Another description of the "Anson Northup" on the Red River is included in an article entitled "The-Man-That-Draws-the-Handcart," which Eggleston wrote for *Harper's New Monthly Magazine* of February, 1894. "Nothing could have been more awkward than that tub of a boat," according to Eggleston, "plunging every now and again headlong into the banks despite the frantic exertions of the pilot, aided by the long steering-oar on the bow. We steamed some three hundred miles, according to the estimate of the boatmen, without seeing on the banks a human being or a house."

aboard the "Anson Northup" and ready to land at Fort
Garry, with the vessel carrying the Stars and Stripes at the
bow and the Union Jack at the stern.   He had much to
say of the obstacles of river navigation.

The river above the mouth of Red Lake River is very narrow and
is so exceedingly crooked that it is not unusual for the boat to run
toward every point of the compass in the distance of two miles. Two
men stand constantly by the steering oar, that is on the bow, to which
I alluded before.   If there is a very short bend to the right the pilot
sings out "right," which is repeated by the captain to the hands at
the oar, when the blade of the oar is immediately turned to the right
of the bow and dipped.   When the boat is turned sufficiently the pilot
calls out "that'll do!" — when the oar is lifted.   In some parts of
the river the oar is kept constantly at work and even then it is impossible to turn the boat quick enough.

Indeed, the mate Hutchinson felt so strongly about the constant twisting of the channel that he ordered the stoker to
use crooked sticks to assist the vessel around the bends!
Eggelston had warm praise for all the officers of the little
craft, the captain, the pilot, the clerk, and the mate.   But
the most interesting character he encountered on the trip
was young George Northrup, already widely renowned as
scout, frontiersman, and Indian fighter.   Northrup, about
whom Eggleston later wrote a long magazine article, was
the "Kit Carson of the Northwest," amiable, soft-spoken,
and unusually cultivated for one in his environment.   The
traveler described Northrup as an authority on Indian life
and linguistics and altogether one of the most remarkable
men he had ever met.[16]

Eggleston closed his letters to the *Minnesotian* with several comments on the people and the topography of the
region.

I have seen Pembina.   Five houses and a Cree wigwam compose the
metropolis. — As your readers nearly all know the principal part of
the settlers live at St. Josephs 31 miles up the Pembina river.   There
are some settlements above Pembina on the Red river and some on the
Pembina river, containing in all about 40 families.

---

[16] "The-Man-That-Draws-the-Handcart" is essentially a biographical
sketch of Northrup, who was watchman on the "Anson Northup."

The Red River, he observed, abounded in fish, notably sturgeon and catfish of enormous size, buffalo still came within thirty miles of the water, while elk and deer frequented its tributaries. The Red Lake River he described as larger than its neighbor with its banks better timbered. The land of its watershed was almost all tillable too, but navigation on the stream was difficult because of the frequent rapids.[17]

At Fort Garry Eggleston left the party of scientists, presumably returning by the same route as that already described. Why he did not continue the whole distance to the Saskatchewan River is a matter of conjecture. Possibly he feared the hazards and the exposure of the remainder of the trip; more likely he was too conscientious to remain away from his congregation for an extended period. At any rate the latter part of July found him once more in St. Paul, and on July 21 the *Minnesotian* remarked: " Rev. Edward Egglestone, pastor of the Market street Methodist Church, who has been absent during the past few weeks, has returned, and will preach as usual tomorrow [*Sunday*]."

Shortly after the young minister resumed his parochial duties he was transferred, this time to Stillwater, where he served during the remainder of 1860 and for most of 1861. The *Stillwater Messenger* for September 4, 1860, announced that Eggleston had been appointed Methodist minister, and subsequent issues of the paper refer to his performance of various routine duties: conducting prayer meetings, officiating at funerals and weddings, preaching on certain occasions. Moreover, because the young clergyman's term of service in Stillwater coincided roughly with the opening of the Civil War, his name was linked with various efforts to exhort and provide for the comfort of recruits for the army. One highly interesting memory of Eggleston's sojourn in the St. Croix Valley town is a sermon which he delivered shortly after the firing on Fort Sumter. His congregation liked it so well that they prevailed upon the editor

[17] *Minnesotian*, July 18, 1860.

of the *Messenger* to reprint it in the issue of May 28, 1861.
In this sermon Eggleston spoke on " Christian Patriotism "
and declared that although he disliked flinging the weight of
the pulpit into political strife, he felt that government was
ordained by God and that a revolt against government
was a crime against God.   He professed a hatred for war
but he asserted that even Christians were allowed to protect
themselves, and that anarchy, despotism, and slavery were
worse evils than war.   Finally, he affirmed that it was the
duty of good Americans to defend their country, and he expressed himself wholeheartedly in favor of the North.

Although few other details of his life in Stillwater survive, there are several allusions to his intense love of literature while he was quartered on the shores of the St. Croix
and to the extensive reading (and the somewhat abortive
writing) which he did at the time.   " I remember particularly," he wrote in after years, " a paper on Beranger and
his songs, which I published while trying to evangelize the
red-shirted lumbermen on the St. Croix."   His first meeting with Milton's poetry is also, curiously enough, inextri-
cably linked with the primitive background of the lumbering
country.   For one night as he stopped for a lodging at a
hut near the river he found a copy of " L'Allegro," and he
records how he looked out of the window at the " deep
trap-rock dalles through which the dark, pine-stained waters
of the St. Croix River run swifty," and how he saw a raft
with several red-shirted lumbermen aboard emerge from the
gorge into the open reaches below, at the same time that he
was allowing his fancy to dwell on the lines of the great
Puritan poet.[18]

During this time Eggleston was also becoming more
prominent in the administration of his church. At the annual conference held at Red Wing in the autumn following
his return from the Red River Valley he was chosen an

[18] Eggleston, in *The Forum,* 10:290; Meredith Nicholson, *The Provincial American and Other Papers,* 41 (Boston and New York, 1912).

elder; he had already been named to two standing committees, those on Sunday schools and on periodical literature.
The *Minutes* of the session contain two reports signed by
Eggleston in his capicity of committeeman, one recommend-
ing the establishment of a church paper in "one, and, if
possible, in both the Scandinavian dialects," and the other
suggesting that Methodist ministers be dissuaded from establishing independent periodicals in opposition to those
edited by the church boards.   In particular Eggleston recognized the increasing utility of newspapers and magazines
in proselytism and urged that even greater use be made of
such organs.[19]   At this same Red Wing conference he was
appointed a deacon and was selected as a member of the
visiting committee to Hamline University for 1861.

After his service of a year as resident minister in Stillwater, Eggleston requested that he be granted a superannuated relationship for 1861–62; consequently he was not
assigned a station and was listed instead among fifteen superannuated preachers.   It may seem odd that a man of
twenty-five should be included in a group composed of the
old and infirm, but Eggleston's health was never robust and
he expended it so recklessly that he was obliged to take
periodic rests in order to continue at all.

The years 1862 and 1863 found him in St. Paul again,
this time as pastor of the Jackson Street Methodist Church.
Eggleston returned to the capital with considerable eagerness.   He had just recovered from a long illness, his family was well, and his congregation welcomed him sincerely.
In a letter to Thomas Simpson, dated November 10, 1862,
he remarked optimistically about his position and recounted
how his parishioners had recently presented Mrs. Eggleston
with "an elegant cloak and bonnet" and himself with "a
splendid overcoat, cap, gloves & overshoes."   Moreover,
"All these articles are in about as costly a style as they could

[19] Minnesota Annual Conference of the Methodist Episcopal Church,
Minutes, 1860, p. 25, 26.

be. You can imagine that such a manifestation of kindly feeling at the beginning of my year is very grateful." In the same letter Eggleston referred to a recent visit in Winona during the annual conference of the Methodist church and commended the hospitality of the Simpsons. "As it was I lacked only you in order to [have] the highest possible enjoyment of the session. I never felt so much how pleasant a place Winona was until then. I think a year there would cure me." [20]

The Jackson Street church in St. Paul was perhaps the most important Methodist church in the state, what with a hundred and twenty members and five probationers and property valued in excess of five thousand dollars. Eggleston's own salary, his "estimated claim," was six hundred dollars. During his incumbency there was a marked increase in Sunday school activity, "Mr. Eggleston being known as a Sunday School man." He was also given the credit for having first devised the Sunday school railroad excursion. One other detail of his second St. Paul pastorate is worth recording, since it connects Eggleston as a minister with the Sioux Outbreak of 1862. On November 4 of that year he and the Reverend J. D. Pope conducted funeral services for seven members of Eggleston's congregation who had been killed in Indian campaigns. [21]

At the annual meeting of the Methodist church which was held in St. Paul in the fall of 1863, Eggleston submitted a report on the spread of Methodism among the Scandinavian populace and pointed out the fruitful field which awaited missionary activity. But he counseled great expedition lest "the ascendancy of the pure doctrines of Wesleyanism" be successfully challenged by "the effete

[20] The letter is in the Larson-Town collection, in the possession of the Minnesota Historical Society. Thomas Simpson was a prominent lawyer and banker in Winona.

[21] Hobart, *Methodism in Minnesota*, 168; Earnest C. Parish, *A Brief History of the Church Known as Market Street, Jackson Street, Central Park* (St. Paul, 1933).

superstitions of pseudo-Lutheranism." Among his recommendations to gain the desired objective were field work, added financial support, and foreign-language periodicals.[22]

At the end of his pastorate in St. Paul Eggleston again pleaded to be excused from parochial bonds because of ill health, and he was not assigned to another pastorate until the end of 1864. But meanwhile he played rather an important role in the municipal life of St. Paul. Temporarily freed from his ministerial duties he found it necessary to cast about for some other form of employment which would be remunerative without exacting so much of his vitality. Throughout 1864 he was agent for the Home Life Insurance Company; in addition he became a kind of expert showman, giving illustrated stereopticon lectures on travel or about celebrated men at various halls and churches in the Twin Cities; finally, he was instrumental in organizing a municipal free library and he served as the first public librarian in St. Paul.[23]

Various newspaper notices testify to public interest in Eggleston's stereopticon ventures. The *Saint Paul Press* of January 3, 1864, announced that Eggleston would give a display at Ingersoll's Hall, using a large canvas of 225 square feet and presenting views of Windsor Castle, Melrose Abbey, and other famous scenes. Two days later the *Press* reported that the exhibition was disappointing because the supply of gas, which Eggleston apparently manufactured himself, had leaked away and that as a consequence the projection was blurred and dim. Later in the month, however, these technical difficulties had apparently been overcome, for the *Press* of January 27 pronounced the en-

[22] Minnesota Annual Conference of the Methodist Episcopal Church, *Minutes*, 1863, p. 29.

[23] The following notice was inserted in the *Saint Paul Daily Press* and the *Saint Paul Pioneer* at intervals throughout 1863 and 1864: " Home Life Insurance Company, New York, offers the most liberal advantages to parties desiring to effect insurance." It was signed by the " Rev. Edward Eggleston, State Agent for Minnesota."

tertainment an unqualified success: "He has got his instrument in complete working order now, and it threw up the views on the canvass last night with wonderful effect, to which the spectators testified by their frequent applause." Throughout January and February Eggleston used his stereopticon to great advantage, educating and delighting his audiences at the same time.   His first displays were apparently free, but with the perfecting of the instrument he began to charge admission, twenty-five cents for adults, fifteen cents for children.   The money was presumably used to defray necessary expenses, since Eggleston showed some local views which had been specially prepared for stereopticon projection.   He even went so far as to take photographs of living celebrities, some of them local personages, and to present them to his enraptured audiences.[24]

More important than Eggleston's lecture work, however, was his effort to establish a public library.   Up to the fall of 1863 St. Paul had had no institution of the sort, although both the Mercantile Library Association and the Y.M.C.A. maintained libraries for their own members.   On October 30, however, the directors of both organizations convened in the rooms of the Ingersoll Block and formed the St. Paul Library Association.   The officers for the remainder of 1863 included D. W. Ingersoll as president, D. A. Robertson as vice president, C. E. Mayo as recording secretary, William Dawson as treasurer, and Edward Eggleston as corresponding secretary and librarian.   Shares in the new library association were valued at five dollars and businessmen were urged to contribute.   By a fusion of the resources of the older institutions, the infant library began with about a thousand volumes, and it was agreed that a lease should be taken on the Y.M.C.A. rooms on the third floor of the Ingersoll Block at Bridge Square.[25]

[24] *Press,* January 28, 31, February 4, 6, 23, 1864.
[25] E. D. Neill, *History of Ramsey County and the City of St. Paul,* 400 (Minneapolis, 1881); *Press,* October 31, 1863.

Naturally the work of organizing and unifying took some little time, but on November 11, 1863, the local papers carried the following notice anent the library:

The St. Paul library will be opened to-day. The Library and Reading Room will be kept open every day except Sunday, from 2 o'clock P. M., till 9 o'clock P. M. There are now about 2,000 volumes, and as many more will be added in the spring. After the first of January the Reading Room will be supplied with the best European and American periodicals. The payment of $2.00 per annum entitles the person paying to take books from the library under the restrictions of the By-laws, and to all the privileges of the Reading Room.

EDWARD EGGLESTON, Librarian.

Eggleston's work in directing the library and in making its facilities generally available was not unappreciated. The *Press* for December 11, 1863, remarked that the institution was progressing admirably and praised its head. "Mr. Eggleston, who has charge of the arrangement and classification of the volumes, has peculiar talents as a librarian. We wish his services may be secured permanently in that capacity." But the first librarian did not remain long at his work. Late in January another meeting of the board was held at which Eggleston was named a director, but no mention of a librarian was made in the press; and by June of 1864 E. E. Edwards had become the librarian.[26]

At the annual conference of the Methodist church in 1864 Eggleston was again assigned to a pastorate, this time in Winona, and late in the same year he began his service in his last Minnesota station. The Winona church was also an important one; its congregation numbered a hundred and sixty-five members and twenty-two probationers, and the church property was valued at four thousand dollars. The minister was paid an annual salary of eight hundred and fifty dollars and was allowed a hundred dollars for rental of the parsonage. During his residence in southern Minnesota, Eggleston figured rather prominently in community

[26] *Pioneer,* November 11, 1863; *Press,* November 11, 1863, January 21, June 8, 1864.

life. In the winter of 1866, for example, he was one of the speakers chosen to give a series of lectures at Court House Hall under the auspices of the Young Men's Library Association; among the other lecturers were Judge Arthur Mac Arthur of Milwaukee and Bishop Henry B. Whipple. Even in his strictly ecclesiastical duties, it is of interest to note, Eggleston mingled the secular with the religious, for the subject of one of his Sunday evening sermons was " The Popular Literature of the Day." At the annual church conference for 1865 he served on several committees, continuing his work on Scandinavian proselytism and helping in the commemorative services in honor of the centenary of American Methodism.[27]

Further evidence of Eggleston's energy during his Minnesota residence is his active participation in the Sanitary Fair held at Chicago in May and June of 1865. The proceeds of this exhibition were devoted to the hospitalization of Union soldiers. Early in the winter of 1865 Eggleston, who later was appointed special agent for the Northwest, urged that Minnesota citizens contribute either in money or in goods so as to make the exposition a success. On February 18 he wrote to Governor Stephen Miller from Winona, urging him to institute legislation similar to that recently enacted in Illinois so that the Minnesota exhibit would have legislative endorsement and funds. " I trust your Excellency will pardon me for burdening one so busy as yourself with so voluminous a correspondence," Eggleston remarked to the governor. " If I had one whit less confidence in your interest in the soldier's welfare I would hesitate to do it." In a second letter to Governor Miller, written from Winona on April 1, 1865, Eggleston spoke optimistically about the Sanitary Fair and noted that agricultural products were already arriving for exhibition.[28] Thus the final Minnesota

[27] *Winona Daily Republican,* January 27, 30, 1866; Minnesota Annual Conference of the Methodist Episcopal Church, *Minutes,* 1865.
[28] The letters are in the Governors' Archives, in the custody of the Minnesota Historical Society.

display in Chicago probably was to a large extent Eggleston's achievement.

Until the late spring of 1866 Eggleston remained in Winona, but then ill health compelled him to resign his pastorate. At this time, too, he severed his connections with the church militant, for he never again occupied a denominational pulpit. His later Brooklyn pastorate, from 1874 to 1879, was strictly nonsectarian. His name remained on the rolls of the Minnesota conference until 1876, first as supernumerary and later as superannuated preacher. But when he left Minnesota for Evanston, Illinois, in April of 1866 to become associate editor of the *Little Corporal,* a widely circulated juvenile paper, he definitely abandoned the ministry in favor of journalism. He did not leave Winona unheralded. According to the *Republican,* " Ill health compelled him to relinquish his ministerial profession some time ago, and seek an avocation better adapted to his feeble constitution." After noting Eggleston's new location, the paper remarked:

This is a position to which Mr. Eggleston, by virtue of his admirable talents as a writer for the young, is peculiarly adapted, and we do not doubt that he will achieve success in the path thus chosen. His many friends in this city will regret that he has determined to leave them, yet they will find frequent occasion, doubtless, to rejoice at the opportunity afforded by his new position to listen to his pleasant and entertaining contributions to the periodical literature of the day. Success attend him.[29]

---

[29] *Republican,* April 24, August 11, 1866. Eggleston was still nominally pastor of the Winona Methodist Episcopal Church as late as August 11 and probably until the annual meeting convened. On January 16, 1875, he returned to Winona to present a lecture on " The Paradise of Childhood." The following comment on his appearance is from the *Republican* of January 18: " Dr. Eggleston is a rapid and entertaining talker, thoroughly imbued with the sentiment of his lecture, which he impresses upon the minds of his auditors. It was a thoroughly satisfactory and enjoyable lecture and left much food for thought. At the close a number of his old friends pressed forward to shake him cordially by the hand and congratulate him upon his fine address." Eggleston later presented the same lecture at Mankato as one of a series given during the winter of 1874–75. It is reported in the *Mankato Weekly Record* for January 30, 1875.

In all his work Eggleston was notable for his sincerity and his enthusiasm.   Yet it was only natural that the young minister's departure from religious circles was not accepted with equanimity by his co-workers.   While according him full credit for his fervent labors and while loath to impute his resignation to mercenary motives, they nevertheless found it difficult to reconcile the writing of fiction with ministerial dignity.   Novels, even in the decade of the Civil War, were not wholly respectable, especially in a community settled at least in part by New England stock.   Thus the Reverend Cyrus Brooks, long Eggleston's colleague in the field, could praise him warmly for his brilliance and persistence but could not excise a word of blame from his tribute:

He had grand capabilities for Sunday School work, and in this field won his greenest and most enduring laurels.   It must have been for his success here, that he was made a Doctor of Divinity.   His present occupation, novel writing, seems out of harmony with the ministerial calling, and has brought upon him severe, and perhaps not wholly unmerited, censure.   But those who know him best, will be slow to believe him mercenary, or false to his convictions of right.

McKinley, more magnanimous, failed to mention Eggleston's later pursuits, but implied that it was infirmity of health only that drove him out of the ministry.[30]   It is quite obvious to any student of Eggleston, however, that he always nursed secretly the desire to write.   As a boy he experimented with type and essayed to learn the printer's trade. His early letters show distinct literary talent, and his official reports to the hierarchy of the church are couched in a style far superior to that of the average circuit rider.   No doubt circumstances drove him to literature the more quickly, but one infers that such was his destination regardless of other temporary interests.   Such a supposition is strengthened, moreover, by the apathy which Eggleston in later life experienced toward Methodism and indeed toward any regular church.   In the final result it was neither ill health nor finan-

[30] Hobart, *Methodism in Minnesota*, 232; McKinley, *Minnesota Methodism*, 65.

cial return which impelled him to letters as a profession; Eggleston would have been happy nowhere else.

Seven years after Eggleston left Minnesota he published the *Mystery of Metropolisville,* his one novel with a Minnesota setting.[31]   His purpose in this book was to sketch the land mania that had seized the people of the Northwest in 1856 and especially to portray the shyster lawyers and the land sharks who battened on the gullibility and cupidity of the immigrants.   At his town of Red Owl in the spring of that year money was worth five and six per cent per month, corner lots doubled in value overnight, and town property was estimated at a hundred dollars a front foot.   Speculation was ubiquitous.   The mushroom growth of villages and their equally sudden obsolescence—as witness Ignatius Donnelly's Nininger—Eggleston portrayed well.   His character Plausaby, moreover, had many counterparts in real life. Plausaby later became a director of the St. Paul and Big Gun River Valley Land Grant Railroad and, thus launched on a business career, entered into inflated schemes which were eventually too much even for him.   His policy was like the fashion of 1856, "to invest everything you had in first payments, and then to sell out at an advance before the second became due."   In sketching such a character Eggleston was only representing what he himself had seen on his earliest visit to Minnesota.   Thus the incident in the novel in which the citizens of Metropolisville remove the county seat from Perritaut is a fictional reworking of the events of 1855, when the county seat of Rice County, originally established at Cannon City, was removed to Faribault.[32]   The historical rivalry of the two towns is well depicted in the novel.

Even as an experienced novelist, Eggleston did not shine

[31] The *Mystery of Metropolisville* (New York, 1873) was published originally as a serial in *Hearth and Home* from December 7, 1872, through April 26, 1873.

[32] *Mystery of Metropolisville,* 153; Franklyn Curtiss-Wedge, *History of Rice and Steele Counties,* 1: 332 (Chicago, 1910).

in the construction of plots, and there is no point in recounting the episodic structure of the *Mystery of Metropolisville.* The romance which lends a specious unity to the book and the characters of the lovers are alike sentimental and conventional. His forte lay not in such matters. But as a realist Eggleston was meticulous and consistent. If his hero and his villain are stereotyped, he took great care to make the stage driver Whiskey Jim, the frontiersman from Indiana, and the speculator Plausaby good genre portraits. Scenes and incidents are likewise full of verisimilitude: the sod tavern at which the Red Owl-Metropolisville stage paused; the occasional homestead where the owner provided the traveler a breakfast of coffee, fried salt pork, and biscuits of various degrees of hardness; the midwinter sleigh ride from the Fuller House in St. Paul to the penitentiary in Stillwater with the manacled prisoner buried in furs. Vivid too is the description of early newspapers, symbolized by the *Wheat County Weakly Windmill.*

As a novel the *Mystery of Metropolisville* has the faults which Eggleston never completely eliminated from his writing — didacticism, rambling structure, characters which lack passion and blood. But as a reflection of frontier conditions it is as truthful an account of early Minnesota as the *Hoosier Schoolmaster* is of early Indiana. Eggleston was a careful observer and a skilled artist, even if an innovator, in the use of dialect. His books furnish an unsurpassed record of a way of life and of a race of people now completely departed.

Nevertheless, one novel seems a small result of nine years of strenuous life in a pioneer community. At the time of Eggleston's death the *St. Paul Dispatch* in its issue of September 5, 1902, remarked succinctly: "He stayed throughout the period of the Indian outbreak, but the event did not burn into his literary soul." The great Sioux revolt of 1862 he allowed to go unchronicled, together with other stirring events in the youth of Minnesota. Indeed, save for a few desultory references to Indians and pioneer customs, the only other fictional use Eggleston made of his residence in the upper Mississippi Valley was in a short story entitled "The Gunpowder Plot." [33]   Obviously the scenes of his boyhood, the charming village of Vevay and the forests of the Ohio, had more artistic appeal for him than the surroundings of his adopted home.   Yet it is not hard to believe that his Minnesota sojourn left an indelible imprint upon Edward Eggleston.   Restored to health by an active life in a more salubrious climate, he won wide recognition; and when he left Minnesota, mature and experienced, he was prominent throughout the state in religious, educational, and philanthropic work.[34]   Indeed it might be said that Eggleston and Minnesota grew up together.

[33] *Scribner's Magazine,* 2: 252–259 (July, 1871).   This story concerns a practical joke and a stereotyped romance, but the setting is the country near the Pomme de Terre River and the valley of the Sauk and the characters include half-breeds, Indians, and settlers.

[34] One anecdote about Eggleston as a Sunday school teacher even got into the "Editor's Drawer" of *Harper's Magazine,* 30: 400 (February, 1865).   "Rev. Mr. E—, of St. Paul, Minnesota, was inimitable as a child's orator," it reads, "and was never as we know of disconcerted in addressing the little folks but once.   He was addressing some Sunday-school scholars, and was in his usual popular and effective way enforcing the duty of gratitude to God for His blessing.   'What,' said he, 'would you say to me if I were to give each one of you a fine new suit of clothes?'   From every part of his youthful audience bright eyes twinkled with delight, and a chorus of boyish voices answered, 'Bully for you!'"

Bayard Taylor.

BAYARD TAYLOR'S MINNESOTA VISITS

WHEN BAYARD TAYLOR RETURNED from Europe in December, 1853, after two years of foreign travel which had included visits to England, Spain, India, China, and Japan, he was already recognized as one of the greatest of American travelers. Ever since he began, as a lad of nineteen, those wanderings which he later chronicled in *Views Afoot,* he had been an almost constant globe-trotter. Indeed an unkind observer once remarked that Taylor had traveled more and seen less than any man alive! Nevertheless, his fame was widespread, and on his return to the United States he was deluged with invitations to lecture and to appear in lyceum courses throughout the country. Taylor at first was hesitant about plunging into this kind of work, but those who had read his travel correspondence in the columns of the *New York Tribune* would not be denied. Moreover, Taylor had recently saddled himself with an enormous country estate, Cedarcroft, near his native Kennett in Pennsylvania. There was no better way to liquidate his debts than to mount the public rostrum, and mount the rostrum he did.

It is hard to realize today the endurance required by a popular lyceum speaker of the fifties and sixties. Lectures in all kinds of places ranging from auditoriums to dimly lighted and poorly heated barns, innumerable introductions to strangers, poor accommodations, bad food, almost incessant travel — this was the portion of Emerson, of Wendell Phillips, and particularly of Bayard Taylor. One wonders if any other lecturer of the time spoke as frequently and in as many places as did Taylor. On his first tour, which lasted from January to May, 1854, he fulfilled ninety engagements, for which he was paid fifty dollars apiece. In the nine-year period between 1858 and 1867 he spoke over six hundred times and, lest his lecturing be considered as a minor activity, found time as well to publish nine books.[1] In these extensive peregrinations, which took Taylor to almost every important city in the land, he could not well have missed Minnesota, and it is interesting to note that he paid the state three visits, in 1859, in 1871, and in 1874.

Taylor's first appearance in Minnesota was the result of his willingness to help the growth of infant libraries. In the spring of 1859 he announced that he would lecture before any literary society which would pay his expenses and a small fee (usually fifty dollars), the balance of the proceeds to be devoted to the benefit of the society which sponsored his appearance. As a result the Young Men's Christian Association of St. Paul induced Taylor to give six lectures in Minnesota, guaranteeing him three hundred dollars plus expenses. Two of these lectures were delivered in St. Paul, and one each in St. Anthony, Minneapolis, Stillwater, and Winona.[2]

Taylor arrived in St. Paul on the evening of May 21, 1859. He and his wife made the last part of their journey by steamboat and they both enjoyed greatly the voyage up the Mississippi. Taylor himself left no record of his impressions of this, his earliest visit to the Northwest, but there is an interesting description of St. Paul in the book which Marie Hansen-Taylor later wrote about her husband.

On the evening of the second day we went aboard the small steamer which was to carry us up the Mississippi to St. Paul. The trip, which occupied several days — the boat steamed between the low and sparsely settled banks of the river and past numerous small green islands — was not without its charm. . . . Saturday evening we finally arrived in St. Paul. The ten-year-old city, with its 10,000 inhabitants, rises in a series of terraces on both sides of the broad river. As in all these new towns of the West, the dwelling houses are built separately, scattered over a disproportionately large area. Here also everything is still in the rough and incomplete; it is evident that the buildings were put up in haste, and that the settlers had an eye more to business

---

[1] Albert H. Smyth, *Bayard Taylor,* 102, 178 (Boston, 1896).
[2] *Daily Pioneer and Democrat* (St. Paul), May 27, 1859.

profit than to comfort and convenience. I know of nothing more uncongenial than such a youthful city, much as I admire the courage and energy to which it owes its existence.

Mrs. Taylor concluded her account with two blunt sentences about St. Paul's neighbors to the west.

St. Anthony, not far distant, with its falls of the Mississippi reminding me of the Rhine falls at Schaffhausen, and the four-year-old town of Minneapolis across the river, are situated at the end of civilisation. North of these two places the only inhabitants are Indians, bears and wolves.[3]

Some days before the lecturer's arrival the St. Paul papers had printed announcements of his appearance as well as the subjects of his two local lectures, "Moscow" and "Life in the North." Tickets sold for fifty cents apiece, and it was understood that the net proceeds would be devoted to the library fund of the Young Men's Christian Association.[4] The *Pioneer and Democrat* of May 21 announced that Taylor would speak that evening at the First Presbyterian Church and feared that the audience might tax the capacity of the building. The paper especially solicited "the sympathy and kind forbearance of the ladies," and it respectfully requested "that their scope be made to correspond to the pressing exigencies of the occasion." The *Minnesotian* of the same date saluted Taylor in verse, the "Lines to Bayard Taylor" being written expressly for the event by a poetess who signed herself A. N. S.

> A hearty welcome we would give
> Thee and thy stranger bride;
> Thou art in all thy wanderings,
> Our country's joy and pride.

Later Taylor was apostrophized as

> A traveler with thy sandals on,
> 'Tis thus we think of thee,

[3] Marie Hansen-Taylor, *On Two Continents,* 72 (New York, 1905). Marie Hansen, daughter of a Danish mathematician, was Taylor's second wife. Mary Agnew, whom he married on October 24, 1850, died in December of the same year.

[4] *Pioneer and Democrat,* May 7, 12, 17, 18, 1859.

and was asked whether he had found any spot, in frigid or torrid zone, which he preferred to Minnesota.

Taylor's lectures in St. Paul were well attended. According to the *Daily Times* of May 25 both occasions were interesting and profitable.

Those who heard his lecture on Moscow, the once proud capital of a mighty empire, were charmed with the artistic and finished style of the lecturer, and the gorgeous manner in which he painted with words its splendor and magnificence. His lecture upon the Arctic Regions, all were delighted with, and regretted that the time passed so quickly during its delivery.

The fullest account of Taylor's first St. Paul visit appeared in the *Minnesotian* of May 23. In an editorial commenting on the lecture on Moscow the paper observed:

Mr. Taylor is not as large a man as many had been led to expect from previous descriptions. He might be called handsome; of a light complexion and somewhat browned by travel. This lecture was wisely adapted to the public requirements — preserving the proper medium between shallowness and profundity. It was made up of a perfect *melange* of facts, fancies, anecdotes, picturesque descriptions, and lively historical allusions.

Taylor's language, the *Minnesotian* remarked, was "what the women call beautiful" — in other words almost too rococo and sparkling. Yet the lecturer impressed his audience by his good sense in shaping and adapting his material, by his judicious arrangement of what he had to say, and by his pleasant delivery. The paper predicted that the lecture would live in the memory of its hearers as "a glittering, glancing, moving panorama of genius and jewels, tartars, turbans, feathers and frippery." [5]

Following his second lecture in St. Paul on May 23 Taylor went to St. Anthony, where he repeated his talk on Moscow, and to Minneapolis, where he again discussed life

[5] During Taylor's sojourn in St. Paul two local papers reprinted extracts from his writings. The *Pioneer and Democrat* of May 22 printed an article which it captioned "Bayard Taylor's Christmas Ride in Norrland." In the *Daily Times* for the same date appeared Taylor's "First Difficulties with Foreign Tongues."

in northern Europe. In both cities he was welcomed by large and enthusiastic audiences. According to the *Falls Evening News* of May 24,

Taylor is the most genial letter-writer, and resolute traveler America has ever produced, and will draw a larger audience than any other cis Atlantic contemporary. He is in demand the year round, and his presence with us at this time will be received as a most fortunate event, and improved as such a rare circumstance deserves to be.

Later the same paper remarked that Taylor lectured "for F-A-M-E — 'Fifty And My Expenses.' He speaks of St. Anthony Falls as being very grand and picturesque and as far exceeding their reputation." Taylor pleased the editor by praising the Winslow House, a hotel of which St. Anthony was justly proud.[6]

Taylor's Minneapolis appearance, at the Methodist Church on Oregon Street on the evening of May 25, has a special interest today because of the lecturer's connection with the formation of the Minneapolis Athenaeum. Earlier in the month a group of Minneapolis citizens had resolved to organize a literary association and to avail themselves of Taylor's offer to lecture. The result of this meeting was the appointment of a committee, which eventually recommended the adoption of a constitution. The Young Men's Literary Association of Minneapolis was then organized, and it adopted a constitution and elected officers. When Taylor spoke on May 25 the proceeds grossed $141.75; Taylor was paid $58.25 as fee and expenses, and the balance, $83.50, was turned over to the newly formed association, presumably for the purchase of books.[7] This was the beginning of a municipal library in Minneapolis. On the occasion of Taylor's second visit to Minnesota the *St. Paul Daily Pioneer* of July 27, 1871, recalled the lecturer's earlier visit with its literary associations. "The Athenaeum of today," it re-

[6] *Falls Evening News* (St. Anthony and Minneapolis), May 26, 1859.
[7] *Subject Catalogue of the Minneapolis Athenaeum Library,* iii (Minneapolis, 1884).

marked, "is the harvest that has been gathered from the seed planted at that time."

Twelve years elapsed before Taylor returned to Minnesota, this time not as a lecturer but as a journalist and reporter. In the interim he had visited England and Germany, he had acted as secretary of the legation at St. Petersburg, he had seen Switzerland and the Italian lakes. In addition he had dabbled as a war correspondent, had delivered lectures on German literature at Cornell University, and had covered most of California on a return speaking tour. In the summer of 1871, Taylor once more interrupted his literary work (he was then engaged on the second part of his great translation of *Faust*) to acccept a newspaper commission. At that time the financier Jay Cooke was deeply interested in the construction of the Northern Pacific Railroad, and his house was attempting to float first mortgage gold bonds to finance the work.[8] If the railroad was to be built, it was necessary to win the interest and confidence of the public. Cooke, as a consequence, organized a journalistic tour which included representatives of the leading newspapers of the country and which was planned to acquaint the travelers with the terrain which the new railroad would exploit. Taylor, of course, represented the *New York Tribune*.

The itinerary of the "editorial excursionists," as the party was soon dubbed, included a boat trip from Buffalo to Duluth, then a rail journey to the Twin Cities, and a combined rail, stagecoach, and steamboat excursion to Winnipeg and Fort Garry. Taylor recorded his experiences in a series of eight fascinating letters to the *New York Tribune,* running at intervals through August, 1871, and captioned "The North-West."

[8] For a typical advertisement see the *New York Tribune,* July 19, 1871, in which the bonds are announced as redeemable in gold and secured by a first and only mortgage on the entire road and its equipment, as well as on twenty-three thousand acres of land for every mile of road completed. The bonds were also announced as tax exempt.

The journalists reached Duluth on July 20 on the steamer "R. G. Coburn" after having seen Isle Royale and Thunder Cape en route. Taylor was greatly impressed by the grandiose scenery of the North Shore of Lake Superior, which he compared to the fjords and pinnacles of the Norwegian coast. Duluth also interested him, although he spoke contemptuously of the new epithet which the town's ambitious citizens had recently adopted: "The Zenith City of the Unsalted Seas"![9] "One would think that life was too short, and American nature too practical, for such a phrase; but there it is." But he observed that Duluth had a royal situation; "her houses are so lifted by the slope that they all show, and the first impression is that of a larger place." He praised his hotel for its elegance and comfort, and declared that the city had accomplished a great deal in three short years. Already it was a town of four thousand people, with spacious streets, five churches, and a daily train and steamboat. "When the hideous burnt forests around it shall have been cut away, the ground smoothed, cleaned, and cultivated, and gardens shall have forced the climate to permit their existence," Taylor predicted, Duluth "will be one of the most charming towns in the North-West." He observed the shortage of arable land but prophesied a future prosperity dependent on the slate and granite quarries, the iron mines, and the wheat fields of the Red River Valley. Already that year, he reported, Duluth had shipped half a million bushels of wheat. Railroad connections would amplify and cement this activity.[10]

The citizens of Duluth did not neglect the opportunity to impress their visitors. The journalists were entertained at "a charming hop in their honor . . . gotten up at the Clark House," were regaled with a "splendid supper and dance at the same place," and were taken for a steamboat

[9] *New York Tribune,* July 29, 1871. The epithet is said to have been used first by Dr. Thomas Foster in a speech delivered July 4, 1868. See *Duluth News-Tribune,* July 4, 1937.

[10] *New York Tribune,* August 5, 1871.

excursion around the bay and over to Superior; while for
those who preferred angling there was a fishing expedition
along the shore to Knife and French rivers.   A grand banquet was given with the mayor presiding and Colonel
Charles H. Graves acting as toastmaster.   Taylor, one of
several speakers, chose the sentiment "Round the World."
On the morning of July 22 the party left Duluth for the
Twin Cities, a group of local celebrities escorting the journalists some sixty miles.[11]

The Lake Superior and Mississippi Railroad followed
for some distance the course of the St. Louis River, which
so interested Taylor that he and Dana rode in the cab of
the locomotive.   The dalles, he observed, provided "the
first approach to really fine scenery which we have yet
found."   The narrow river valley soon was transformed
into a gorge, the rapids becoming cataracts and the dark
brown water itself altering to an amber foam.   But from
Thomson onward the country grew poor and ugly.   "Mile
after mile of ragged, ugly, stunted forest," Taylor reported,
"standing in its own rot and ruin, only varied, now and then,
by reedy, stagnant-looking pools or lakes, which had the
effect of blasting the trees nearest to them."   After eighty
miles of this the members of the editorial party reached the
division point of Sicoots, where they were entertained at
lunch by Colonel D. C. Lindsley, chief engineer of the
Northern Pacific Railroad.   The afternoon journey Taylor
found less diverting than the morning travel, although he
observed that in the vicinity of Hinckley the pineries of the
St. Croix began to fade until they were replaced by open,
slightly rolling agricultural country.   Dusk overtook the
travelers near Wyoming so that the approach to the Twin
Cities was utterly obscured, but Taylor was quick to discern
a change in the settlements which he had not seen for twelve
years.[12]

[11] *Duluth Daily Herald, Duluth Minnesotian,* July 22, 1871.
[12] *New York Tribune,* August 16, 1871; *Pioneer,* July 23, 1871.

In St. Paul, he wrote,

We were installed in a hotel [*Metropolitan Hotel*] of metropolitan proportions and character; the streets had become massive and permanent in appearance; the ragged-looking, semi-savage suburbs were wonderfully transformed into sumptuous residences and gardens — in short, St. Paul seemed to be not only fifty years older, but to have been removed three degrees further south.   Its former bleak, Northern aspect had entirely vanished.

Everywhere the traveler observed smooth lawns, pleasant foliage.   In Minneapolis he found to his inextinguishable regret that the beautiful Falls of St. Anthony had been sacrificed to business.   Sight-seeing occupied much of the visitors' time, and Taylor was shown among other spectacles Minnehaha Falls and Colonel William S. King's farm with its famous blooded stock.   He was not greatly impressed by the former, commenting on the fact that its commercial possibilities had not been realized.   But, he reasoned,

After a while Minneapolis will stretch down in that direction, and the gorge will be filled up by an immense manufacturing establishment, with the cascade driving its huge wheels.   Minnehaha is the luckiest waterfall in the world; it has achieved more renown on a smaller capital of performance than any other I ever saw.   Norway has a thousand nameless falls of greater height and beauty; Ithaca, New-York, has two-score, only locally known; but this pretty, unpretending tumble of less than a hundred feet is celebrated all over the world.

The Twin Cities, he asserted, were natural and bitter rivals and would continue to be so because of their proximity to each other until one or the other gained an insurmountable ascendancy.   Taylor did not predict when that time would be or which city would triumph, but he did add one blunt remark: "There is certainly more industry in Minneapolis, and more wealth in St. Paul — more life in the former, more comfort in the latter."   He closed his third *Tribune* letter with praise for the Nicollet House, both for its furnishings and for its food, and with a reference to a dinner and a serenade which the visitors had been tendered.[13]

[13] *New York Tribune,* August 16, 1871.

The morning of July 25 the "editorial excursionists" set out for Fort Garry, a special train conveying them over the St. Paul and Pacific Railroad as far as Morris; from Morris they traveled via stagecoach to Pomme de Terre and thence to Nolan's Tavern, opposite Fort Abercrombie on the Red River. Taylor was immensely pleased and perhaps a bit surprised by the farm land adjoining the Twin Cities.

The belt of carefully-farmed country around Minneapolis is still narrow, but it has all the charm of an older region. The tracts of timber are constantly interrupted by little lakes, from one to three miles in extent; and it is remarkable how a farm-house and a few grain fields give to each of these an air of long-established cultivation and comfort. Lake Minnetonka, 15 or 20 miles from Minneapolis, is a charming sheet of water, about 25 miles long, but with so many indented arms and bays that it has a shore line of nearly 200 miles. There is here a Summer hotel, a little propellor for excursions, and a few sail-boats for fishing parties.

Farther on he noticed that the country grew wilder and more lonely. Farmers were cutting meadow grass for hay, the dry season making the practice profitable. The travelers, speeding along at thirty miles per hour, did not find the trip monotonous but instead enjoyed the varying shades of green and the undulations of the land. "After a number of first faint efforts at towns," Taylor wrote, "we reached Litchfield, aged two years, and already grown into some large frame buildings, an elegant hotel, and $600 lots." He praised the Scandinavians for the readiness with which they adapted themselves to strange conditions and he thought that the country through which he traveled bore a distinct resemblance to the valley of the Platte in central Nebraska. The town of Benson proved to be only a cluster of houses, while Morris, the temporary end of the railroad, was a mere six months old and had many of the earmarks of a portable community. At Morris, where it was necessary to shift to stagecoaches, a considerable redistribution of personal effects was made; and Taylor commented on the changed appearance and the lightened luggage of the travelers. Flannel replaced boiled shirts, sardines and crackers and cigars peeped out from convenient crannies, and fowling pieces were everywhere visible.

The coach ride was at first not unpleasant. Taylor compared the terrain with southern Nebraska, which it fully equaled in richness; in addition it boasted "numberless little lakes, bright, lonely tarns, generally with a timbered bluff on the northern side. All the most attractive situations are being rapidly claimed by settlers." But Taylor remembered Pomme de Terre only for its filth and soot and for the clouds of pestiferous mosquitoes. The stage journey was brought to an end at the banks of the Red River. Across from the travelers loomed Fort Abercrombie, with adjacent Indian lodges silhouetted against the crimson sunset. Even for a man who had seen the Orient the scene was impressive. Taylor was romantic enough not to forget the beauty of the prairie contrast.[14]

At Fort Abercrombie Taylor and his party were welcomed warmly by the officers and were conducted officially around the post. But the correspondent was obviously more interested in the settlers moving rapidly into the new country than he was in the garrison. For one who had been with Commodore Perry in Japan, sailors and soldiers were hardly a novel spectacle. Taylor observed that the tides of immigration were already sweeping in over the great fertile plain of western Minnesota. Between Brainerd and the Red River he estimated that there were thirty thousand people established on the land, and he repeated the comment made to him by a native that in one day twelve hundred wagons had been seen, all bound for the vicinity of Detroit Lakes. Twenty-five miles beyond Fort Abercrombie the party stopped at the hut of a Norwegian settler who had recently augmented his original cabin. "He has laid in a good stock of prairie hay for the Winter," Taylor reported, "but his agriculture is still scanty. He came to the

[14] *New York Tribune,* August 16, 1871.

place between two and three years ago, with $60 in his
pocket, and has already been offered $2,000 for his prop-
erty.   Like every Scandinavian whom I have met in this
region, he is perfectly contented, and prefers the new home
to the old."   But not all the white inhabitants of the country seemed as worthy and as honest.   Before entering Oak
Port, a temporary camp settled mainly by gamblers and
prostitutes, the journalists examined the priming of their
revolvers and loosened the pistols in their holsters.   The
settlement itself proved far less dangerous than they had
anticipated, but later Taylor remembered unpleasantly one
visible sign of barbarism: a man whose ear had been chewed
off in a fight and who kept the loose fragment joined to the
side of his head by a piece of court plaster.[15]

From Frog Point, the head of navigation on the Red
River during periods of low water, to Fort Garry was a distance of four hundred water miles; and Taylor voiced his
surprise at the meandering stream which was to supply the
final route to his destination.   The Red River he found to
be "a deep, swift river, about 70 feet wide, winding between sloping banks of verdure, and elms so old and spread-
ing that their branches almost meet above the water."   But
a little later he was amazed at the shallowness of the stream
and he complained that although the "Selkirk," the little
boat on which his party traveled, drew only two feet of
water, it was in frequent danger of going aground.   Taylor's description of the luxuriant vegetation calls to mind
Chateaubriand's fanciful picture of the Mississippi which he
never saw.

An unbroken mantle of willow and hazel, knotted together with wild
convolvulus and ivy, enveloped both banks down to the water; behind
this foliage stood large, scattering elms, ash and box-elder; and all
were mixed together in such a tangle of riotous growth that we could
well have believed the stream to be the Red River of Louisiana.   The
current was so swift, and the bends so sharp and frequent, that the
steamer was continually bumping against one or the other bank, and

[15] *New York Tribune,* August 17, 1871.

the sun seemed to perform a rapid dance around all quarters of the sky.[16]

After the first shock of surprise, however, the novelty wore away, and Taylor and his companions found the slow voyage to Manitoba rather fatiguing. The fowling pieces laboriously carried this far soon came into play and the travelers shot from the deck at hawks, ducks, owls, pigeons, usually with no great execution. Along the lower reaches of the river, cabins were seldom seen and even the solitary canoe of Indian or voyageur seldom dotted the surface. At Fort Pembina the party was received by the commandant. But Taylor was sadly disappointed by the town of Pembina itself, a straggling, unkempt community of two hundred Chippewa, half-breeds, and soldiers. He found no habitations other than filthy log huts and scant signs of farming or gardening. With the buffalo already three hundred miles westward, he speculated on the food supply of these improvident idlers. The climate he claimed was little different from that of St. Paul, the people were generally enthusiastic about their new home, and if the land seemed deadly monotonous, the monotony was at least fertile! Taylor closed his fifth letter to the *Tribune* with a series of antitheses. Northwestern winters were long and hard like those of Norway, but the land gave signs of growing a plenitude of wheat. Timber was unfortunately wanting, but the soil produced the finest potatoes in the world. Moreover, he gloated with all the zeal for exploitation of Jay Cooke himself, the country was easily accessible by a railroad. "Therefore, it verily hath a future"!

Along the Manitoba shores Taylor saw nothing but half-breeds, who failed to impress him. "Their dark faces, long black hair, gay blankets, and general aspect of dirt and laziness promise nothing for the speedy civilization of the

[16] Taylor's account squares perfectly with the navigation notes made by Eggleston and Thoreau some years earlier on the Red and Minnesota rivers, respectively.

region." Indeed in every way save in their attachment to the soil they resembled the Indians whose blood they shared. Despite the widening of the stream, the "Selkirk" still experienced difficulty in its progress toward Fort Garry, and Taylor again complained of the obstacles confronting navigation. "On approaching a rapid, it was next to impossible to keep her head to the one practicable channel: we grounded at the bow, grounded at the stern, ran against the banks, swung around, ran up stream, swung again, bumped over the rolling bowlders in the river-bed, and so worked our painful way along." Eventually, however, the party reached St. Boniface (like New France, Taylor thought), then Fort Garry and Winnipeg. At this Manitoban village of six hundred souls they were welcomed by the American consul, James W. "Saskatchewan" Taylor, and by a host of citizens eager to fete the visitors. But there was an unpleasant side to the arrival too, since the excitement of the Riel rebellion had only partly subsided, and the settlers tried in vain to mob the attorney general of the province, who had been a passenger on the "Selkirk." Taylor, unfamiliar with the grievances of the métis, expressed his bewilderment at the situation.[17]

During their brief stay, the Americans visited Adams G. Archibald, governor of Manitoba, and Bishop Alexandre Antonin Taché of St. Boniface; they also made a short exploratory trip up the Assiniboine River, a trip which convinced Taylor that the prairie provinces could grow wheat. Indeed he grew so eulogistic about the agricultural possibilities that he deprecated the climatic dangers. He admitted that in winter the extreme cold sometimes touched a temperature of forty degrees below zero, but he claimed that the air was pure and dry and that the snowfall rarely exceeded two feet. Autumn, furthermore, was a delightful season. Indeed, he opined,

[17] *New York Tribune,* August 17, 1871.

Minnesota, Dakota, and Manitoba only require a bridge here and there, and their natural grading does the rest. The rich soil everywhere will carry settlement along as fast as the roads can be built; and it is a very safe prediction to say that some of our party may yet ride in a Pullman car to Slave Lake.[18]

The railroads that Taylor envisaged have since spread their steel web well over the western prairies, and the grassland states have become as he partly foresaw the granary of the nation; but unfortunately even after the lapse of almost seventy years it is still impossible to travel in a Pullman to Slave Lake. And after the economic disappointment of The Pas-Churchill Railroad one must be bold indeed to presage any such rail connection in the immediate future. Yet in the main Taylor's enthusiasm has been vindicated; certainly he was too faithful a reporter to become merely the publicist for Jay Cooke and Company's bonds.

The return up the Red River was a mere repetition of the downward trip with few innovations to prevent boredom. The party detoured slightly so as to visit Oak Lake, Pelican Lake, and Fergus Falls (then a year old, with eighty houses, a newspaper, a sawmill, and a flour mill in prospect) before returning to Morris to board the train. Some of the travelers were enthusiastic about the lake scenery which they had diverged from their itinerary to see, but Taylor's comments are petulant and reveal weariness. In particular he protested against the use of classic names for frontier beauty spots. "A little pond near St. Paul is called 'Como,' from its total unlikeness, let us hope. So a cluster of shanties is called Constantinople, and a miserable station where the refreshments are a lingering death, Paris." [19]

Taylor was obviously glad to return to civilization. Great traveler that he was, the privations of the western frontier and the slow river boats vexed him considerably, and he was eager to be done with this whole western inter-

[18] *New York Tribune,* August 23, 1871.
[19] *New York Tribune,* August 30, 1871.

lude. On Thursday afternoon, August 10, 1871, the citizens of St. Paul gave a grand dinner for the visitors, among the guests being Henry H. Sibley and Governor Horace Austin. The "collation," said the *Pioneer* of August 11, included "peaches, pears, apples and grapes, in abundance." The speeches were as numerous as the fruits and were duly reported by the local newspapers, but Taylor was conspicuously absent. On the morning of August 11, almost before his fellow travelers had left the Twin Cities, he was in Chicago eager to return to Cedarcroft and his family.

Taylor's final Minnesota visit, on one of his last lecture tours, came in the fall of 1874. The preceding winter and spring he had spent in Europe, chiefly in Italy and Germany with a short excursion into Egypt. Then, on the request of Whitelaw Reid of the *Tribune,* he had gone to Iceland to write a series of letters dealing with the millennial celebration of the settling of the island. Early in September he was in America once more, his head buzzing with literary plans. But, as usual, he found it necessary to earn some ready cash before he could execute any of his projects. Once more then he turned to lecturing.[20] This tour began on October 20, 1874, and lasted with intermittent pauses until the middle of the following April. Taylor spoke in many of the middle-western cities and at least four times in Minnesota. His subject was invariably "Ancient Egypt."

The *Pioneer* enthusiastically announced the return of the "greatest traveler and lecturer of modern times" and declared that no person of intelligence would want to miss "his finished and instructive lecture." Taylor was to speak on Thanksgiving Day, and the *Pioneer* of that morning reminded its readers of the double treat in store for them: the turkey and the lecture. The *Press* took a similar attitude. "Everybody is acquainted with Bayard Taylor's writ-

[20] Marie Hansen-Taylor and Horace E. Scudder, *Life and Letters of Bayard Taylor,* 2: 652, 655–657 (Boston, 1885).

ings, but it is worth while to *see and hear talk* one who writes
so much and so well." [21]

Taylor's talk was delivered in the Opera House.   H. Knox
Taylor, who introduced him, reminded the audience that the
lecturer had been one of the earliest friends of the St. Paul
Library Association and that he had been the organization's
first speaker fifteen years before.   Since his last appearance
in St. Paul, the *Press* reported, Bayard Taylor had become
more rotund and obviously grayer; but his enunciation was
clear and distinct, and for an hour and a half he captivated
his audience by his review of discoveries among the ruins of
ancient Egypt.   The *Dispatch* was much more explicit.

His forehead is high, his complexion florid, his nose aquiline.   He
wears a moustache, whiskers upon his chin and spectacles upon his
nose.   He talks he doesn't lecture.   His manner is easy, graceful and
refined.   He speaks with an evident familiarity with his text and
carries his hearers to the scene of his remarks in an irresistible manner, making in all one of the most charming and interesting lecturers
before the public.

Taylor's lecture, according to the *Dispatch,* was entertaining and instructive.   His thesis apparently was that ancient
Egypt provided the genesis of religion, morals, and art, and
in exposition of that thesis he touched on many facets of
Egyptology: Champolion and the Rosetta stone, domestic
life, mythology, literature, Moses, and the Hebrew captivity.
"The speaker closed with a fine apostrophe to the spirit of
progress and research which now animates the thinking
world." [22]

The day following his St. Paul address, on November 27,
Taylor repeated his lecture in Minneapolis, before eight
hundred people at the Academy of Music.   The *Tribune*
praised the lecturer highly for his concise and orderly arrangement and for his interesting delivery.   "Mr. Taylor
is a very clear, impressive speaker, and passages of his lec-

[21] *Pioneer,* November 22, 26, 1874; *Press,* November 26, 1874.
[22] See the issues of the *Press,* the *Dispatch,* and the *Pioneer* for November 28, 1874.

ture were full of natural eloquence. His audience was delighted with the rich, scholarly treat he presented." Before leaving the state he delivered his talk on Egypt in two southern Minnesota towns, Mankato on November 28, and Faribault on November 30. According to the *Faribault Republican* of December 2, "He has the appearance of one who enjoys life, and could relish a hearty meal. He has a very pleasant and happy style of delivery, and held the attention of his audience very closely throughout." Taylor's address was so successful that the Reading Room Association, which sponsored his appearance, cleared nearly a hundred dollars.[23] In an interesting letter which he wrote to Martha Kimber from Mankato on November 29, Taylor pictured himself in southern Minnesota "on the borders of civilization, on a still, sunny day, and temperature at zero."

He told his correspondent that his audiences were larger than ever before and that his fees averaged a hundred and ten dollars an engagement. Nevertheless, he expressed his dissatisfaction with hot cars, cold rooms, bad dinners, committees, and autograph seekers, the bane of any lecturer's life.[24]

At the completion of the lecture tour of 1874–75 Taylor returned to the East to resume his literary work. His labor in translating *Faust* had stirred in him the desire to write biographies of Goethe and Schiller, and he was already collecting material. For a short time the gods smiled on him, and when he was appointed minister to Germany in February, 1878, he could hardly realize his good fortune. But he had spent his energy carelessly; as correspondent, lec-

[23] *Minneapolis Tribune*, November 28, 1874; *Mankato Weekly Record*, December 5, 1874; *Review* (Mankato), November 24, 1874; *Press*, December 5, 1874.

[24] John R. Schultz, ed., *Unpublished Letters of Bayard Taylor in the Huntington Library*, 183 (San Marino, 1937). In Mankato Taylor met the son of the poet Ferdinand Freiligrath, whom he had known years before in Germany. Writing to his wife, he remarked: "He is settled here as a fur-trader and seems to be doing well. He is quite handsome, remarkably like his father." Hansen-Taylor, *On Two Continents*, 256.

turer, and author he had been indefatigable; and when the crowning honor of his life came his health failed.   During the summer and early fall of 1878 he was able to fulfill his duties, but disease slowly sapped his vitality, and on December 19 he died, crying out almost in his last breath, "I want, oh, you know what I mean, that *stuff of life!*" [25]

Little is left today of the fame that was once Bayard Taylor's.   His numerous books have survived only in libraries, his poetry and his fiction have been forgotten, his name no longer connotes cosmopolitanism.   For his great translation of *Faust* alone he is remembered, and carping critics have objected even here to his retention of the original meters in his version of Goethe's dramatic poem.   In general Taylor's contemporaries thought well of him, but even in his own day voices were raised objecting to his superficiality.   Surely the author of the obituary in the *Pioneer Press* of December 20, 1878, showed remarkable discernment and literary taste.   Pointing out Taylor's versatility, he expressed his regret that the life of Goethe was never completed, for he professed to find little among Taylor's productions that bore the stamp of durability.   Indeed, "Mr. Taylor's literary work has not been that of a creative character.   His travels are newspaper letters, his novels commonplace and his poems ephemeral.   His critical faculty was above his creative, and he was greater as an interpreter of thought than as a thinker."

What, then, gave Taylor his pre-eminent reputation as a lecturer?   In the first place, he was a capable reporter; he saw things clearly and in their true perspective, and he sketched them vividly.   Secondly, Taylor was a romanticist on a perpetual tour of the world; he had no ax to grind, he was not interested in politics, he sought chiefly the exotic and the novel.   In the third place, he had a flair for descriptive language.   He could picture clearly and freshly the

[25] Hansen-Taylor and Scudder, *Life and Letters of Bayard Taylor,* 2:765.

scenes he had viewed, and he could impart details of costume, accounts of strange foods or domestic habits, with little or no loss of verisimilitude. Finally, those of us who depend entirely on the motion picture for our knowledge of foreign lands and people can scarcely realize what a travel lecture meant to a community deprived of intimate contact with other nations. Taylor and his ilk brought the bizarre and the romantic close to home. His present obscurity is not to be deprecated. He fulfilled his function in his own time and his books have since lost their vitality. But life in the sixties and seventies would have been much more insular without the contact with foreign cultures which he provided.

Henry D. Thoreau.

THOREAU IN MINNESOTA[1]

In 1861, a short year before his death, Henry David Thoreau was already a sick man. A certain consumptive tendency, no doubt inherited from his grandfather, had become less and less dormant; and the disdain for weather and exposure which Thoreau had evinced for years had resulted in a dread affliction of the legs and lungs. Contrary to general belief, Thoreau was not possessed of a strong constitution. His walking feats, his mountain bivouacs, and his rigorous outdoor life are to be attributed more to an iron will which scorned fatigue than to a naturally tireless physique.

As a result of Thoreau's illness, his physician advised him early in 1861 to see what a change of climate would do for him. For once the patient was tractable and consented. At first he desired Ellery Channing, an old Concord friend and companion on many a long ramble, to accompany him on a journey to the West. Channing had lived on the Illinois prairie and could have given Thoreau valuable information about the mode of western life. But Channing was unable to go, and as a result Thoreau chose as a companion Horace Mann, Jr., a son of the distinguished educator and a botanist in his own right. In the early part of May these two departed from Concord on the long trek westward, planning to make their journey by easy stages.[2]

From a letter to Harrison Blake of Worcester, written by Thoreau barely a week before the departure, one may sketch the itinerary of the two travelers. After stating that

[1] A paper read at the afternoon session of the eighty-sixth annual meeting of the Minnesota Historical Society on January 21, 1935, in the Historical Building, St. Paul. *Ed.*

[2] Annie R. Marble, *Thoreau: His Home, Friends and Books,* 174 (New York, 1902); Franklin B. Sanborn, *Henry D. Thoreau,* 310 (Boston, 1882); H. S. Salt, *Life of Henry David Thoreau,* 202 (London, 1890).

"it will be most expedient for me to try the air of Minnesota, say somewhere about St. Paul's," Thoreau wrote that
he planned to purchase a through ticket to Chicago with
stop-over privileges, as he was especially eager to break
his journey at Niagara Falls and Detroit. From Chicago
he meant to strike west to Dunleith on the Mississippi, and
thence go by boat to St. Paul. On May 11, 1861, he left
Concord with about a hundred and fifty dollars in his
pocket and personal equipment consisting of such traveling
accessories as "a half-thick coat, a thin coat, 'best pants,'
three shirts, a flannel shirt, three pairs of socks, slippers,
underclothing, five handkerchiefs, a waistcoat, towel and
soap." [3]   Nor must one forget the indispensable equipment
of the naturalist: spy glass, notebook, measuring tape, botanical manual, in fact all the paraphernalia which made
Thoreau's pockets bulge as he rambled around Concord.

Various notations in Thoreau's journals indicate the stops
that the naturalist and Mann made, as well as the impressions they received of the western towns which both saw
for the first time. Thoreau, for example, noted the scenery
about Schenectady and along the Mohawk, the rumble and
spray of Niagara, and the flowers on Goat Island. Chicago, he observed, "is built chiefly of limestone from 40
miles southwest. Lake Street is the chief business one.
The water is milky." In northwest Illinois Thoreau first
saw the prairie, and on May 23 at Dunleith he watched the
great flood of the Mississippi as it swept southward. The
following day he embarked for St. Paul. [4]

The traffic on the Mississippi interested Thoreau tremen-
dously. The navigable part of the stream was some sixty
rods wide, but the valley between the bluffs stretched for al-

[3] Franklin B. Sanborn, ed., *Familiar Letters of Henry David Thoreau*,
444 (Boston, 1894), and *The First and Last Journeys of Thoreau*,
2: 108 (Boston, 1905). Dunleith is now known as East Dubuque,
Illinois.
   [4] Franklin B. Sanborn, *The Life of Henry David Thoreau*, 396
(Boston, 1917).

most a mile. Thoreau observed few boats, but he saw many huge lumber rafts floating quietly down the current. Passengers disembarked from the steamer by means of planks thrown toward the shore, and at the various landings men piled cords of wood on the deck.[5] His description of a river town is particularly vivid:

The steamer approaching whistles, then strikes a bell about six times funereally, with a pause after the third bell; and then you see the whole village making haste to the landing, — commonly the raw, stony, or sandy shore, — the post-master with his mailbag, the passenger, and almost every dog and pig in the town. That is commonly one narrow street and back-yards, at an angle of about forty-five degrees with the horizon. If there is more flat space between the water and the bluff, it is almost sure to be occupied by a flourishing and larger town.

About the only larger town that impressed Thoreau was Prairie du Chien, which he reached on May 24. This he termed "the smartest town on the river," and added that "it exports the most wheat of any town between St. Paul and St. Louis. There is wheat in sacks, great heaps of them, at Prairie du Chien, — covered at night, and all on the ground."[6] On the twenty-fifth he saw La Crosse and on May 26 he reached St. Paul. The capital city apparently did not impress Thoreau greatly, for after breakfasting at the principal hostelry, the American House, he took stage for St. Anthony. "At St. Paul," he observed, "they dig their building stone out of the cellar; but it is apparently poor stuff." He also noted that wood sold for from three to four dollars a cord.[7]

The following two weeks Thoreau spent in and around St. Anthony and Minneapolis, largely in the company of the

[5] Sanborn, *Life of Thoreau*, 397.
[6] *Journeys*, 2: 25, 27.
[7] *Journeys*, 2: 28. The American House is advertised in the *Pioneer and Democrat* (St. Paul) for May 8, 1861, as follows: "This popular Hotel has long since passed the period when a 'puff' could add to its reputation. All that is necessary to satisfy one's mind that Mr. Spencer 'knows how to keep a hotel' is to take a seat, at his table, or look into his sleeping rooms."

state geologist, Dr. Charles L. Anderson. Together they roamed through the woods and around the shores of Lake Calhoun, botanizing and culling specimens of plant and animal life. Near Minnehaha Falls Thoreau saw the rosebreasted grosbeak eating the seeds of the slippery elm, and on the edge of Lake Harriet he stumbled across the nest of a wild pigeon. Of the flowers he found on Nicollet Island he made a long list in botanical Latin. The birds he was able to identify included among the more common species the pewee, redstart, catbird, goldfinch, oriole, tanager, horned lark, flicker, and killdeer. Rattlesnakes were visible in the small stretches of prairie. But chiefly appealing to the naturalist in Thoreau were the wild crab apple and the prairie gopher, or spermophile, both of which had hitherto been beyond the pale of his experience. Only after much diligent and careful search was Thoreau able to find the crab apple, but the gopher became very familiar to him. His description of the animal which was to become the symbol of the state of Minnesota is meticulously vivid:

Dirty grayish-white beneath, — above, dirty brown, with six dirty, tawny or clay-colored, very light-brown lines, alternating with broad, dark-brown lines or stripes (three times as broad), — the last having an interrupted line or square spot of the same color with the first-mentioned, running down their middle; reminding me of the rude pattern of some Indian work, — porcupine quills, "gopher-work" in baskets and pottery.[8]

It is obvious that Thoreau viewed the settlements along the upper Mississippi not as hamlets struggling to achieve fame and prosperity, but as happy hunting grounds for a naturalist and wanderer who had hitherto been limited to a different terrain with other flora and fauna. More interested in the wild pigeon, the basswood, and the hyssop than in the strange wild life of the primitive civilization that surrounded him, he practically ignored the traders, soldiers, pioneer settlers, and Indians of the region, and contented

[8] Sanborn, *Life of Thoreau*, 402–409; *Journeys*, 2: 29–37.

himself with a persistent survey of that tangled region of woods and marshes which has since become a prominent residential district of Minneapolis. Yet despite his preoccupation with the things of the naturalist, Thoreau did jot down a few comments on the white man's life around him, comments which reveal a pleasing sharpness of perception.

He noticed that both the Mississippi and the Minnesota rivers were high, and that at the angle of the two streams rose the "tawny or butterish" limestone walls of Fort Snelling. "The government buildings are handsome," he remarked. The University of Minnesota, he averred, "is set in the midst of . . . an oak opening, and it looks quite artificial." As for the towns at the Falls of St. Anthony, he noted that "St. Anthony was settled about 1847; Minneapolis in 1851. Its main streets are the unaltered prairie, with bur and other oaks left standing." Eighteen or nineteen years earlier, he declared, the mill occupied the main position; at the time of his visit Minneapolis boasted five drugstores.[9]

The one event of Thoreau's Minnesota sojourn, however, which compelled him to observe carefully the people and the country, since it deprived him of the opportunity to ramble in the woods, was a trip up the Minnesota River to the Redwood agency, the scene of a payment of annuities to the Sioux Indians. This trip was a gala affair in the annals of the frontier communities, long prepared for and invested with much factitious brilliance. For days before the departure of the boats for the agency, the local papers carried announcements in rather florid terms. On June 12, 1861, the *Pioneer and Democrat* of St. Paul informed its readers that on the following Monday an excursion up the river would take place and that several thousand Indians would be assembled at the agency. "We would inform strangers who

[9] *Journeys,* 2: 32, 37, 41, 42.

may be amongst us that this excursion will give them a better opportunity of seeing wild, frontier life, and the sports
of the red men than they could otherwise have.   There will
doubtless be a large attendance from this city."   And four
days later the same paper declared with a bold flourish:
"HO! FOR THE PAYMENT!—Remember that the Frank
Steele and Favorite leave for Red Wood, at 4 o'clock, on
Monday afternoon, accompanied with the Great Western
Band, and a bevy of beautiful ladies and brave men."   But
perhaps the peak of the enthusiasm was reached by a writer
in the Minneapolis *State Atlas* of July 3, who described the
party on the "Frank Steele":

> We had a very choice and select company, among whom were Gov.
> and Mrs. Ramsey . . . Horace Mann, Jun., son of the lamented
> statesman, Samuel May, Esq., Henry D. Thoreau, Esq. the celebrated
> abolitionist, &c.—there being about 25 or 30 ladies.   It is very
> rarely that an excursion party is assembled combining such a degree
> of sociability, refinement, intelligence and culture as this.   It was, in
> fact, composed mainly of the *creme de la creme*—the rich yellow
> skim from the mottled milk of frontier society.   In all the trip, I
> heard hardly one profane or boisterous word, and did not see one
> rude loafer, nor one tipsy man.

This quotation is of special importance since, so far as the
writer knows, it is the only direct reference to Thoreau
made by the Minnesota press.   With this solitary exception,
the journalists of St. Paul, St. Anthony, and Minneapolis
were apparently ignorant of the fact that a "celebrated
abolitionist" was in their midst.

On June 17 the "Frank Steele" started up the Minnesota River for the Redwood agency, carrying Governor
Ramsey, Thoreau, the Indian agents, and a German band
from St. Paul, also "a small cannon for salutes, and the
money for the Indians (ay, and the gamblers, it was said,
who were to bring it back in another boat)."[10]   Thoreau's
comments on the trip are of special interest today since they
indicate vividly the importance and kind of navigation that

[10] Thoreau, *Familiar Letters,* 451.

was common on the Minnesota when drouth had not shrunk the river to a pitiful skeleton of its earlier magnitude; and they also reveal the quickness of an eye which had hitherto been focused largely on the streams of New England. The Minnesota River, Thoreau said in a letter to Frank Sanborn, "flows through a very fertile country, destined to be famous for its wheat; but it is a remarkably winding stream, so that Redwood is only half as far from its mouth by land as by water." He observed that in the whole distance covered by the boat there was not a straight reach of water a mile in length; as a consequence, "the boat was steadily turning this way or that." At some of the bends, indeed, it was customary for the passengers to alight and walk over the intervening land, as more than one isthmus measured only a stone's throw in width but two or three miles around.[11]

To one accustomed to piloting an Indian canoe along Maine rivers or rowing and drifting along the lazy Musketaquit, the navigation practiced on the Minnesota River was strange indeed. The "Frank Steele" was a large boat, a hundred and sixty feet long, and the water was lower than normal. "In making a short turn," Thoreau said, "we repeatedly and designedly ran square into the steep and soft bank, taking in a cart-load of earth, — this being more effectual than the rudder to fetch us about again; or the deeper water was so narrow and close to the shore, that we were obliged to run into and break down at least fifty trees which overhung the water, when we did not cut them off, repeatedly losing a part of our outworks, though the most exposed had been taken in." Frequently the boat grounded, and in such a predicament a windlass and cable would be fastened to a convenient tree. But before the vessel was straightened out once more upon its course, it often swung sideways and completely blocked the stream. "It was one consolation to know that in such a case we were all the while

[11] Thoreau, *Familiar Letters,* 448.

damming the river, and so raising it." Snags and sawyers were so numerous that the hull of the boat scraping against them made a constant and peculiar music, and on one occasion the steamer collided with a large rock. But as long as the boiler did its work nothing serious could happen. Thoreau saw too that the singular navigableness of the Minnesota River was due to its very crookedness. "Ditch it straight, and it would not only be very swift, but would soon run out." At some seasons of the year, he learned, navigation was practicable as far as Big Stone Lake, and in times of high water steamers might even pass into the Red River.[12]

Thoreau estimated the distance by water up the "long and crooked river" from St. Paul to the Redwood agency as between two hundred and fifty and three hundred miles, whereas the proverbial crow need not fly more than a hundred and twenty miles between these points. En route he observed many forms of bird and animal life, noting especially the wild pigeon in enormous flocks, swallows, kingfishers, and jays, turkey buzzards and herons, ducks and turtles. By the evening of the second day, the boat had reached Fort Ridgely, and by nine o'clock on the morning of June 20 it docked at the agency. The last settlement Thoreau saw before reaching Redwood was New Ulm, which consisted largely of Germans. "We left them a hundred barrels of salt, which will be worth something more when the water is lowest, than at present." [13]

At the Redwood agency, Thoreau found a mere Indian village, with a store and a few houses thrown in for good measure. Although it was barely on the edge of the plains, he reported that he walked three miles and could see no tree on the horizon. He was told that buffaloes were feeding some thirty miles away, yet he failed to see any — a

[12] Thoreau, *Familiar Letters*, 449.
[13] *Jouneys*, 2: 46–53; Sanborn, *Life of Thoreau*, 410–412; Thoreau, *Familiar Letters*, 451.

failure which must have been one of the disappointments of his trip. If one is to judge by the paucity of comment, the Indian council, ostensibly the reason for the excursion, failed to impress Thoreau. This is the more surprising when one recalls the eagerness with which he studied relics of the red man around Concord, as well as his interest in the Indian lore of the Maine woods. But it must be remembered that he was a sick man and was probably unable to indulge all his natural inclinations. At any rate, he heard the Sioux eloquence, candidly observing that in comparison with that of the white man it had the advantage of truth and earnestness, and he saw the principal chief, Little Crow. Furthermore, he noted the apparent restlessness of the Indians and attributed it to the cavalier treatment accorded them by the whites. "They were quite dissatisfied with the white man's treatment of them, and probably have reason to be so." Thoreau's observation gains added significance when one recalls that the Sioux Outbreak of August, 1862, occurred little more than a year after the naturalist's visit. His sharpness of perception and his suggestion that there was something deeper than the usual unrest among the Sioux seem almost prophetic today. After the ceremonies were concluded the Indians performed a dance, about which Thoreau, beyond expressing a mild interest, says little. About thirty dancers participated, he noted, "and twelve musicians with drums; others struck their arrows against their bows. Some dancers blew flutes and kept good time, moving their feet or their shoulders, — sometimes one, sometimes both. They wore no shirts." [14] One cannot help feeling that Thoreau looked upon the dance as an excrescence, that he would have much preferred seeing the Sioux in the intimacy of village and wigwam life. Men on dress parade never appealed to the philosopher of simplicity. Yet the western Indians as a whole failed to impress Thoreau as did the red

[14] *Journeys,* 2: 54–56; Thoreau, *Familiar Letters,* 452; Sanborn, *Life of Thoreau,* 412.

men of Maine and eastern Canada. He was more interested in itemizing in botanical nomenclature the flowers and
plants that he found around Redwood than in dissecting the
peculiarities of the followers of Little Crow.

Thoreau remained at the agency only one day. On the
night of June 20 the "Frank Steele" lay halfway between
Redwood and Fort Ridgely, and it paused half of the following night some fifteen miles above Mankato. "Our
boat had pushed over a tree," Thoreau recorded in his journal, "and disturbed the bats, which were beaten out. We
take in a cartload of earth, then swing round the river-bars,
and pull off by the capstan." June 23 found him at Red
Wing, safely back from his five hundred mile cruise deep
into Indian country—a week's excursion for which the
round-trip fare was ten dollars.[15]

At Red Wing Thoreau wrote a long letter to Frank Sanborn, his friend and biographer, detailing his adventures
briefly and indicating his desire to return to Concord. He
informed Sanborn that he was reading his mail on top of
the great isolated bluff that overlooks the valley and that
remains the most conspicuous feature of the landscape at
Red Wing today. The height of the bluff he estimated at
four hundred and fifty feet and its length at half a mile.
"The top, as you know," he wrote, "rises to the general
level of the surrounding country, the river having eaten out
so much. Yet the valley just above and below this (we are
at the head of Lake Pepin) must be three or four miles
wide." Like many travelers before and since, Thoreau
was deeply impressed by the magnitude of the Mississippi
River, which he termed "the grand feature hereabouts."
He thought that too much could not be said about its grandeur and beauty. He was particularly impressed by the
physical dimensions of the stream, as well as by its comparative freedom from rapids. "Steamers go up to the

[15] *Journeys,* 2: 58, 119.

Sauk Rapids," he remarked, "above the Falls, near a hundred miles farther, and then you are fairly in the pinewoods and lumbering country. Thus it flows from the pine to the palm." Finally, Thoreau, all his life a woodsman and a surveyor, was impressed by the forests of the trans-Mississippi country, and he saw clearly that the early prosperity of towns like St. Anthony and Minneapolis was due to the lumber industry. Talking, as was his wont, with lumberjacks and timber cruisers, he came across many Maine men who had migrated westward and who liked to compare the streams and forests of Minnesota with those of their homeland. One woodsman told Thoreau that the Mississippi and its tributaries made the floating of logs relatively easy, but the timber was knottier than that in Maine.[16]

When Thoreau and Mann left Concord they intended to be away three months, but time palled, and the end of June found the travelers ready to resume their homeward trip. On the twenty-sixth the two left Red Wing on the "War Eagle" for Prairie du Chien, whence they took the train to Milwaukee. June 30 found them at Mackinac, where they lodged at the Mackinaw House and rested for five days. They returned to Concord via Toronto, Ogdensburg, Vermont, and New Hampshire.[17]

One can only conjecture the reason for this abbreviation of the stay in the West. Thoreau returned to Concord in the middle of July, 1861, somewhat improved in health but still far from well. In a letter to Daniel Ricketson he alluded to the Minnesota trip but complained that his cough continued and intimated that he might have to resort to travel again.[18] Possibly he was homesick, weary of strange scenes and unfamiliar topography, he who preferred Concord to all the world. The avidity with which he read letters from home would suggest such a conclusion. The

[16] Thoreau, *Familiar Letters*, 446–448.
[17] Marble, *Thoreau*, 174; Sanborn, *Life of Thoreau*, 415.
[18] Thoreau, *Familiar Letters*, 455.

journey to Minnesota, an excursion of some thirty-five hundred miles, was the longest that Thoreau had ever made, and it is probable that he tired of constant travel by train and boat; he would have preferred his own legs as a means of locomotion. Possibly also he realized that there was no cure for him, and he desired to spend his final lingering days in the setting endeared to him by nature and man. In any event, he never left home again. In the ensuing winter the disease made terrifying inroads upon a weakening constitution, and on May 6, 1862, he died.

Thoreau's visit to Minnesota is of significance only when one considers what materials it might have afforded him for future books. Unfortunately there are few literary echoes of his penetration into the trans-Mississippi frontier settlements. But even his affliction with an incurable illness could not prevent him from taking pleasure in familiarizing himself with flora and fauna which did not flourish in his native New England. And there is the testimony of Sanborn that despite Thoreau's apparent apathy toward the habits and environment of a strange race of red men, one of the chief disappointments of his life was that he did not live to include his Minnesota notes on the Sioux in a volume dealing with the American Indian. Furthermore, it is known that Thoreau read with great interest not only the accounts of early travelers in Minnesota, but the publications of the Minnesota Historical Society as well.[19] Even in sickness, his comments suggest an intelligence of observation and a sharpness of judgment which few men of the time were able to focus on a pioneer environment. It is indeed a heavy loss that Thoreau did not live to do for the woods of Minnesota and the land of the Sioux what he had already done for Concord and for Maine.

[19] *Journeys,* 1: xxxvi, 2: 68–72.

Hamlin Garland.

HAMLIN GARLAND, OCCASIONAL MINNESOTAN

IN THE SPRING of 1939 I had the pleasure of conversing with Hamlin Garland on the terrace of his home on De Mille Drive, Hollywood. Garland then seemed in good health, a short but stocky man with a white mane of hair and stubby fingers. His garrulousness, his accurate memory for details belonging to another century, and his physical energy belied his seventy-eight years. Our conversation ran naturally to books, to his experiences in the Middle West, to his meetings with western writers like Joseph Kirkland and Edward Eggleston, and to his own ideals as a novelist. He remarked that he could not stomach the fiction of John Steinbeck, nor the work of any writer who limited himself to the evil and ugly aspects of life. To him, the novelist who wrote of nothing but the seamy and the revolting was guilty of gross distortion. He admitted that of late years his interest had gradually narrowed and that it was now focused largely on spiritualism. When I left him I carried away with me the impression of an old man who realized that it was time to take in sail, but who still believed his earlier credo and who was unashamed of his life or his work. A year later Hamlin Garland was dead.

Thus departed the man who became known as the type-symbol of the pioneer in American literature, the dirt farmer who for a time moved westward with his emigrant family but eventually chose to become a back-trailer and created the literary Middle Border. In Garland's chronicles the Middle Border means the four states that bound Minnesota, Wisconsin, Iowa, and the Dakotas. Yet the term is much more inclusive than this simple geographical definition. Like the phrase "the frontier," it can be explained or interpreted in a multiplicity of ways. Even in Garland's own books the Middle Border is richly connotative; it suggests not merely a periphery of settlement nor a strip of farm land confronting the prairie, but a large, amorphous area in which the settlers are restless, ever turning their eyes westward, in which the population is polyglot and unstable, speculating in land like the family of Herbert Quick, groping in a half-blind way for education and culture, practicing democracy in society and government and religion.[1] Geographically the Middle Border is still a useful term; chronologically it is obsolete.

Hamlin Garland was never for long a resident of Minnesota. His restless family never attempted to operate a Minnesota farm. Yet the westward migrations of the Garlands followed the rim of the state so that the Minnesota bluffs and prairies were seldom far beyond the horizon. From their homes in Winneshiek and Mitchell counties, Iowa, the Garland children could easily ride northward across the border. As Hamlin Garland himself declared long afterward, "In my boy-hood it [*Minnesota*] was a strange wild country of Big Woods, the home of panthers, bears and Indians. Without doubt the stories my father told of it form a part of the substratum on which much of my earlier fiction is based."[2] In his early maturity Garland visited Minnesota frequently, occasionally as an advocate of Henry George's single-tax theory and of Populism, and later as a lecturer. The friends of his adult years included Cordenio Severance, lawyer, and Richard Burton, late professor of English in the University of Minnesota.

Hamlin Garland was born in 1860, and spent the early years of his boyhood on a farm in Green's Coulee in western Wisconsin not far from La Crosse. On occasional visits to the post office at Onalaska, the boy discovered the Missis-

[1] Herbert Quick's *One Man's Life* (Indianapolis, 1925) gives a vivid picture of an Iowa pioneer family which suffered from western land fever.
[2] Personal letter from Garland to the writer, February 25, 1938.

sippi River and the bluffs of Minnesota beyond, for him and especially for his adventurous father the beckoning gateway to the West.   Garland later remarked that these Minnesota hills "were mysterious and majestic features in a land bounded only by the sunset." [3]   The elder Garland had crossed the great river before the Civil War and remembered fondly the fertile grassy prairies which contrasted so sharply with the tilted and eroded farms of the Wisconsin coulees.   Thus, when a La Crosse merchant in 1868 offered to buy the farm, he could not resist the temptation to sell out and move westward.   The refrain of a marching song pelted his ears:

> Then o'er the hills in legions, boys,
> Fair freedom's star
> Points to the sunset regions, boys,
> Ha, ha, ha-ha! [4]

In this way the Garland family began that series of migratory jumps from farm to farm which terminated only in what was then Dakota Territory.

To reach their first destination, Iowa, the Garlands traversed Houston County, Minnesota, crossing the Mississippi at La Crescent, lodging for the night at Hokah, pausing again at Caledonia, and finally entering Winneshiek County, Iowa, and stopping on a farm near Hesper.   But even this remove did not satisfy the pioneer desire for change.   Within a few months the Garlands had substituted a farm at Burroak for the one near Hesper, and some time later they migrated to Osage in Mitchell County.

The period spent in Osage was important, for it was there that Hamlin Garland had the opportunity to attend school at the Cedar Valley Seminary.   He finished the four-year course in 1881, excelling in declamation and oratory and

[3] Garland, *A Son of the Middle Border*, 12, 27 (New York, 1923); Garland to the writer, February 25, 1938.

[4] *A Son of the Middle Border*, 45.

preparing himself for schoolteaching. In one of his earliest novels, *A Spoil of Office,* Garland pictured such an academy in the corn country as he himself had attended and sketched the earnest students and the mortifications brought on by ignorance. The callow farm laborer avidly seeking an education who is the protagonist, Bradley Talcott, is in more than one respect reminiscent of his creator.

Following graduation Garland vainly attempted to find a school which would welcome his untried abilities. He himself has narrated his experiences in the summer and fall of 1881, when he wandered through Minnesota in search of work at Faribault, Farmington, Chaska, Granite Falls. At Faribault he stood beside the "Cannonball River," as he designated the Cannon, and thought of his predecessor, Edward Eggleston, who as a young man had also come to Minnesota and had written a novel about his new environment, *The Mystery of Metropolisville.* No doubt Garland's own Boomtown of later years owed something to Eggleston's picture of land speculation on the frontier. But while Hamlin Garland was thus striving to profit financially from his course at the Cedar Valley Seminary, Richard Garland, obsessed with the idea that richer land lay where the sun set, had determined to make one more move westward; and soon the son followed his family to the new homestead near Ordway in what is now South Dakota, traveling the last twelve miles from Aberdeen on foot.[5]

His first visit to Dakota Territory was of short duration. After a fortnight's work shingling a double house, the twenty-one year old Garland, consciously proud of his legal maturity, gathered up his wages and headed eastward. At Hastings he was tempted by the river packets, so that when the "War Eagle" arrived from St. Paul he bought passage for Red Wing, the picturesque strip of water impressing him somewhat as the Nile impresses the traveler at Cairo. Red Wing

[5] South Dakota Writers' League, *Hamlin Garland Memorial,* 10 (Mitchell, South Dakota, 1939); *A Son of the Middle Border,* 243.

to him was an exciting town, and he described the bluffs surrounding it in terms that he later applied to the peaks of Wyoming. But unfortunately his money did not allow an extended stay to appreciate the scenery, and shortly he departed for Wabasha and then for the hamlet of Byron, where his mother's relatives lived. Again a search for a school was futile. Garland remained until December on the farm of William Harris, plowing, threshing, and husking, but at the end of 1881 he left Olmsted County to revisit Onalaska and the scenes of his boyhood. Well over a year later, after an interval of carpentry and schoolteaching, Garland again traversed Minnesota en route to the family homestead near Ordway.[6]

For some time thereafter he remained at least nominally a Dakotan, pre-empting a claim in McPherson County, enduring the vicious prairie winter in a frail shanty, and earning more money at manual labor than at teaching. Then in the fall of 1884 he mortgaged his claim for two hundred dollars and started for Boston, determined to carve out a career for himself away from the privations of prairie farming. It was in Boston that he fitted himself for the dual work of writing and lecturing that allowed him to return to the Middle Border as a successful man of letters.

For the next fifty years Garland made frequent visits to the Middle West, to see his parents who clung to the Ordway farm for some years longer, to observe agrarian discontent for B. O. Flower's *Arena,* or to speak to various audiences on political or literary topics. On numerous occasions he came to Minnesota, particularly to Worthington, where his mother's sister resided and where his grandfather, Hugh McClintock, spent his declining years, to Winona, and to the Twin Cities. Several times in the early 1890's he spoke in the state in an attempt to convert Minnesotans to the support of Henry George's single-tax doctrine or as an

[6]*A Son of the Middle Border,* 249–255; Garland, *Roadside Meetings,* 1–4 (London, 1931); *Hamlin Garland Memorial,* 12–15.

earnest advocate of Populism.[7]   The *St. Paul Daily Globe* for January 1, 1891, announced Garland's arrival on one of these visits and outlined his engagements.

Prof. Hamlin Garland, of the Boston School of Oratory, is visiting Minneapolis, and while here will read his famous play, *Under the Wheel,* and deliver several addresses.   At the Unitarian church on Friday evening of this week *Under the Wheel* will be read.   On Sunday evening next Prof. Garland will address Mr. Sample's congregation in All Souls church on the East Side, and on Wednesday evening of next week he will address the Single Tax League at Labor Temple on "The Third House."   The public generally is invited to all these entertainments.

According to the *Minneapolis Tribune* for January 6, the title of Garland's address at Labor Temple was changed to "How the People's Franchises are Stolen"!   In 1891, however, Garland was still young and relatively unknown, so that probably none of these speeches attracted much attention.

It was a different matter when Garland was invited to speak at the national convention of Populists at Omaha in 1892.   There had assembled the lean, hollow-eyed farm wives and the bitter, militant, exacerbated farmers who fill the pages of Garland's better stories.   "Before this whispering, restless, respectably threadbare throng, young Mr. Garland rose to read a story which he called 'Under the Lion's Paw.'   The horrors of farm debt hung over many in the audience; they *knew*."[8]

The decade of the 1890's brought fame and recognition to Garland.   It was the period of *Main Travelled Roads* and *Rose of Dutcher's Coolly,* of numerous articles in national magazines, and of successful lecture tours.   Consequently, when Garland returned to Minneapolis in the winter of 1900 he was received as a distinguished man of letters.   The *Min-*

[7] For Garland's political beliefs at this time see his articles in the *Arena* (Boston), notably the following: "A New Declaration of Rights," 3: 157–184 (January, 1891); "The Single Tax in Actual Application," 10: 52–58 (June, 1894); and "The Land Question, and Its Relation to Art and Literature," 9: 165–175 (January, 1894).

[8] George R. Leighton, "Omaha, Nebraska," in *Harper's Magazine,* 177: 128 (July, 1938).

neapolis Journal for February 14 announced his lecture on "Tales of the Trail" at the Lyceum Theater on February 21, printed a biographical sketch, and hailed him as in every way a western man.   It referred to Garland's literary theory that a man's subjects should be chosen from his immediate surroundings and it praised him most highly as a writer of short stories.   Moreover, the paper remarked that Garland had inherited sturdy ideals from his Scotch Presbyterian fore-bears and that a life of hard work and privation on the farm had developed his natural bent as a reformer.

In subsequent issues the *Journal* kept Garland's name before the public.   He was described as a new form of local colorist, as an intimate student of the upper Mississippi Valley and of the frontier in Dakota, as a poet and historian, as an authority on U. S. Grant — Garland had recently finished a biography of the great general.   "He was and has remained a realist of the strong, healthy type — not the naturalist of morbidity."   Again, Garland was pictured as a veritist, one who faithfully followed his literary creed and who, despite criticism, was widely read and admired.   In its last preliminary announcement of Garland's lecture, the *Journal* eulogized the speaker not only as a student and lover of the western country but as a distinguished orator.[9]

At the Lyceum Theater on February 21 Garland was introduced by Richard Burton.   His lecture was apparently very successful, and he was praised for his sincere interpretation of outdoor life.

As an original recital, his discourse with the spirit of freedom and unconventionality it involved, was of a very pleasing character, and his audience found great enjoyment in following him.   He described a condition of nature and civilization peculiar to the Western country, and the fact that it is rapidly being superseded, lends individual interest to the literature that concerns it.   Mr. Garland is a natural lover of the Western life and has reveled in his study of its phases.[10]

---

[9] *Minneapolis Journal,* February 17, 19, 20, 1900.
[10] *Minneapolis Tribune,* February 22, 1900.   The *Journal* for the same date alluded to Garland's poetic treatment of his theme.

Professor Burton became one of Garland's warmest friends. From 1906 to 1925 head of the English department at the University of Minnesota, Burton was generally liked and esteemed. Garland especially had high respect for Burton's genial scholarship. He compared him to Professor William Lyon Phelps of Yale for his ability to interest and at the same time to educate his students, and he pronounced the two men as outstanding among American lecturers on literary themes.[11]

But no Minnesotans were closer to Hamlin Garland than Cordenio and Maidie Severance, whose intimacy he valued highly and whose home he praised for its opulence and luxury. The Severances had bought the old Harriman farm near Cottage Grove and had added wings and ells to the house until it was transformed into a veritable rural mansion, complete with pipe organ and picture gallery. In *Companions of the Trail* Garland recounts how the Severances had descended upon him in 1906 while he was at work on a novel in West Salem, Wisconsin, and how they had given him his first ride in an automobile, an adventurous, bumpy excursion along the Minnesota bluffs. Four years later he enjoyed the hospitality of the Severances at their baronial farm. It was during this visit that he occupied a box at the St. Paul Auditorium with Charles Flandrau while Theodore Roosevelt addressed the audience, and probably Garland was also a guest at the dinner which Colonel Alexander O. Brodie gave at the St. Paul Hotel in honor of the ex-president. On many later occasions Garland was entertained by the Severances; it is doubtful, indeed, if he ever passed through the Twin Cities without visiting Cedarhurst, Cottage Grove.[12]

In the years preceding his California retirement Garland

---

[11] Garland, *Companions of the Trail*, 422 (New York, 1931).

[12] Garland, *Companions of the Trail*, 312. The *St. Paul Pioneer Press* for September 7, 1910, states that Cordenio Severance and Frank B. Kellogg were among Brodie's guests, but makes no mention of Garland. On November 13, 1923, the Severances entertained Garland at a luncheon at the Minnesota Club. See *Minneapolis Tribune*, November 15, 1923.

was an inveterate lecturer and even something of a cosmopolite. His many tours sent him up and down the country, so that he became as well known as the great lyceum speakers of the past. To trace these tours would be both difficult and fruitless, since Garland became so familiar a figure that editors no longer considered his appearance as news. But if one may select a single series of lectures as having special importance, it must be that of 1923, for it was then that Garland returned to the Middle West after a long absence only to realize that some of his earlier impressions were unpleasantly accurate. After speaking at various places, including Valley City, North Dakota, on November 14 and Albert Lea, Minnesota, on November 19, Garland asserted that his observations had softened his original resentment at Sinclair Lewis' *Main Street*. "I here confess with sorrow that this tour has been a painful revelation of the ugliness, crudity and monotony which still characterizes most of our Mid-West homes. . . . Everywhere I went, I saw neglected gardens, unhoused machinery, heaps of garbage, weedy fields and boxlike graceless homes. These are my outstanding memories." [13] It should be pointed out, of course, that this reintroduction to the West occurred after the publication of *A Son of the Middle Border*, not only his most famous book but the book which marked Garland's return to the authentic realism of his earlier writings.

Perhaps a more pleasant memory to Garland in later years was a convocation address at the University of Minnesota on May 24, 1928, when he spoke on the topic, "The Westward March of the Pioneer." In the afternoon he was en-

[13] Hamlin Garland, *Afternoon Neighbors,* 129 (New York, 1934). The lecture at Albert Lea is reported in the *Albert Lea Tribune* for November 20, 1923. The account states that Garland read his address, and observes that neither his delivery nor his lecture was anything to become excited about. In fact, the paper concludes, Garland was hardly equal as an entertainer to the "high class talent" which went to Albert Lea in those days! Garland also spoke at Hamline University in St. Paul at chapel exercises on November 19, choosing the subject "Two Summers in England." *Pioneer Press,* November 20, 1923.

tertained at tea by Dean and Mrs. Melvin E. Haggerty, and in the evening he was the principal speaker at the annual banquet of the college of education held in the Minnesota Union.   Choosing the subject "Getting a Start," Garland stressed such essential pioneer qualities as self-reliance, independence, and the desire to establish a home.[14]

The fact that Hamlin Garland never lived in Minnesota for any length of time may explain his failure to use the state as a locale for his more important work.   It is significant that when he chose to describe a Middle Border farm hand or a western boom town, his prototypes were an Iowa laborer and a Dakota village.   Yet he knew Minnesota not only from personal experience but vicariously from the adventures of his father.   He had traveled across it; he had talked with its people.   Moreover, he recognized its literary possibilities.   In that little-known but stimulating plea for literary regionalism, *Crumbling Idols,* Garland asserted that "themes are crying out to be written," notably northern lumbering.   He observed that novelists did not need to look far for suitable material, that the life in sawmills and shingle mills, the vicissitudes of the river, and specifically the changes engendered by the rise of cities like St. Paul and Minneapolis offered interesting potential themes.[15]   And he pleaded passionately for veritism, his neologism for sincere, blunt, and penetrating expression of what the writer saw.

The actual appearance of Minnesota material in Garland's books is infrequent.   One of the stories in *Main Traveled Roads,* "A Day's Pleasure," was suggested by a visit to Worthington in 1891.[16]   Unhappily, the theme of

[14] Garland's convocation fee was a hundred dollars.   An editorial in the *Minnesota Daily,* the campus newspaper, rebuking students for their discourtesies to convocation speakers, suggests that Garland's speech was not too well received.   *Minnesota Daily,* May 24, 25, 1928; *Tribune,* May 24, 25, 1928.

[15] Garland, *Crumbling Idols,* 14, 21 (Chicago, 1894).   Compare an article entitled "The West in Literature" in the *Arena,* 6: 669–676 (November, 1892).

[16] Garland to the writer, February 25, 1938.

the story, although thus localized in Minnesota, is characteristic of many a farming community of the Middle West. Scarcely a village but knows women like Mrs. Markham, gaunt, work-tired farm wives, to whom a monthly visit to the nearest shopping center is "a day's pleasure." The romantic hero of *Jason Edwards,* Garland's crude novel of poverty in the Boston slums and on the Dakota prairies, traverses Minnesota en route to Boomtown to meet his fiancee.[17] Allusions to Minnesota are scattered throughout Garland's best-known book, *A Son of the Middle Border,* including wistful glances westward across the level uplands, scenes of cornhusking on an Olmsted County farm, and fruitless attempts to find a rural school. A chapter in *Trail-Makers of the Middle Border,* a thinly veiled picture of Richard Garland's life, gives an idyllic glimpse of Minnesota soil before the Civil War and of an attempt at homesteading which was frustrated by federal troops acting to prevent Sioux depredations on the squatters. Garland himself admitted that a handful of tales and poems was also the result of Minnesota observations or episodes.[18] As a whole, it cannot be said that Garland's work was greatly shaped or stimulated by his Minnesota experiences.

Nevertheless, Minnesota is intrinsically part of the Middle Border, and Minnesota was the land that Hamlin Garland saw when his boyish dreams pictured fabulously fertile soil and pampas inhabited by Indians and deer and buffalo. If Richard Garland's path westward had been straight as the crow flies, he would have crossed Minnesota rather than Iowa en route to his Dakota paradise, much as the pilgrims of *Giants in the Earth* toiled through Fairmont and Worthington and Luverne — or their embryos. And if Hamlin Garland had lived out his life as poetic destiny would seem to have outlined it, he would have died in a big log house on one of the Minnesota bluffs overlooking La Crosse. But

[17] Garland, *Jason Edwards: An Average Man,* 118 (New York, 1897).
[18] Garland to the writer, February 25, 1938.

as he himself remarked to the writer, he felt unable any longer to endure the isolation and rigor of a northern winter, and instead of surveying the great Mississippi in his waning years he was "doomed" to finish his life "in a Monterey Colonial house in a city of perpetual sun and perennial flowers."

Oscar Wilde.

OSCAR WILDE'S TWIN CITY
APPEARANCES

When Oscar Wilde arrived in New York Harbor on January 2, 1882, ready to begin an American lecturing tour which was to occupy nearly twelve months and which was to include appearances in cities as far separated as Chicago, Denver, and San Francisco, he was a young man of twenty-seven, striking in appearance, somewhat eccentric in dress, and famous rather for his aesthetic doctrines than for any tangible achievements in art. To be sure, he had to his credit a book of poems, published the year before but in the main consisting of verse which had already seen print in obscure periodicals. Perhaps the best known of these fugitive bits were two sonnets which he had dedicated to Ellen Terry. But Wilde's career as playwright and novelist was still in the future, and America accepted the young Irish aesthete more as an emissary of a peculiar cult than as a distinguished man of letters. Nevertheless, American audiences were eager to hear at first hand what all this pother about aestheticism actually was, and curiosity if nothing else impelled them to see what Oscar Wilde had to say.

Originally planning to spend only a few months in the United States, Wilde was induced by the popularity of his first lectures to remain for a longer time. His initial appearance at Chickering Hall, New York, on January 9, 1882, was followed by readings in Baltimore, Washington, and Boston.[1] His Boston lecture, the fourth of the series, was attended by a demonstration on the part of Harvard students which had reverberations throughout the country.

[1] See an account of Wilde's "American Lectures " by the manager of his tour, W. F. Morse, in Oscar Wilde, *Writings,* 1: 75, 79 (London and New York, 1907). There is some doubt about the sequence of these lectures, but Morse is obviously the best authority.

Stimulated by the unconventional dress which Wilde usually wore on the platform and no doubt incited by some rather insolent newspaper notices of the speaker, sixty collegians trooped in to their allotted seats with absurd clothes and even more absurd demeanor.   To quote one of Wilde's biographers: ". . . all were dressed in swallow-tail coats, knee-breeches, flowing wigs and green ties.   They all wore large lilies in their buttonholes, and each man carried a huge sunflower as he limped along." [2]   But the point of the jest was lost, since Wilde had been warned of the imminent demonstration and turned the tables on his hecklers by appearing in ordinary evening clothes.   The story of this lecture, however, did not lose in the newspaper retelling, and to its perpetuation Wilde no doubt owed some of the curious audiences which paid to hear their own artistic accomplishments belittled and their pretensions vilified.

From Boston Wilde went to Philadelphia, thence to Albany, Rochester, and Buffalo, and finally, striking definitely westward, to Chicago, where he spoke twice to rather small audiences.   The next leg of his journey brought him to the Twin Cities, where he delivered addresses in Minneapolis on March 15 and in St. Paul on March 16.   But before discussing his Minnesota reception it will be of interest to notice the first repercussions of the new cult of aestheticism as revealed in the local press.

The day after Wilde's arrival in New York the St. Paul and Minneapolis *Pioneer Press* carried an announcement of the newcomer's landing, with a subhead as follows: "The Distinguished Lily-Consumer of England, Oscar Wilde, Reached New York — An Interview With the Utterly Utter Young Man."   Copying the report of one of the eastern papers, the *Pioneer Press* declared that "Mr. Wilde appeared like a good natured, tall, well dressed, somewhat enthusiastic young man who was not at all averse to the

[2] Robert H. Sherard, *The Life of Oscar Wilde,* 202 (New York, 1928).

American process of interviewing." Following this description appeared a detailed account of Wilde's life and forebears.

On January 4 the Emma Abbott Grand Opera Company was to give a production in St. Paul of the Gilbert and Sullivan work *Patience*. The *Pioneer Press* had already advertised this performance in a notice which described *Patience* as "the intensely utter." Now it will be remembered that this particular operetta had as the butt of its innocuous satire the very cult of aestheticism which Wilde represented; and, further, that the character of Reginald Bunthorne was popularly conceived to be drawn directly from Wilde himself. As a consequence, the first real contact that Minnesota audiences had with the new gospel was one hardly calculated to inspire respect for it. As the *Pioneer Press* aptly remarked:

Although the aesthetic craze has not yet reached St. Paul, everybody is familiar with the manifestations of it through the columns of descriptions of the actions and utterances of the aesthetes which have appeared in the newspapers, and consequently there will be no lack of appreciation of the delicate satire as well as of the palpable hits of the amusing burlesque.[3]

During the weeks following the St. Paul production of *Patience*, reports of Wilde's eastern lectures or remarks about the personality of the new celebrity were constantly filtering into the local papers. Thus on January 8 the *Pioneer Press* contained a detailed account of Wilde's arrival, together with comments from New York and Chicago journals. A week later the same paper printed two columns of extracts from the *Boston Herald* and from Wilde's own lectures. As a whole the tone of these excerpts was laudatory; Wilde's personal mannerisms and affectations were discounted and his technical ability praised. On January 16 the *Pioneer Press* quoted the *Chicago Tribune's* account of the lecturer and on January 22 it referred editorially to

[3] *Pioneer Press* (St. Paul and Minneapolis), January 2, 4, 1882.

Wilde's experiences in New York. Also scattered through
the various issues of the same paper about this time were
personal items of the following tenor: "Oscar Wilde, the
aesthetic apostle, is making money by his alleged lectures."
And "A Washington paper sizes up Oscar Wide as 'an
emasculator of ideas.'"[4] It is not hard to trace a growing
contempt in the allusions to the Irish aesthete as his ideas
and his peccadilloes became more familiar. Thus on January 31 the *Pioneer Press* remarked: "The wild aesthete
exhibited his thin legs and ample locks to an agravating
[*sic*] array of empty benches in Baltimore, which would
indicate an elevated social scale in the Monumental city."
And a few weeks later, in the Washington's birthday issue:
"Oscar Wilde says the American newspapers are comic
without being amusing. Fact is they have been treating
a comical subject, and it isn't singular that the subject isn't
amused." The *Duluth Tribune* joined the chorus of criticism too. The issue of February 17 commented on Wilde's
Chicago appearance and pointed out that "the aesthetic Chi-
cagoans forgot their pork-sticking and grain-gambling to go
hear him." If the spectators were not pleased, they were
at least attentive.

Oscar's knee-breeches and flowing hair were novel sights, and the
audience feasted their eyes upon them, but the lecturer didn't seem
to "take" half as well as vaccination. Oscar, of course, spoke of the
"beautiful in art," and the "joy in art," and it was all Greek to the
men and women who listened to him. Had he spoken of the "beautiful in grain" or the "joy in pork" he would have been understood
and appreciated, but Chicago knows only one art — that of making
money. The Apostle of the Utter evidently has not learned how to
suit himself to his audience.

Obviously, then, the more publicity that Wilde received,
the more satirical became the allusions to him. Rarely
were his ideas seriously analyzed or considered; the whole
attention was focused on his eccentric deportment and his
freakish dress. No modern press agent or propagandist

[4] *Pioneer Press*, January 25, 29, 1882.

could have done a better job of inciting popular disfavor toward an individual or a movement than the press of the eighties did toward Oscar Wilde. As a result, when the lecturer himself stepped off the train in Minneapolis on the afternoon of March 15, 1882, and went directly to the Nicollet House, the general reaction of the public toward him was one of curiosity and not always too polite contempt.

The advance notice of Wilde's lecture in the *Minneapolis Tribune* of March 14, 1882, was hardly of the most complimentary nature:

This "boss English sunflower" will appear Wednesday evening in the Academy of Music "in full bloom," and tell his audience — should he be fortunate enough to have one — what he knows about "The English Renaissance."

But much more forthright was the comment of the *St. Paul Globe*, which had appeared the previous Sunday, March 12:

Oscar is the best advertised menagerie this country has ever enjoyed. . . . This utterly, all but and entirely if, concentrated too too young man has secured more gratuitous notoriety than any Wilde animal which has heretofore landed on these hospitable shores.

Following an official announcement of Wilde's lecture, the *Globe* critic vented his contempt in verse of a sort:

> He's happy as a big sunflower,
> He rides upon a lily,
> Feeds on daffadowndilly
> And rakes in the ducats — by jimminy.

The *Pioneer Press,* too, seized the opportunity and editorialized in the issue of March 15 on the "Apostle of the Utter," a tart discussion in which the true aestheticism of Ruskin, as revealed in *Fors Clavigera,* was upheld and praised, whereas the pseudo aestheticism of Wilde was ridiculed. "It becomes a hodge-podge of oddities in gesture and expression, and loses all squeamishness as to the scrap bag from which they are drawn." The *Pioneer Press* even denied Wilde ability in his own field, opining that his poetry "has no more gleams of the genuine aestheticism than has that of Bunthorne whom he, or his manager rather, chooses to send before him as an advertising agent. It is all a farce; and since nobody can be deceived, everybody is happy while the receipts come in handsomely."

Wilde's first Twin City lecture was given Wednesday evening, March 15, at the Academy of Music in Minneapolis. To a small but curious audience numbering about two hundred and fifty the lecturer spoke on "The English Renaissance," a subject which he again discussed the following night at the St. Paul Opera House.[5] Journalistic comment on this lecture was almost embarrassingly candid. The *Globe* curtly said that "Wilde Oscar amused the young Minneapolitan aesthetes at the Academy of Music last evening," but the other local papers were both more splenetic and more loquacious. The *Tribune* of March 16 printed a long review entitled in part "An 'Ass-Thete,' " which was at once an account of an interview with Wilde and a report of his lecture. Thus the writer began by sneering at the aesthete's dress and physique. In his hotel room Wilde had arisen languidly to greet the reporter and had extended a "lily white hand." Wilde's appearance was also made somewhat less leonine, according to the *Tribune,* by the fact that he was pigeon-toed. As for the lecture itself, it was flat and insipid.

From the time the speaker commenced to his closing sentence, he kept up the same unvarying endless drawl, without modulating his voice or making a single gesture, giving one the impression that he was a prize monkey wound up, and warranted to talk for an hour and a half without stopping.

Wilde's reception, the *Tribune* noted, was cold and apathetic. Indeed, his English was hard to understand. In regard to the substance of the talk the review did not go into great detail. Wilde said, briefly, that the truths of art cannot be taught; they must be revealed. He thought

[5] Since Wilde's fee was two hundred and fifty dollars and the admission prices ranged from seventy-five cents to a dollar, it is obvious that the sponsor of the lecture lost money.

that beauty must be introduced into common life and a love of art be inculcated among the peasantry.   As beauty is the one thing worth living for, the beautiful and the useful must be combined.   These scattered impressions the *Tribune* reported succinctly, and without further comment.

The digest of the same lecture in the *Pioneer Press* was somewhat more detailed and stressed even more the personal peculiarities of the speaker.   The account began by stating that "The audience was bright and appreciative, but they were cultured enough to know that the lecture would be a series of artistic platitudes without the slightest trace of artistic revolution."   Then the reviewer criticized the plainness of the stage setting, which, with its bad drops, its two lonely looking chairs, and its heavy table on which reposed the inevitable glass of water, must have been dingy indeed.   But the lecturer himself furnished the necessary color, for Wilde did not choose to abandon in the West the eccentric evening garb which had brought him so much notoriety in the East.

His long and bushy hair crowded in front of his ears and nearly to his eyes, but it was brushed well off his forehead.   He wore a low-necked shirt with a turned-down collar and large white necktie, a black velvet cut-away coat, and vest of the same material, knee breeches, long, black stockings and low shoes with bows, a heavy gold seal hung to a watch guard from a fob pocket.   The poet had no flower in the lappel [*sic*] of his coat.

In addition Wilde flaunted white kid gloves, and spoke monotonously with a strongly English pronunciation.   According to the *Pioneer Press,* the difficulty of understanding him kept the audience from being lulled to sleep.

Nevertheless, the report intimated that Wilde's ideas were worth serious consideration, since it went to some length to recount the more striking suggestions.   Wilde, the *Pioneer Press* declared, urged bright and simple dress for both sexes, pleaded for soft and harmonious color schemes, and spoke in favor of a distinctive but simple native architecture. Great art is local, the lecturer insisted, and should be autochthonous as well. He advised Americans desirous of improving their artistic life to go to the meadows or the docks of a great city for subjects, and to use the buffalo and the wild deer as judiciously and as effectively as the Japanese had used the stork. Finally, Wilde opined, America should use liberally and with taste the quantities of native marble which were free to the taker and which excelled even the Greek stone in variety of color; or America should go back to the painful red brick of the Puritan fathers.

Wilde's final Minnesota appearance was at the St. Paul Opera House on Thursday evening, March 16. He did not change his subject but apparently he did allow certain small variations to creep into his discourse, and he certainly "refined" his costume. According to the report which appeared in the *Globe* the following day, Wilde "was dressed in purple silk velvet, wide sleeves, cut away coat and knee breeches. One hand was encased in a white kid glove and the other sported a lace handkerchief. A long lace neck tie, with bow in front, encircled his neck." Such extravagance of dress, one may be sure, was not lost on the audience and unquestionably did much to vitiate whatever truths Wilde could bring across the Atlantic. Nor did it help matters much to remember, as one of Wilde's biographers apologetically suggests, that the lecturer's garb had much in common with the court dress of the English gentleman.[6]

The substance of this address was again mainly art. According to the *Globe,* Wilde "was shocked by our buildings, by the mud in the streets, and especially by the rooms and furniture in the hotels." The lecture was described in general as well worded, melodious, and without annoying mental stimulation. The "smooth sentences of a languid poet" were pleasing aurally, and certainly must have been profit-

[6] Morse, in Wilde, *Writings,* 1:77.

able. This view was echoed by the *Pioneer Press* in a short squib which appeared on March 17, the paper apparently disdaining to allot any more of its valuable space to the foibles of Wilde:

Oscar Wilde claimed the usual privilege of the peripatetic foreigner, and made several slighting references to American institutions. We are used to that sort of thing, however, and the only time he really trod on St. Paul toes was when he asserted that our streets were dirty. That is a sensitive point with all St. Paul people, except the city authorities, whose business it is to keep the streets clean.

From such reviews it is not impossible to conclude that whatever Wilde's visit did mean to the Twin Cities, it certainly had no lasting effect, and it obviously did nothing to put into more favorable light the gospel of aestheticism. The *Globe* did end its report of the lecture with the apathetic admission that America could stand more art in its daily life, but implied very strongly that Wilde was not the man to bring about that consummation. Indeed, one feels that when Wilde donned his famous fur-collared, green overcoat and boarded the train for Omaha to spread his cult of the new art across the Missouri, his final impression on Minnesotans was that of a personable charlatan, amused and amusing.

Several factors tend toward this conclusion. In the first place, the newspaper publicity that Wilde received almost as soon as he landed in the United States was not calculated to impress favorably the people who were to hear him. Almost invariably the press notices emphasized his witticisms and his personal appearance rather than his ideas. Such a remark as he made upon disembarking in New York, to the effect that he was disappointed in the Atlantic Ocean, received more attention than his really keen appraisal of art in daily life. His affectations of dress (for no one apparently ever thought that a sane man might wear knee breeches and silk stockings because he sincerely believed in them), his "languid" airs, his condemnation of American taste—

all these made juicy copy; and the journalists were not slow in taking advantage of the fact.

Secondly, Wilde's own attitude was hardly conducive to effective proselyting. Originally he had planned to give only one lecture, "The English Renaissance," but soon he compromised and alternated that with "The Decorative Arts." [7] Nevertheless, by the time Wilde had gone half way across the country, both lectures had been so quoted and commented on that their substance must have been reasonably familiar to a majority of every audience that he faced. The fact that this familiarity did not decrease appreciably the numbers of people who thronged to hear him must be interpreted to mean that curiosity and not a genuine interest in his doctrine impelled his hearers. Furthermore, although he must have known that his words were already a subject for comment, he made no effort to win his audiences by either gesture or vocal charm. All the Minnesota reports of his lectures agree that the speaker was monotonous and stiff in delivery; yet at Oxford Wilde had been known for his "golden voice." [8] Obviously a man who would not take the trouble to be either original or pleasing and who seemed to glory in eccentricity was fair game.

Yet the Minnesota press did not make the mistake of undervaluing Wilde's intellectual ability. As the *Pioneer Press* for March 14 stated: "Whoever argues that Mr. Wilde lacks intelligence is most decidedly mistaken. He is a thoroughly educated and very bright man and has made an impression wonderful in one so young." Indeed the *Pioneer Press* was fairer in its digest of Wilde's artistic ideas than the eastern papers often had been. But even though Minnesota journalists were frank to admit that Wilde's message was worth taking to heart, they found it almost impossible to divorce that message from the man

[7] Morse, in Wilde, *Writings*, 1: 95.
[8] G. J. Renier, *Oscar Wilde*, 7 (Edinburgh, 1933).

himself.[9]   On his American tour Wilde revealed himself as clever and tactless, amusing but simpering, half poseur and half iconoclast.   It is no wonder that Twin City audiences dismissed him as a harmless gentleman, not so far removed from the level of Barnum's freaks.

[9] A provincial reverberation of Wilde's visit appears in the *Dodge Center Index* of December 30, 1882, which carries an account of a Christmas masquerade that had been given in the community and had been attended by dancers in motley dress. "The best impersonation costume present," reads the account, "was that representing Oscar Wilde, worn by Cordy Severance, of Mantorville. He was dressed a la Wild[e], knee breeches, big buckled shoes, low collar, sunflower and all, and got around with the esthetic, languid air of the champion of lah dadahism in a style that was button-bursting to see."

Mark Twain.

MARK TWAIN ON THE UPPER MISSISSIPPI

In the fall of 1874 William Dean Howells, then editor of the *Atlantic Monthly,* importuned Mark Twain for something to put into the columns of that periodical for the coming year.   Twain at first demurred, but later informed Howells that a mutual friend, the Reverend Joseph H. Twichell, had suggested that his early experiences as a pilot on the Mississippi would be "a virgin subject to hurl into a magazine!" [1]   Acting upon this hint Twain sent an experimental paper to the editor of the *Atlantic.* Howells was enraptured and begged for more.   The result was the series of papers printed monthly from January to June and in August of 1875 under the caption, "Old Times on the Mississippi."   Thus it is interesting to note that neither the conception of nor the early stimulus for one of Mark Twain's greatest books was original with the author.

It was a labor of love, this setting down on paper the experiences of a cub pilot on the Father of Waters before the Civil War marked the end of the steamboating era.   But Mark Twain was not content with mining in the treasure trove of reminiscence.   He wished to revisit the great river, to write a book about it, to perpetuate in so far as he was able its history, its multiplicity of existence, its captivation. As early as 1875 he had urged Howells to accompany him on an exploratory trip, but Howells found the press of

[1] Quoted by Albert Bigelow Paine, in *Mark Twain, A Biography,* 2: 531 (New York and London, Harper and Brothers, 1912).

affairs too exacting.[2]   Delay followed delay, and it was
not until April, 1882, that the desire was finally realized.
Twain's companions then were his publisher, James R. Os-
good, and a Hartford stenographer, Roswell Phelps.[3]

The plan of the party was to travel by rail to St. Louis,
then to transfer to a steamer and descend the river as far as
New Orleans.   After a brief visit there, including a talk
with Joel Chandler Harris (whom Twain had futilely tried
to induce to accompany him on a lecture tour), they were to
ascend the Mississippi as far as St. Paul, the terminus of
their trip.   Originally Twain had intended to travel incog-
nito, hoping by that method to observe the better and to
gather the necessary information.   He even went to the
trouble of inventing an alias, C. L. Samuel, but found that
neither the pseudonym nor his own reticence was a satisfactory disguise.[4]   When he reached St. Paul he dropped both.

For a large part of the journey Twain was very happy.
Besides renewing old acquaintances en route he stopped off
at Hannibal, his boyhood home, and lingered there for three
days in a kind of sentimental haze.   But soon after, the
weariness incident to a long trip of any kind began to tell
on him, and even though he had never seen the upper river
he commenced to show petulant irritation.   Writing to his
wife from Quincy on May 17, he admitted his homesickness
and his fatigue; particularly he spoke of "this hideous trip
to St. Paul."[5]   The great sweep of the channel, however,
still exerted a fascination over the old riverman, and he
could not resist penning a tribute to the color that engulfed
him.   "The water above Dubuque is olive green, beautiful
and semi-transparent with the sun on it.   Upper Mississippi
the home of superb sunsets."   Nor was he unimpressed by
the famous valley as his boat, the "Minneapolis," steamed

[2] Paine, *Mark Twain*, 2: 532.
[3] Paine, *Mark Twain*, 2: 735.
[4] Paine, ed., *Mark Twain's Letters*, 1: 417 (New York and London,
Harper and Brothers, 1917).
[5] Paine, *Mark Twain*, 2: 740; Twain, *Letters*, 1: 419.

toward the Falls of St. Anthony.   He commented later on
the exquisite beauty of the bluffs above St. Paul:

Where the rough broken turreted rocks stand up against a sky above
the steep verdant slope, they are inexpressibly rich and mellow in
color — soft dark brown mingled with dull green — the very place to
make an artist worship.   Remind one of the old houses in Spanish
New Orleans.

But even the scenery did not make Mark Twain forget his
perennial interest, humanity, and he has left in his notebook
a graphic picture of an immigrant family, impoverished and
lonely:

Wretched poor family on boat going to the frontier — man on deck
with wagon; woman and several little children allowed in cabin for
charity's sake.   They slept on sofas and floor in glare of lamps and
without covering, must have frozen last night.

Perhaps these very immigrants recalled to the old pilot the
days when the river teemed with life and when steamboat
captains had difficulty in stowing away the cargoes that
awaited them everywhere.   How different things were in
1882!   Empty landings greeted the traveler and the whistle
of the arriving vessel produced no thunderous reception.
"The romance of boating is gone now," Twain wrote sadly
in his journal.   "In Hannibal the steamboatman is no longer
a god."[6]

The humorist arrived in St. Paul at seven o'clock in the
morning on Sunday, May 21.   Frigid weather welcomed him,
the mercury having dropped to thirty-seven degrees, and in
Iowa shortly afterward three inches of snow fell.   The
newspaper brethren were as a whole laconic about his presence, being much more interested in the arrival of the Duke
of Manchester and a party of English nobles en route to
Manitoba on a land-purchasing expedition.   Thus the *Minneapolis Tribune* of May 21 devoted considerable space to
the foreign party and seemed much impressed by the fact

[6] Paine, ed., *Mark Twain's Notebook,* 163, 164, 165 (New York and
London, Harper and Brothers, 1935).

that the duke had engaged almost a whole floor at the Metropolitan Hotel; Mark Twain's registration in the same hostelry was apparently overlooked.   One lone reporter penetrated the meaning of the signature "S. L. Clemens, Hartford" and under the caption "Mark Twain — Not Misrepresented" wrote a short account of his meeting with the humorist.

All along his present Mississippi river tour, Clemens has refused to be interviewed by newspaper men, on the ground that he has been misrepresented so many times, and that newspaper men in general were chronic fabricators.   The reporter found the gentleman in bed at a late hour last evening, but discovered that the gentleman is of medium height, with full face, heavy moustache and hair tinged with gray; drawling in speech, but entertaining to the highest degree.   No questions were asked, but voluntarily Mr. Clemens gave the desired information.

An explanation of his motives for undertaking the long journey followed.   Questioned about St. Paul, Twain had "nothing to say, as he had seen but little of the city, but he is disgusted with yesterday's climate, and will leave to-day for his home in the East." [7]   Apparently even fifty years ago the vagaries of Minnesota weather annoyed strangers!

The result of this journey in the spring of 1882 was *Life on the Mississippi* (1883), a book in which were reprinted with some alteration the chapters that had already appeared in the *Atlantic* supplemented by an account of the more recent voyage.   Every reader of Mark Twain is aware of the difference between the two halves of the book, the one transfigured by memory, the other factual and specific.   As Bernard De Voto well said, "Eight years elapsed between the writing of the two parts and in the second he could not recapture the glamour of the first, which is romance." [8]   Nevertheless, despite his brief visit to the upper river, the humorist recorded some interesting opinions of Minnesota.

[7] *St. Paul and Minneapolis Pioneer Press,* May 22, 1882.
[8] Bernard De Voto, *Mark Twain's America,* 107 (Chautauqua, New York, 1933).

His first impression was unfavorable, particularly since he had left New Orleans ten days before in the midst of roses and magnolias, only to find the northern river valley ornamented with snow.   "In New Orleans we had caught an occasional withering breath from over a crater, apparently; here in St. Paul we caught a frequent benumbing one from over a glacier, apparently." [9]   One infers that Twain, Missouri-born and Missouri-bred, preferred the crater.

St. Paul he held to be " a wonderful town."

It is put together in solid blocks of honest brick and stone, and has the air of intending to stay.   Its post-office was established thirty-six years ago; and by and by, when the postmaster received a letter, he carried it to Washington, horseback, to inquire what was to be done with it.

In addition to similar facetious remarks Twain larded his account with statistics — statistics of population, of housing, of finance.

St. Paul's strength lies in her commerce — I mean his commerce.   He is a manufacturing city, of course — all the cities of that region are — but he is peculiarly strong in the matter of commerce.   Last year his jobbing trade amounted to upwards of $52,000,000.

The city's schools, libraries, and churches, the new capitol then being constructed to replace the one which had recently burned — all these drew the writer's attention.   Also, Twain observed,

There is an unusually fine railway station; so large is it, in fact, that it seemed somewhat overdone, in the matter of size, at first; but at the end of a few months it was perceived that the mistake was distinctly the other way.   The error is to be corrected.

He noted that St. Paul was still being made, that building material littered the streets and was being transformed into houses as fast as possible.   And then he began to philosophize upon the forces that produced civilization.   The pioneer of culture, he said, was not the steamboat, nor the railroad, nor the newspaper, nor even the missionary — but whisky!

[9] *Life on the Mississippi,* 583 (Boston, 1883).

The missionary comes after the whiskey — I mean he arrives after the whiskey has arrived; next comes the poor immigrant, with axe and hoe and rifle; next, the trader; next, the miscellaneous rush; next, the gambler, the desperado, the highwayman, and all their kindred in sin of both sexes; and next, the smart chap who has bought up an old grant that covers all the land; this brings the lawyer tribe; the vigilance committee brings the undertaker. All these interests bring the newspaper; the newspaper starts up politics and a railroad; all hands turn to and build a church and a jail, — and behold, civilization is established forever in the land. But whiskey, you see, was the van-leader in this beneficent work. It always is. It was like a foreigner — and excusable in a foreigner — to be ignorant of this great truth, and wander off into astronomy to borrow a symbol. But if he had been conversant with the facts, he would have said, —

Westward the Jug of Empire takes its way.

And so Twain asserted that the arrival of Pierre Parrant, with a jug of civilizing liquid, marked the beginning of a progressive movement the fruition of which is to be found in the capital city of Minnesota.[10]

Of Minneapolis he was similarly observant, pointing out that it was already larger than its neighbor and growing fast, and predicting that the Siamese twins would eventually rival in prestige and numbers the metropolis at the other end of the great waterway, New Orleans. Twain then listed the sawmills, newspapers, schools, and railroads native to Minneapolis and praised the university, then numbering as many as four hundred students, because it was "not confined to enlightening the one sex." [11] The environs of the Twin Cities also drew the visitor's eye, and he singled out for terse comment such spots as Fort Snelling, Minnehaha Falls, and White Bear Lake. The book ends with the narration of a legend connected with the last-named place, followed by some remarks on the story characteristic of the humorist.

Mark Twain's next visit to Minnesota came in 1886 when he chose the Great Lakes route to visit his aged mother,

[10] *Life on the Mississippi*, 584–587. Parrant arrived at Mendota in 1832, and he opened a whisky shop near Fountain Cave in 1838.
[11] *Life on the Mississippi*, 588, 589.

then living with Orion Clemens at Keokuk.   Accompanied
by his three daughters, Susie, Clara, and Jean,[12] the humorist traveled from Buffalo on the "India," a vessel carrying
both passengers and merchandise.   He arrived at Duluth
on Monday, June 28, stopping at the St. Louis Hotel and
again evading prospective interviewers.   Indeed, the Duluth press commented on his inaccessibility:

Mark Twain is too old a bird to be caught with chaff, and he managed to avoid all newspaper men yesterday, but we would warn Mr.
Clemmens [sic] that some enterprising reporter will catch him before
he leaves Duluth, even if he has to black his face and sling hash at
the Hotel St. Louis for a day.[13]

Apparently no such reporter was found before Twain left
the head of the lakes, but upon his arrival in the Twin Cities
on June 29 the press had been duly warned and he found
further escape impossible.   To the Ryan Hotel, where the
Clemens family stopped, came emissaries from three Twin
City newspapers, each eager to depict the visiting celebrity.

The *St. Paul Daily Globe* published no interview, but
instead a rambling account of the humorist and his background.   Twain's "lectures and readings for the present are
at an end," said the *Globe* for June 30, "either as the whole
show or a companion with G. W. Cable of New Orleans.
He is now enjoying himself and will not enter the lecture
field before next winter."   The other local newspapers were
more specific.   The *Minneapolis Tribune* commented with
acerbity on the handwriting of his signature, then described
Twain as he lounged around the lobby of the Ryan: "a quiet
man of medium height, attired in alligator slippers, a light
gray suit, and a pearl colored high hat.   In his mouth he had
the stem of a corn cob pipe."   In reply to questions about
his destination Twain said that he had come west partly for
the sake of a vacation but chiefly to see his mother, then

[12] So entered on the register of the St. Louis Hotel, according to the
Duluth Tribune of June 29, 1886.
[13] *Duluth Tribune,* June 29, 1886.

eighty-three, and that he was leaving for Keokuk shortly. The talk then inevitably shifted to his work.

Mr. Clemens said that his intimate acquaintance, "Mark Twain," was now in the publishing business and consequently did not have much time for writing. Still he contemplated building a new book this summer. His contracts to publish other works ran four years ahead, and if issued, his book must be published by some one else. Said he: "I never wrote for the sake of publishing my books. I usually have two or three books on hand in an unfinished state, and I work on the one I am most interested in." [14]

A similar account save for certain discrepancies in detail appeared in the *Pioneer Press* for June 30. "White plug hat, gray, bushy hair, gray moustache, gray suit of clothes and an Arkansas corn cob pipe in his mouth, from which came wreathing curls of smoke" — thus was Mark Twain pictured. The account of the ensuing dialogue between Twain and his interviewer savors a little of the humorist's own writing:

Glad to meet you (puff). I and my family are on their way to Keokuk (puff), Iowa, to visit my mother, and we have chosen the lake route as the most pleasant by which to reach there, (Puff.) The benefit of coming by the lakes was that I got no news. I was (puff) five days in the heart of the United States, and did not see a newspaper. It was refreshing. That's what people take sea (puff) voyages for. To get away from the news; and when the New York Herald (puff) proposed to establish ocean life and news bureaus a thrill (puff) of horror went through the minds of many people, because the (puff) news would then go with them on their voyage.

Commenting on modern journalism, Twain remarked that "the metropolitan journalism of my day is the village journalism of to-day." The *Pioneer Press* account ended with the statement that the Clemens family had spent the preceding day driving around the city and out to Minnehaha Falls and that they were to depart on the "War Eagle" for Keokuk.

[14] *Minneapolis Tribune,* June 30, 1886. Twain at this time was interested in the Charles L. Webster and Company publishing firm and in the Paige typesetting machine. The Webster house had just issued General Grant's memoirs, which proved an extremely profitable venture.

Thus ended the second of Mark Twain's visits to the upper river. Despite the numerous packet ships that plied the great waterway in the eighties, traffic on the Mississippi was a far cry from what it had been in its heyday before the Civil War and the era of the railroads. Twain saw a declining medium of trade and a waning of interest in the river per se, but he was obviously impressed by the beauties of the valley, in many ways so different from the broad reaches farther south. Moreover, he envisaged a day when the Twin Cities and New Orleans would be the two termini of a great internal artery; and, if he never mastered the bars and snags north of St. Louis as well as those below the mouth of the Missouri, he at least became familiar with a river system that stretched full two thousand miles, at once dividing and uniting a continent.

Albert Bigelow Paine, Twain's official biographer, recounts an amusing anecdote of his trip from St. Paul to Keokuk. As the "War Eagle" steamed slowly down the Mississippi in the evening of that first day of July, 1886, it encountered a shoal crossing. Soon the leadsman, in reply to the booming of the forward bell, began to chant out the depth. As the water grew shallower the measurement came closer to the famous pseudonym of the vessel's most distinguished passenger. Suddenly the exact figure was reached and the cry "Mark twain" reverberated through the gloom. As the humorist stood on the hurricane deck, no doubt steeped in recollections of a long distant past, the figure of his small daughter Clara emerged from the shadows and called out reprovingly: "Papa, I have hunted all over the boat for you. Don't you know they are calling for you?" [15]

Mark Twain's first two visits to Minnesota were made chiefly as a traveler interested in new country and as a vacationist. But when he saw the upper Mississippi for the last time, in the summer of 1895, he came in the capacity of a

[15] Paine, *Mark Twain,* 3: 845.

public lecturer.   A great change had taken place in his
personal fortunes in the intervening years.   The Webster
publishing firm, in which he had invested his own money together with sixty thousand dollars furnished by his wife, had
failed in April, 1894, with liabilities of two hundred thousand dollars; and the typesetting machine, which he had
backed with all the promoting fervor of a Colonel Sellers,
had proved to be far too complicated for daily use.[16]   In
addition, his health was shaken, and he had become percep-
tibly grayer.   Nevertheless, like Sir Walter Scott over a
half century before him, he resolved to shoulder the burdens
of the bankrupt company as if they were his own.   Twice
before, in 1872 and in 1884, when in severe financial straits
he had resorted to the lecture platform and had profited
handsomely.   And so once again he resolved to appear before the public as an entertainer and in this manner liquidate
his obligations.   He had always had an aversion to the formal lecture; he chose instead to give a series of readings
from his own works, relying no doubt on his delivery and
his infectious drawl as much as on the material for his
effect.[17]   In the spring of 1895, consequently, he arranged
with Major J. B. Pond for an extensive lecture tour, one
which was to take him not merely across the United States
but around the world as well.   It was in the course of this
tour that he appeared before audiences in Duluth, Minneapolis, and St. Paul.

Once more Twain chose the Great Lakes route westward,
embarking at Cleveland on the steamer "North West."
He reached Duluth late on Monday, July 22, so late indeed
that his audience in the First Methodist Church was kept
waiting over an hour.   The Duluth papers had printed various comments in anticipation of his coming, largely quota-
tions from eastern journals relative to his platform behavior
and to his readings.   Proclaiming Mark Twain as "prob-

[16] Paine, *Mark Twain,* 3: 969, 984.
[17] Paine, *Mark Twain,* 2: 783.

ably the greatest of all American humorists," the *Duluth Evening Herald* for July 20 declared:

Few men have ever written whose humor has so many sides, such breadth or reach. His passages provoke the joyous laughter of young and old, of learned and unlearned, and may be read or heard the hundredth time without losing, but rather multiplying in power. Sentences and phrases that seem at first only made for the heartiest laughter yield, at closer view, a sanity and wisdom that is good for the soul. He is, too, a wonderful story-teller, and many will bear testimony that the very humor which has made him known around the world is sometimes swept along like the debris of a freshet by the current of his fascinating narrative. As a reader and speaker Mr. Clemens is utterly outside and beyond the reach of all conventional rule. But coming from his own lips his lines gather and convey innumerable new and charming significances.

The *News Tribune* for July 21 described Twain's entrance upon the stage.

The look upon his own features suggests that he has mislaid his eyeglasses and returned to look for them. Finding a number of persons present, he stops and has a long talk with them, during which they are the most willing listeners in the world. To describe his voice is next to impossible. It is a thoroughly down East nasal tone. There is not a sentence but what conceals a mirth provoker of some kind that jumps out at the most unexpected time and place.

Later Twain's awkwardness of gait, his homely language, and his peculiar drawl were remarked, as well as his facial inflexibility while recounting his inimitable stories. In an advertisement for his Duluth reading, his performance was captioned "Ninety Minutes Chat and Character Sketches." Prices ranged from a dollar to seventy-five and fifty cents a seat.[18]

As the Clemens party, including Mrs. Clemens, Clara Clemens, and Major and Mrs. Pond, reached the Duluth wharf, they spied Deacon R. R. Briggs feverishly awaiting their arrival. Hurrying them off the boat, he bundled them into a hackney coach and drove as fast as possible to the First Methodist Church. There the Reverend J. M. Thoburn escorted Twain to the platform, and the humorist al-

[18] *News Tribune* (Duluth), July 22, 1895.

luded to his delay in the briefest of introductions. "It looked for a time," said he, "as if I would be a few minutes late." The various selections followed without intermission, the story of the jumping frog, his boyhood visit to the office of his father late one night only to be horrified by the presence of a corpse on the floor, and several more anecdotes.[19]

The *Herald* described Twain as "a man of medium height and size with a rather calm and serene looking countenance. He wears an iron grey moustache and a bushy head of decidedly grey hair that makes one believe Twain is trying to rival Paderewski." The lecturer's drawl was also conspicuous. As to the effect of the entertainment, the *Herald* was skeptical. Perhaps, the account intimated, the anticipation had been too great.

The people started in to laugh at once as though they were there for that purpose and thought they ought to. After he had narrated a couple of his yarns, however, they subsided somewhat, and only occasionally broke out again. Twain did not seem to be able to get the audience under his control although he had the opportunity to do it very easily at the beginning.

The ease and informality of Twain's style were readily apparent, but not all his stories impressed one as being really funny. Some fell rather flat.[20]

Almost immediately after his Duluth lecture Mark Twain took the night train for Minneapolis, arriving there Tuesday morning, July 23, and stopping at the West Hotel. He was flooded with offers of entertainment and sight-seeing from loyal Minneapolitans who wished to do their share in feting their famous visitor, but he declined all on the score of ill health. Indeed he spent the time before his evening lecture in bed. The *Minneapolis Tribune* announced Twain's coming with a great flourish and predicted a splendid audience for "the most celebrated and widely known literateur that has ever visited this city in many years." But

[19] *News Tribune,* July 23, 1895.
[20] *Duluth Evening Herald,* July 23, 1895.

to a *Journal* reporter who visited Twain at his room and found him suffering from a carbuncle on his leg, the distinguished visitor did not seem very brilliant.

To the casual observer, as he lay there, running his fingers through his long, curly locks, now almost gray, he was anything but a humorist.   On the contrary, he appeared to be a gentleman of great gravity, a statesman or a man of vast business interests.   The dark blue eyes are as clear as crystal and the keenest of glances shoots from them whenever he speaks.

To his interviewer Twain spoke about his travels and about his plan to visit the Sandwich Islands, Australia, and Europe before returning to Hartford to spend the balance of his life in peace and quiet.   Asked whether his daughter Clara was the one who had claimed she had never read her father's works, Twain smiled:

All my daughters ought to be pretty familiar with my works, seeing that they have edited my manuscript since they were 7 years old. They always sided with me whenever Mrs. Clemens thought that I had used some sentence or word that was a little too strong.   But we never stood on that, because Madame was always in the majority, anyway.[21]

A large audience greeted the humorist at the Metropolitan Opera House the same evening, "one of the most brilliant audiences that ever crowded into the Metropolitan and sweltered in the heat of midsummer."   Twain began with a short talk on moral courage, illustrating it with the account of his boyhood experience in Hannibal.   The jumping frog story and excerpts from *Huckleberry Finn* followed in sequence.   According to the *Journal,* the program excited no boisterous merriment but rather a quiet mirth which was often permeated by a rather unorthodox moral.   Yet the audience was greatly pleased and felt that the ninety-minute program was too brief.   As an encore Twain gave the "Whistling Story" and remained standing and bowing on the rostrum as the people filed out.   Following the reading

[21] *Minneapolis Tribune,* July 23, 1895; *Minneapolis Journal,* July 23, 1895.

Twain was the guest of the Minneapolis Press Club and the Commercial Club at the quarters of the latter in the Kasota Block, where he was welcomed by Mayor Robert Pratt and other dignitaries and introduced to a score of the curious. The attendance at the reception was less than had been expected because of a misunderstanding of its semiprivate nature, but one can infer that the guest of honor, in anything but robust health, did not feel slighted. After refreshments had been served, the entertainment broke up and Twain was escorted back to his hotel.[22]

His final platform appearance in Minnesota was made at the People's Church in St. Paul, Wednesday evening, July 24. A reporter from the *St. Paul Dispatch,* finding him at the Ryan Hotel, questioned him about his lecture tour and observed that he was in need of rest and quiet.

His health is not what it once was, and his luck has not been of the best; but even these would be bearable were it not for the carbuncle that insists upon being his compagnon de voyage. A man does not fully realize what trouble is until he has entertained a carbuncle or a boil, and at present Mark is having a good deal of experience. Nevertheless, he is in trim to amuse and he is able to do it as few men can.

The *Pioneer Press,* too, praised the lecturer and announced his reading in enthusiastic tones. "An American author of universal fame should draw an American audience, even in summer, with his stories of American life." [23]

The program Wednesday evening included the familiar selections and found a large audience responsive. But the newspaper reports emphasized Twain's changed appearance and analyzed his humor. According to the *Pioneer Press* he seemed visibly older and rather less animated; yet his delivery had lost neither charm nor effect. The account of

---

[22] *Tribune,* July 24, 1895; *Journal,* July 24, 1895.

[23] *St. Paul Dispatch,* July 24, 1895; *St. Paul Pioneer Press,* July 24, 1895. In the issue of July 23, the *Pioneer Press* announced Twain's appearance and urged its readers to benefit by getting a little of the " philosophy of laughter." Moreover, it said, " Mr. Clemens will teach many new lessons and his musical Yankee drawl will put in fun where printer's ink has failed to make it appear."

his reading concluded with a shrewd discussion of his material.

Twain has never been classed so much with the wits as with the humorists. His function has been rather to say amusing things and put things in grotesque and telling ways than to be brilliant. One seldom finds him brilliant, and one never finds him dull.[24]

In other words, Twain's humor consisted of sudden changes from the commonplace to the ridiculous and of discrepancies of circumstance. Swift, revealing thrusts and the surprise ending so dear to O. Henry brought about his effects.

The Clemens itinerary, after the St. Paul program, included a side trip to Winnipeg and stops at Helena and Butte. On the Pacific coast Major and Mrs. Pond left the party, and Mark Twain, with his wife and daughter Clara, set out on the long trip to the Orient which was to occupy nearly a year. Minnesota never saw him again.

Minnesotans who heard Mark Twain in 1895 must have realized that their entertainer was a tired and ailing man. Harassed by financial pressure and physically weak, he obviously was in no condition to appear at his best on the rostrum. Yet there were few disgruntled murmurs from his auditors. People in general realized his plight and admired the courage which drove him back to the public platform in an effort to recoup his fortunes. Moreover, they liked the man himself and appreciated the pleasure which his books had given to multitudes. Twain, of course, was sincere in his effort to entertain and no doubt endured stoically a great many burdens under which a lesser man would have quailed. But curiously enough he never changed his program throughout his American tour, rarely even altered the sequence in which the selections were given. Instead of novelty he relied on the effects of delivery, of manner and tone.[25] And despite the fact that his material was ex-

[24] *Pioneer Press,* July 25, 1895.
[25] *Dispatch,* July 24, 1895. In the issue for July 20, Twain's complete program appears: " My First Theft," " The Jumping Frog," " Character

tremely familiar his readings were unqualified successes. One concludes, too, that many of the patrons, partly because of Twain's reputation and partly because of the advance advertising, came to laugh at the witticisms of the speaker whether they were really funny or not.   A humorist, his fame once established, will seem amusing even when he is talking seriously.   Twain's delivery, furthermore, was well calculated to appeal to his audiences, who delighted in the twinkling eye, the slow, pleasing drawl, and the simple language of this Yankee from Missouri.   At any rate the lecture trip was highly profitable and gratified the impresario, Major Pond, as much as it satisfied the auditors.

Thus Mark Twain visited Minnesota and the upper river three times, twice as a traveler and once as a platform entertainer.   His sojourns on each occasion were brief and probably, in perspective, not especially important.   Nevertheless they merit more than the reticence or the casual allusions which are their portion in all the Clemens biographies.   For they afford additional evidence of his humor, his alertness, his geniality and shrewdness, and they prove that he formed at least a partial acquaintanceship with the whole of that great river, a large section of which he learned to know in detail through Horace Bixby several years before the Civil War.   Wherever Mark Twain went he made friends, and the above evidence suggests that Minnesota was not backward in welcoming one of the most magnetic men who ever trod the public rostrum.

of the Bluejay," "A Fancy Dress Incident," " Bit Off More than He Could Chaw," and " Tom Sawyer's Crusade."   A writer in the *Minneapolis Tribune* of July 24 considered the humorist's alteration of the order of his selections a change of major importance.   Twain himself planned to make no change until he reached Australia.

Knut Hamsun.

KNUT HAMSUN'S EARLY YEARS IN THE NORTHWEST

IF ONE CHANCES to turn the pages of *Who's Who* to the name of Knut Hamsun one will find, curiously enough, that Hamsun's first mark of distinction is his title of farmer. If one reads farther, one discovers that his surname was originally not Hamsun but Pedersen, that he had little formal education, and that he divided his early years among farming, clerking, school teaching, and various other occupations. It is only toward the end of the brief notice that one learns that Knut Hamsun won the Nobel Prize for literature in 1920 and that he is the author of such distinguished novels as *Hunger* and *Growth of the Soil*.

Most people today know Hamsun's fame as a writer rather than his success as a farmer. But what is not common knowledge is Hamsun's four and a half years in the United States when, a callow, ignorant youth, he crossed the Atlantic to bring poetry to the lives of the Norwegian emigrants to America. Nor is it remembered that his first published book, *Fra det moderne Amerikas aandsliv*, was a violent diatribe against American materialism which the author never re-published and which he would not allow to be translated into English.[1] To all intents and purposes, when Hamsun left New York in the summer of 1888 he severed his American connections permanently.

Hamsun's early life on the Lofoten Islands and on farms was not only hard; it also promised little escape as the boy grew older. The portion of a laborer did not appeal to him, yet he could see no other work ahead. According to one story, a boyhood friend, Nils Fröisland, took Hamsun

[1] Edwin Bjorkman owned a copy of this book in which Hamsun had written the following inscription: "A youthful work. It has ceased to represent my opinion of America. May 28, 1903." See *Hunger*, vii (New York, 1924).

home during the Christmas season of 1881 and Mrs. Fröisland, impressed with the boy's earnestness, offered to lend
him four hundred kroner to continue his studies.   Hamsun
replied that he would prefer to use the money in traveling
to America, a place in which he expected to find a fresh and
clean society.   According to another story, Hamsun was
given free passage on the North German Lloyd ship "Oder"
from Germany to New York on condition that he later write
an account of his trip for publication.   At any rate Knut
Hamsun left Bremerhaven shortly after New Year's, 1882,
and carried with him letters of introduction supplied by
Björnsterne Björnson.[2]

For some time after his arrival he worked on eastern
farms, tending the scanty livestock of the Yankee husband-
men.   But later in the winter he traveled westward into
Wisconsin and shortly presented himself at the home of
Rasmus B. Anderson in Madison.   Years later Anderson
wrote that the family had been at table that day when the
doorbell rang.   Anderson himself opened the door, to find
standing before him "a tall, slender, smooth-faced young
man with a large growth of hair on his head.   You could
not look at this youth with a forest of brown hair without
thinking of Björnsterne Björnson in his palmiest days."[3]
Hamsun presented his letters of introduction, which were
directed not to Anderson but to an infantry captain with
whom Hamsun had worked, and the two men talked briefly.[4]

[2] Walter A. Berendsohn, *Knut Hamsun: Das unbändige ich und die
menschliche Gemeinschaft,* 34 (Munich, 1929); Einar Skavlan, *Knut
Hamsun,* 95 (Oslo, 1929).

[3] Rasmus B. Anderson, *Life Story of Rasmus B. Anderson,* 305 (Madison, 1915).   All Anderson's comments on Hamsun are to be taken *cum
grano salis.*   For specific corrections of errors in Anderson's account, see
Hamsun's "Nogen faa svar" ("A Few Answers"), manuscript notes
written on January 18, 1915, and now in the library of the University of
Minnesota.   Hamsun even declared that his hair was *cendré,* not brown!

[4] Hamsun remarked that, although the letters were not addressed to
Anderson, he begged to be allowed to keep them, as they contained words
highly favorable to him.   Hamsun consented.   See Hamsun, "Nogen faa
svar."

The next definite information about Hamsun's life concerns a period spent in Elroy, Wisconsin, where he went to visit an older brother, Per Pedersen, who had preceded him to the United States. "I travelled to my brother who lived at Elroy," Hamsun later wrote. The young emigrant was having some trouble about this time deciding the orthography of his name, as he advised his family in Norway to address him as Knut Hamsund but put in parentheses, Knut Pedersen. He also recorded later that he had fallen in love three times in two months, but did not establish the identity of his inamoratas. For a time, probably, Hamsun worked on farms near Elroy. Later he was employed by local merchants as a clerk. "I worked first in the shop of E. Hart, later in that of J. G. Wighman, from neither of which was I discharged," he declared long afterward.[5] During his residence of a year and a half at Elroy, Hamsun tried to learn English, a village schoolmaster by the name of Johnston giving him instructions in the evenings. Even as a village clerk he hungered for the intellectual life and hoped to give lectures. Rasmus Anderson alleged that Hamsun studied so much late at night that he found it impossible to arise in the morning and that his employer was obliged to discharge him for unpunctuality; but Hamsun, as we have already seen, specifically denied this charge. More plausible is the story that Hamsun made himself ill by overwork and that Johnston lent him forty dollars in order to go to Colorado for his health. This journey he never made, but years later he repaid the money.[6]

Some time afterward Johnston began to operate a woodyard at Madelia, Minnesota, and urged Hamsun to run the business while he and his wife traveled east. Hamsun accepted the offer and soon established himself in the little prairie town. The great loneliness of the open spaces

[5] Hamsun, " Nogen faa svar "; Skavlan, *Knut Hamsun,* 96.
[6] " I was never in Colorado," Hamsun declared in a personal letter to the writer, November 9, 1938.

began to prey upon him, but he had ample time for composition and with deliberate care he experimented with writing. It was at Madelia, too, that Hamsun met Kristofer Janson.[7]

Janson was a Norwegian intellectual who had espoused Unitarianism and as a result of various inducements had emigrated to America to establish a liberal church for his countrymen. In Minneapolis he organized the Nazareth Unitarian Church, located at Twelfth Avenue and Ninth Street, and he also served two outlying parishes, one at Hudson, Wisconsin, and one at Madelia. Janson was immediately attracted by the tall young Norwegian with the aristocratic figure who wore gold-rimmed glasses while working in the woodyard. After some acquaintance Janson offered Hamsun a position as his secretary. Hamsun admitted no predilections toward religion and particularly none toward Unitarianism, but he quickly grasped the opportunity to do work other than manual.[8] Thus in the spring of 1884 Hamsun was installed in Minneapolis as the rather inefficient secretary of Kristofer Janson.

At first Hamsun fitted well into his new sphere. Living in Janson's home he was modest and retiring, proved a good friend to the children, and exerted a peculiar charm over Mrs. Drude Janson. He reveled in the library of his new friend and was said to stand constantly before the book-filled shelves, reaching down volume after volume and rapidly paging through them. He seldom sat down or read a book through. Instead he had a certain intuitive faculty

[7] Martin B. Ruud, "Knut Hamsun," in Society for the Advancement of Scandinavian Study, *Publications,* 3: 241 (1916); Skavlan, *Knut Hamsun,* 98.
[8] In 1888 Hamsun declared: " Janson's Christianity is perplexing to me, a delicate mixture of reason and Turkish superstition (*Tyrkertro*), with a touch of mysticism "; and in the next year he referred scathingly to " that incomprehensible assemblage of ignorant culture and half radicalism which some people call Unitarianism." See Skavlan, *Knut Hamsun,* 100, which quotes from *Ny jord* (Copenhagen); and Hamsun, *Fra det moderne Amerikas aandsliv,* 87 (Copenhagen, 1889).

for getting the gist from a volume even while reading it superficially.   Moreover, he was valuable to the pastor in various ways, although his obsession with reading and writing and his occasional fits of abstraction must have proved difficult.   In small gatherings he spoke effectively, was successful at a *lutefiskfest* in the basement of the church, and even filled in at the pulpit when Janson was absent addressing his missionary congregations.   But when he preached he usually eschewed theology entirely and was not above injecting a satirical note into his discourse.   Rasmus Anderson, always hostile to Hamsun, remarked that he had heard Hamsun preach, "but I must confess that I did not have the slightest idea of what he talked about.   It seemed to me like nonsensical and incoherent twaddle.   There was a superabundance of words that gushed from him like peas poured from a bag." [9]

After about a year of this association Hamsun and Janson began to drift apart.   Hamsun was much more interested in literature than in theology and had no stomach for the pastor's attempt to make a clergyman of him.   The rift would no doubt have widened immeasurably had not Hamsun at this time fallen sick.   An observer who saw him act as auctioneer at a charity bazaar reported that he suddenly began to spit blood and shortly afterward collapsed. He was examined by Dr. Tonnes Thams, who pronounced his condition serious and apparently convinced the patient that he was a victim of consumption.   Rasmus Anderson, who visited Minneapolis at this time, remarked that Hamsun was pale, emaciated, and quite despondent, and that Professor August Weenaas of Red Wing had even administered the last sacrament to him.   According to this account Hamsun repented his treason to the Lutheran faith and wished only to return to Norway so that he might die in his

[9] Skavlan, *Knut Hamsun,* 99; Anderson, *Life Story,* 308. Hamsun declared flatly in 1915 that Anderson had never heard him preach! "Nogen faa svar."

homeland.   But Hamsun himself later declared that he did
not call Professor Weenaas, and that Weenaas came to
visit him chiefly because the two men had known each other
in Norway.   Hamsun denied that he either confessed or
received the last sacrament.   At any rate, a group of Hamsun's friends raised a small purse, and not long afterward
the sick man was on a train bound for New York.   The
change of climate and the smell of sea air worked wonders
on him, and by the time he saw the shores of Norway once
more he was quite restored to health.[10]

Soon after his arrival in Christiania in the autumn of
1885 he met Lars Holst, editor of the *Dagbladet,* for
whom he did some journalistic work.   He remained in Norway about a year, serving as postmaster at Valders, doing
some editorial chores, and lecturing occasionally on such
literary figures as Strindberg and Kielland.   The exact reason for his return to the United States is obscure.   Perhaps
his reception at home had not been quite what he desired,
perhaps the wanderlust still seized him.   Probably his commission as correspondent for a Norwegian newspaper emboldened him to face a strange country and a strange
language a second time.   But if this conjecture is true, his
disappointment must have been bitter.   Einar Skavlan has
chosen a peculiarly suitable title for his chapter dealing with
Hamsun's life at this time: "Years of Distress in America
and at Home."

In August, 1886, Hamsun was once more on the high
seas headed for New York, this time in the Danish emigrant
ship "Geiser."   He was determined to be a success in literature, and he declared to himself: "I am a literary artist.
People shall yet come to celebrate me in Norway!"[11]   But
his position as correspondent paid him little, and once more
he was forced to resort to manual labor for a living.   There
is an apocryphal story about his having spent several months

[10] Anderson, *Life Story,* 309; Skavlan, *Knut Hamsun,* 101–103.
[11] Quoted by Skavlan, *Knut Hamsun,* 112.

aboard a Russian fishing schooner on the Newfoundland banks in the company of ignorant and brutalized companions, an experience which reputedly is the basis of the sketch "Paa Bankerne." It is more likely that Hamsun simply utilized memories of his Lofoten days and transferred the locale from the Norwegian to the American coast.[12] Christmas of 1886 found him a conductor on a Chicago horsecar, where his difficulties were many. Nearsighted and lacking completely a sense of location, Hamsun conscientiously learned the sequence of streets forward and backward, but after nightfall he would simply begin to call out the names somewhere in the middle of the sequence and continue to the end. People who remembered him on the Halstead Street line affirmed that he was distinguished by a perpetual stare into the horizon and that he usually wore clothes with the elbows out. One passenger, perhaps stimulated by early proximity to a famous man, wrote in 1920:

I still remember Knut's chapped, red wrists, where his coat-sleeves forgot to meet his mittens. And he carried books in his pockets. Always books, Euripides, Aristotle, Thackeray. Such a dreamer! The passengers used to get mad. He would forget to pull the rope. They missed their corners.[13]

At any rate the passengers, infuriated at missing their stops, complained to the company, and Hamsun lost his job.

From Chicago he apparently drifted to Minneapolis, where he re-entered the Norwegian society that he had known earlier. He had rather a conspicuous part in the Seventeenth of May celebration which the Scandinavians of the Twin Cities organized in 1887. A grand parade with delegations from surrounding communities began the day, and Mayor Albert A. Ames of Minneapolis addressed the

[12] " I never compose after living or dead models. *Zachaeus* and *Paa Bankerne* are merely localized in the United States, but are not created therefrom." Hamsun to the writer, November 9, 1938.

[13] " The Horse-car Conductor Who Wins the Nobel Prize," in the *Literary Digest*, 67:35 (November 20, 1920), quotes the reminiscences of Dr. Anders Doe of Chicago.

people. Later at Dania Hall the Norwegian Total Ab-
stinence Society held its festivities. According to the *Minneapolis Tribune* of May 18,

The most notable event of the evening was a lecture on the origin and
history of Norway's day of independence by Knud Hamson [*sic*].
The lecture throughout was full of interest to the audience and full
of bright and happy sayings which took the Scandinavian heart by
storm.

In the early summer of 1887 Hamsun went to the Red
River Valley in search of work in the grain fields. In an
interesting letter written to Kristofer Janson from Casselton, Dakota Territory, July 16, 1887, he recounted his attempts to find employment and pictured the great prairie
wheat country.[14] Hamsun went first to Fargo, where for a
few days he probably lived the life of any migrant farm
laborer. He told Janson of shaving himself and making
his toilet under a convenient bridge. He and two other
field workers celebrated the Fourth of July with a flask of
beer and some rye bread. The next day they walked six
miles to a "storfarm," or bonanza farm, seeking work, but
soon went on to Casselton and there walked from one huge
grain farm to another until they found employment.

During the era of bonanza farms — roughly from the
panic of 1873, when land could be purchased cheaply, until
about 1890 — Casselton was the headquarters of the Oliver
Dalrymple farm and was also a kind of supply center for
the entire Red River Valley. Dalrymple himself had begun
wheat farming as a kind of resident manager on a small
scale, but by 1878 he had thirteen thousand acres under cultivation, and in 1895 he is said to have farmed sixty-five
thousand acres.[15] It is impossible to ascertain today exactly where Knut Hamsun was employed. If it was not on

[14] Kristofer Janson, *Hvad jeg har oplevet,* 222–224 (Christiania,
1913).
[15] Lewis F. Crawford, *History of North Dakota,* 470–472 (Chicago
and New York, 1931). See also *North Dakota: A Guide to the
Northern Prairie State,* 278 (Fargo, 1938).

the Dalrymple farm, it could have been either on the farm of the Amenia and Sharon Land Company, which operated thirty thousand acres north of Casselton, or on the Watson farm, a bonanza project of twenty thousand acres which lay south of the town. At any rate, Dakota filled him with wonder. "Fy for et land dette Dakota!" ("Fie, what a country, this Dakota!") he exclaimed, half in bewilderment, half in admiration.

To Janson he wrote his impressions of the isolation of the prairies and the endless sea of wheat; he remarked the cloudless sky, the long day without shade, the vistas in every direction unbroken save by an occasional thicket or "tree claim"; and he particularly observed the unequaled sunset, blood-red in hue and of an intensity almost defying description. To judge by his reminiscences of his Dakota life, these were happy days.[16] He was liked by his fellow workers and he wrote Sunday letters for them. Together with them he sat on plows as on a stool, with wheels replacing legs, and talked and sang as the machines crawled along the furrows. But Hamsun was never a great success as a manual laborer. As one critic expressed it,

For general farm labor and work on the street-cars he had no ability at all. He had earned anything but praise this summer in Dakota. He had strength enough, he was as powerful as a lion, and he was not altogether an idiot, either, but if a certain kind of work could not completely engage his attention, his thoughts ran off with him.[17]

His overpowering ambition was, of course, to write, and only intellectual work could ever satisfy him. His work on a Chicago streetcar and a Dakota plow was only a stopgap, something to tide him over temporarily. His real interest lay in literature, in reading the sentences of other people and in polishing and shaping his own.

[16] Two semi-autobiographical sketches by Hamsun, "Zachaeus" and "Paa praerien," both of which reflect his North Dakota experiences, are included in *Kratskog: Historier og skitser*, 51–78, 117–131 (Copenhagen, 1903). They are as yet untranslated.

[17] Joseph Wiehr, "Knut Hamsun," in *Smith College Studies in Modern Languages*, 3:5 (1921–22).

It may have been during this latter period of Hamsun's stay in the United States that he experienced the close contact with the Indians that he speaks of in *Fra det moderne Amerikas aandsliv*. Twice, he declared, he lived in the wigwams of the red men for short periods, probably to gather material for literary purposes, but in both cases the result was unsatisfactory. The Indians were shabby, dirty, unheroic people; they were not even a fit source for a short article. Hamsun, of course, was temperamentally a realist and he had only contempt for the doctrine of the noble savage. For him the romantic pictures supplied by "holy Longfellow" and other apologists were only a stultification of the truth. Intimate contact with the domestic life of the Indians naturally failed to stimulate his interest.[18]

In the autumn of 1887 he collected what money he had saved and set out for Minneapolis to rejoin Kristofer Janson. Janson opened his parish house to the young Norwegian and Hamsun gave several lectures there for a nominal fee, his audience seldom including more than thirty or forty listeners. Hamsun discussed in rather iconoclastic fashion the work of the chief Scandinavian writers, as well as that of Zola and Maupassant. He also ventured to comment on American literature, but he held such antagonistic views about Longfellow and Emerson (he found it possible, he said, to read parts of Poe, Whitman, and Hawthorne!) that he alienated his hearers, who were quick to resent any slurs on their adopted country.[19] In later years Hamsun rather regretted the arbitrary judgments passed in these lectures. As he remarked in a letter to the present writer, "These lectures were very imperfect, I was myself ignorant."

Some time after Hamsun's return to Minneapolis the

[18] "I have been among the Indians, on two occasions have stayed for a considerable period in their wigwams," writes Hamsun in *Fra det moderne Amerikas aandsliv*, 60.

[19] Hanna Astrup Larsen, *Knut Hamsun*, 23 (New York, 1922).

journalist Kröger Johansen met him and interviewed him, remarking on Hamsun's "refined and well-chiseled features, his tall, strong figure, his lively manners and animated conversation, his whole unique personality," all of which contrasted strongly with his surroundings. It was Hamsun's wish, the journalist asserted, to charge only ten cents admission to his literary talks; he hoped to get advertising for these meetings from the less bigoted Scandinavian papers and from Kristofer Janson's pulpit.[20]

Hamsun's activities from the fall of 1887 to his departure for Denmark in 1888 are not altogether clear. Apparently he spent a large portion of that time in Minneapolis. The *Minneapolis City Directory* for 1888–89 lists "Knute Hamsum" as a clerk with rooms at 904 North Fourth, whereas the directory for the previous year contains no such name. It was probably during the winter of 1887–88 that Andreas Ueland encountered Hamsun. Ueland related that Kristofer and Mrs. Janson were in the habit of holding Thursday evening sessions at their home, when literature and art were discussed and there was often singing and instrumental music.

On those occasions my wife and I often met a young Norwegian with hair *à la* Björnson in somewhat threadbare clothes, who was intensely interested in what Janson had to say about literature. We understood he was working for the street-car company, but of that I have no personal knowledge. He was, at all events, earning his livelihood by some common labor, and was meanwhile absorbing everything he got hold of in literature. Janson would say that like a girl practicing the scales on a piano, the young man was practicing on sentences in Norwegian, writing and rewriting to find a satisfactory form; and according to the late Dr. Thams, his most intimate friend, he would say: "Some day I shall *pinedöd* show them how to write." And he did. It was Knut Hamsun.[21]

---

[20] *Dagbladet* (Christiania), January 18, 1905, quoted by Wiehr, in *Smith College Studies,* 3:5. Johansen used the pseudonym of Cecil Kröger.

[21] Andreas Ueland, *Recollections of an Immigrant,* 63 (New York, 1929).

Halvard Askeland, the editor of *Felt raabet,* a Norwegian temperance weekly published in Minneapolis, recalls that on one occasion Hamsun accompanied him to Trinity Church and pumped the organ while Askeland played and the Reverend M. Falk Gjertsen delivered his Thursday evening sermon. During intervals in the service Hamsun crouched down behind the organ and wrote notes for a satiric sketch entitled "Flies, a Speech at a Strawberry Festival in the Nazareth Church." Hamsun occasionally wrote editorials for *Felt raabet* and, after his departure for Europe, sent several letters to John Hansen, the business manager of the weekly, which were duly published. He also played some part in the Minneapolis celebration of the Norwegian national holiday in 1888, although festivities were apparently on a smaller scale than in the previous year. The Norwegians gathered in various halls throughout the city, and the Wergeland Lodge met at Turner Hall, Washington Avenue and Fifth Avenue North, the morning of May 17. There were toasts, exhibition drills, and music, and addresses were made by Judge Lars Rand and Knut Hamsun.[22]

Before leaving Minneapolis Hamsun gave a kind of valedictory address at Dania Hall, a bold and violent speech in which he flayed American materialism and ridiculed American culture. Undoubtedly it epitomized the book which he was soon to publish on his experiences and observations in the United States. Once more Hamsun's friends had to assist him to return home. John Hansen aided him to reach Chicago, and there he was helped by Professor N. C. Frederiksen, then a wealthy land agent. Hamsun sailed from New York for Denmark in the steamer "Thingvalla."

One of the last anecdotes relating to Hamsun's sojourn in America is told by Rasmus Anderson. In the summer of

[22] Personal conversation with Halvard Askeland; *Felt raabet,* July 1, March 9, 1887, October 5, 1888; *Minneapolis Tribune,* May 17, 1888; *Minneapolis Journal,* May 16, 1888. There are probably articles by Hamsun in *Felt raabet* that have not been located, as he rarely signed his contributions and identification is therefore difficult.

1888 Anderson, then American minister to Denmark, was in the United States on vacation and by chance happened to return to Copenhagen on the very vessel that was carrying Hamsun. Anderson tells in his autobiography how one day, as he walked through the steerage, he saw four young men, all badly clad and dirty, playing cards. One of them he recognized as the young Norwegian who had rung his doorbell in Madison six years before. Anderson engaged him in conversation and Hamsun replied that he had spent some time in Chicago, North Dakota, and the Minnesota pineries, and that he was now bound for Copenhagen to find a publisher for his book. Thereupon Hamsun produced his manuscript, bulky enough according to the narrator to make a volume of a thousand pages, and urged Anderson to read it. Anderson declined. Then, noticing that Hamsun was wearing a black ribbon on his lapel, Anderson inquired whether he was in mourning for any member of his family. Hamsun said no; he was simply honoring the Chicago anarchists! "From that moment," Anderson wrote, "Knut Hamsun was in my mind an anarchist and I had no use for people of that ilk." When Hamsun later applied at the American legation at Copenhagen, he found the doors closed. Even after the publication of *Hunger* in 1890 had made the author famous, almost overnight, Anderson did not relent in his animosity. Years later when Hamsun was established as one of the outstanding European novelists, Anderson wrote: "There are passages in his books too coarse and indecent to be read aloud even where only men are present. Such writers as Hamsun are a disgrace to the country that tolerates them." [23]

Hamsun's reaction to his American experiences is to be found in the book which he persuaded a publisher to bring

[23] Anderson, *Life Story,* 314–318. Hamsun's final comment on Anderson's remarks may well be found in a sentence taken from "Nogen faa svar": "One lie more or less hurled at me by a man of Rasmus Anderson's caliber is a matter of no consequence."

out the year following his arrival in Copenhagen, *Fra det moderne Amerikas aandsliv*. For this volume is a scathing indictment of almost everything American. Here Hamsun paid his respects to American journalism, the arts, the theater, the legal system, schools and churches, morals and etiquette, and particularly patriotism, which was to him rather chauvinism, and the national antagonism toward foreigners. Everywhere he found materialism rampant. The newspapers gloried in sensationalism, although he admired the trickiness of their advertising, and printed whatever the newsboys could best yell out on the streets; the ministers kotowed to the common passion by quoting statistics in their sermons; the people constantly speculated, whether on the New York stock exchange or in Texas cattle. America, he asserted, had no cultural life at all, the only society which made the pretense of being cultured having been exterminated by the Civil War. He condemned the national prudery and the tendency of American men to submit to feminine domination, and he arraigned the popular devotion to money-getting. Worst of all, he thought, was the ubiquitous patriotism, a kind of national conceit which seemed all the more ridiculous when he realized that the United States had welcomed and naturalized the scum of Europe.[24]

Although the book is largely objective in the sense that there are few personal references, Hamsun did allude occasionally to his residence in Minneapolis. He chose to discuss Minneapolis and Copenhagen, cities comparable in population but in other respects very different. Minneapolis expended three times as much money on schools and education as did the Danish capital, and got poorer results. Minneapolis boasted 146 churches, Copenhagen only 29, a statistical comparison which led Hamsun to remark sarcastically that there was much God in America! He then remarked about the opulence of the Minneapolis churches, the

[24] *Fra det moderne Amerikas aandsliv,* 2, 19, 26, 28.

monstrous organs, the deep carpets, the stained glass windows, one of which alone cost five hundred dollars; the pews, the people, and the word of God were all alike in that all were highly polished! He remarked that the preaching was American, being given over chiefly to Bostonian morals, but he expressed his own preference for American sermons since, if they were sugar-coated, they were at least entertaining. Particularly was he impressed by Minneapolis' deficiencies as a cultural center. It was an important commercial city, it could boast theaters and schools, art galleries and a university, yet it had a negligible library and only *one* bookstore. The Minneapolis Athenaeum he thought was a remarkable building, but one could hardly call it a library. It shelved the works of Scott and Dickens and Dumas and Marryat, but it contained no modern literature. Instead of French and Russian novelists one was given handsomely bound volumes of Congressional debates and patent reports. If one asked for Comte or Schopenhauer, one was handed Emerson. The books of Zola, of course, were not even available in America, since if they were sold they would have to be distributed through cigar stores. Nor was the one bookstore much better supplied. There one could purchase detective stories, calendars, copies of "Yankee Doodle" and "Home Sweet Home," lithographs of Washington, *Uncle Tom's Cabin,* and Grant's memoirs. As an emporium of the latest and best thought it was beneath contempt.[25]

Many of Hamsun's strictures were undoubtedly true, and a few may even still be pertinent. Many, on the other hand, were the direct result of his own unsatisfactory achievements and the unwillingness of a strange land to accept him at his own estimate. It is not hard to understand why Hamsun never allowed the republication of *Fra det moderne Amerikas aandsliv.* There is both irony and

[25] *Fra det moderne Amerikas aandsliv,* 55, 58, 205, 209.

pathos in the spectacle of the young critic parading his animadversions with a kind of wounded arrogance. But the interest of the book today is due to the very candor and forthrightness of the writer.

The years since 1890 are no part of the present story. Hamsun left America embittered and almost as poor as when he arrived; he never returned.[26] For over four years he had worked and suffered privations of all sorts, in the meanwhile learning the countryside and fraternizing with the workers very much as Vachel Lindsay and John Steinbeck have done since. From these experiences he gathered a knowledge and an insight which stood him in good stead as a novelist. Specifically, his use of American material in his fiction is probably not great; he has repeatedly denied his utilization of autobiographical events. But there is no doubt that the years of toil left their imprint on Hamsun. Quite possibly he has transferred to Norway characters and incidents that were indigenous to America. Certainly Miss Larsen is not alone in attributing the success of *Hunger* to Hamsun's American years.[27] The New World was not kind to the young Norwegian; it taught him hard lessons the hard way. But today Americans buy his books and read them with pleasure and admiration. Knut Hamsun may often have wished to forget his experiences in the United States, but Americans have no wish to forget him.

[26] The visit of the Norwegian crown prince and princess to the United States in the spring of 1939 reminded the Norwegian-American press of the earlier visits of distinguished Norwegians, including Hamsun. See a brief account of his American sojourn in *Normanden* (Fargo), June 8, 1939; and two editorials in *Decorah-Posten,* June 23, August 4, 1939.

[27] Larsen, *Knut Hamsun,* 35.

Grimstad, 9 Novbr. 1938.

Mr. John T. Flanagan.
Dear sir,

I am not able to write in English, I have been out of practise in 40 years.

Hvorlange jg var i U.S. förste Gang? Jg var omkring 3 Aar.
— — andre — ? — 3 Aar.

Förste Gang kom jg til Elroy, Wis., arbeidet först paa Farm, derpaa i Butik. Jg husker ikke Aarstal, men fra Elroy reiste jg til Vesten, arbeidet paa Prarien i Red River Valley, reiste til Minneapolis, holdt nogen faa Foredrag i Kr. Jansons Kirke og ellers andre Foredrag i Dania Hall. (Foredragene handlet om Literatur og Kunst. Det var meget ufuldkomne Foredrag, jg var selv uvidende.) Det var under Opholdet hos Janson mine Lunger begyndte at blöde. Jg reiste hjem til Norge, var hjemme ca 2 Aar og drog atter til U.S., denne Gang til Chicago. Var Sporvognskonduktör i et Aars Tid, reiste atter til Janson, indtil jg returnerte hjem for godt.

Jg husker ikke Aarstal, bare Gangen i mit Liv i U.S., og selv dette höist mangelfuldt. Jg var aldrig i Colerado. Jg talte aldrig nogen 17 Mai.

Hvorvidt Opholdet i U.S. har influeret paa min Diktning kan jg ikke svare paa. Saa mange, saa mange har skrevet og spurt herom, men jg er blit svar skyldig. I alle Fald er jg ikke influeret direkte. Jeg dikter aldrig efter levende eller död Model. Zacharas og Paa Bankerne er bare stedfastet til U.S., men er ikke diktet derfra. Jg beder undskylde disse korte Svar.
Deres ærbödige
Knut Hamsun

A French Humorist Visits Minnesota

THE LATE nineteenth century was the heyday of the lecture platform in the United States. Neither before nor since has the public flocked so willingly to gather up the pearls of wit or wisdom flung casually or vigorously from every imaginable kind of rostrum. In the days when radio and television were unknown, the pulpit was declining in influence, and the newspaper was exercising only a sporadic effect, it was the platform sage who came into the most intimate contact with the people. Philosophers like Ralph W. Emerson, temperance polemicists like John B. Gough, emancipated slaves like Frederick Douglass, literary celebrities like George Washington Cable and Mark Twain, evangelists like Dwight L. Moody — all came to the lyceum in an effort to entertain or persuade large audiences, and often of course to replenish a lean purse.

These speakers were Americans who had won their place by professional competence and who frequently held their audiences by rhetorical power. In such circumstances it is all the more remarkable that one of the great successes of the period was gained by a Frenchman, and by a Frenchman, moreover, who ventured to compete with native entertainers on their own ground. Certainly a Minnesota newspaper paid a singular compliment to Paul Blouet when it asserted that of all foreigners he approached most closely to the American humorist.[1]

Today the name of Leon Paul Blouet is relatively unfamiliar, but in the last decade of the nineteenth century it was well known in England and the United States, not to speak of his native France. For Blouet, using the pseudonym of Max O'Rell, had undertaken long lecture tours in the English-speaking countries and had also written several volumes of sharp comments on his travels which achieved a rather wide

circulation. Born in Brittany in 1848, Blouet in his
early maturity entered the army and served as an officer in the Franco-Prussian War. Mustered out because of wounds sustained in that conflict, he migrated
to England where he worked for many years as a
teacher and as a correspondent for French journals.[2]

It was during his English residence that he began
to develop his faculty for perceiving national differ-
ences which he described both humorously and with
acerbity in his books. *John Bull et Son Île,* published
in 1883, and subsequent volumes extended his reputation until, in the autumn of 1887, he was emboldened
to go to the United States. A lecture tour which kept
him busy for six months introduced him to audiences
from Boston to Florida and as far west as Chicago.
In 1890 he repeated his tour, this time enlarging his
itinerary to include Canadian cities, the Middle West,
and the Ohio Valley. One result of this second visit
was *Un Français en Amérique,* published in 1891, perhaps his most widely read book, in which he followed
a long nineteenth-century tradition of European comment upon American manners and customs.[3] Blouet
began a third tour in 1893 which was to have carried
him throughout the English colonies, but ill health
compelled him to relinquish this plan. In 1902 he settled in Paris as the French correspondent for the *New
York Journal,* and the following year he died.

IT WAS DURING his travels in 1890 that Blouet
visited the Twin Cities. Under the direction of the
famous impresario, Major James B. Pond, the Frenchman began his tour in Tremont Temple, Boston, on
January 6 with a lecture entitled "A National Portrait
Gallery of the Anglo-Saxon Races." Some 2,500 people
heard his remarks. Varying his material by topical
allusions but seldom altering his chief thesis, he addressed enthusiastic audiences in New York, Buffalo,
and Pittsburgh. Gradually working his way westward,
he spoke in Chicago, and on February 18 he arrived
at St. Paul to pay, as he remarked, "a professional
visit to the two great sister cities of the north of
America."[4]

---

[1] *St. Paul and Minneapolis Pioneer Press,* February 19, 1890.
[2] For biographical information on Blouet, see *Encyclopaedia
Americana,* 4:118 (New York, 1964); *Dictionary of National
Biography,* Supplement 1901–1911, 1:183 (London, 1939); *La-
rousse Du XXe Siècle,* 1:738 (Paris, 1928).
[3] The English version, *A Frenchman in America* (New York,
1891), bore the subtitle *Recollections of Men and Things.*
[4] *A Frenchman in America,* 214.

It did not take the visitor long, however, to perceive that the vaunted "sisterliness" was highly superficial. His earliest comments relate to the municipal friction that he observed. Minneapolis and St. Paul, he declared, "are near enough to shake hands and kiss each other, but I am afraid they avail themselves of their proximity to scratch each other's faces." He also appended a typical anecdote to substantiate his charges of mutual jealousy — a jealousy, incidentally, which he found characteristic of a great many American cities which were geographically juxtaposed: "St. Paul charges Minneapolis with copying into the census names from tombstones, and it is affirmed that young men living in either one of the cities will marry girls belonging to the other so as to decrease its population by one. The story goes that once a preacher having announced, in a Minneapolis church, that he had taken the text of his sermon from St. Paul, the congregation walked out *en masse*." [5] It is not hard to understand after such stories that American audiences were frequently beguiled into believing that they were hearing a genuine native humorist.

More seriously, Blouet was pleased with the appearance of the Twin Cities. In the published account of his tour he remarked that both Minneapolis and St. Paul "are large and substantially built, with large churches, schools, banks, stores, and all the temples

The grand stairway and lobby of the West Hotel as they appeared in 1887

[5] *A Frenchman in America*, 215.

that modern Christians erect to Jehovah and Mammon." Moreover, he had praise for the hostelries in which he stayed, the Ryan Hotel in St. Paul and the West Hotel in Minneapolis. The latter particularly impressed him, and he compared it favorably with the outstanding caravansaries of the country.[6]

Even his arrival at a time when the thermometer registered thirty degrees of sub-zero temperature did not disconcert him. For Blouet like other foreign observers attributed the energy and prosperity of the Yankee to the bright and bracing climate of North America.[7] He remarked: "The air here is perfectly wonderful, dry and full of electricity. If your fingers come into contact with anything metallic, like the hot-water pipes, the chandeliers, the stopper of your washing basin, they draw a spark, sharp and vivid. One of the reporters who called here [*Minneapolis*], and to whom I mentioned the fact, was able to light my gas with his finger, by merely obtaining an electric spark on the top of the burner. When he said he could thus light the gas, I thought he was joking." [8] He also professed that he did not mind the cold and informed a reporter in St. Paul that professionally an arctic climate suited him admirably as it induced more people to come to hear him.[9]

Blouet gave his first Minnesota lecture at the People's Church in St. Paul, February 18, 1890. His subject as usual was "A National Portrait Gallery of the Anglo-Saxon Races," in which he paid his respects, sometimes politely, sometimes maliciously, to the French, English, Scotch, and Americans (one of his peculiarities was his consistent omission of the Irish). Advertisements had billed him as "the great French wit and satirist" who "will give an amusing talk," and a rather large audience braved sub-zero weather to hear Blouet analyze racial types. After the lecture the humorist was guest of honor at a dinner at the Minnesota Club, a function attended among others by Messrs. Hiram F. Stevens, Christopher D. O'Brien,

The Ryan Hotel,
built in 1884 and
razed in 1962

St. Paul's Minnesota Club
in the late 1880s

---

[6] *A Frenchman in America,* 35, 216. According to the *Minneapolis Tribune* of February 20, 1890, Blouet occupied room number 208 in the West Hotel, the one always reserved for Thomas Lowry when the municipal traction magnate was in the city. The lecturer compared the West Hotel with the Grand Pacific Hotel in Chicago, the Windsor in Montreal, and the Cadillac in Detroit.

[7] *A Frenchman in America,* 216. See also Blouet's earlier book, written in collaboration with Jack Allyn, *Jonathan and His Continent,* 249 (New York, 1889).

[8] *A Frenchman in America,* 219.

[9] *St. Paul Dispatch,* February 18, 1890.

Edwin W. Winter, George H. Moffet, Delos A. Mont-fort, Ambrose Tighe, and Eugene V. Smalley (who had introduced the lecturer to the audience).[10]

THE PRESS REPORTS of Blouet's talk were uni-formly flattering. According to the *Pioneer Press* the Frenchman succeeded where hundreds of foreigners had failed. "His satire, while biting, is honest, good-natured and devoid of offense. John Bull, Sandy Mc-Donald, the typical Frenchman and Brother Jonathan were each and collectively whipped with a lash of small, tingling cords." Blouet centered most of his re-marks on John Bull, and John, said the St. Paul reporter, "being the tougher, is the better able to sus-tain the onslaught." The Scot, on the other hand, was celebrated for his wit, his shrewdness, and his com-mon sense.[11]

The *Globe* critic, while praising the lecturer for his attractive delivery and impervious good humor, pointed out that much of the material was ancedotal. Typical of Blouet's sallies was the remark that the Scots were so thrifty that the Jews could not make a living north of the Tweed: they came, they saw, they left. But the reviewer also commented on the speaker's disparagement of the Yankee. For Blouet declared that Jonathan (his generic name for the American) was not a gentleman: he was talkative as a child, he was inquisitive beyond the pale of good manners, he chewed tobacco, and — *horresco referens* — he spat! The lecturer hastened to add that the uncanny accuracy with which Jonathan found the brass cuspidor partly atoned for the offense of expectoration! [12]

Blouet met the reporters who trooped to the Ryan Hotel to interview him with all the insouciance of his race. In return he was described as a dapper French-man who wore his monocle with the ease of long habit.[13] Furthermore, "The famous satirist is fairly bald and wears a beard which, only a fringe at the sides, tapers into a slender imperial at the chin. He

Jonathan: "What yearly income does your books and lectures bring in?"

---

[10] *St. Paul Daily Globe*, February 19, 1890.
[11] *St. Paul and Minneapolis Pioneer Press*, February 19, 1890. The perennial appeal of such comparisons can be seen in the contemporary popularity of various books by the French wit and satirist, Pierre Daninos. See, for example, *Les Carnets du Major W. Marmaduke Thompson* (Paris, 1954); *Le Secret du Major Thompson* (Paris, 1956); and *Un Certain M. Blot* (Paris, 1960). The second of these books is set partly in New York and contrasts French, English, and American social customs.
[12] *St. Paul Daily Globe*, February 19, 1890.
[13] *St. Paul Daily Globe*, February 19, 1890.

talks with a French accent, although a resident of
London for seventeen years." [14]

In conversation with his interviewers Blouet seemed
unwilling to admit that a book might eventuate from
his current lecture tour. He praised American means
of transportation as more comfortable and more eco-
nomical than European and remarked that he had
often, on his travels throughout the United States,
been mistaken for a drummer. But his Gallic wit never
failed him, and to the inevitable question of what *line*
he carried, he always replied, "French goods!" [15]

A reporter from the *Minneapolis Tribune* who interviewed him at the West Hotel found him amiable
and witty but extraordinarily sensitive about his hat,
which he customarily wore indoors to ward off chills. [16]
He told his interviewer that he did not dislike reporters save when they annoyed him about his head-
gear, adding: "Some times they come in and ask me
if I have anything to say. And then they sit down and
fold their arms and think I must wind myself up
and then talk like a machine, so." Whereupon he gave
a vivid physical demonstration of his point, turning
an imaginary crank in his side. [17]

He then praised the Americans for their friendliness
and warm sympathy. "But," he said, "America to the
traveler is a feeling of monotony. There are long streets
and square blocks in your cities, but all alike. The
telegraph poles stand just so on all the streets, and
overhead there is the web of wires." [18]

Blouet's Minneapolis lecture was as well received as
that in St. Paul. According to the *Minneapolis Journal*

---

[14] *St. Paul and Minneapolis Pioneer Press,* February 19, 1890.
[15] *St. Paul and Minneapolis Pioneer Press,* February 19, 1890.
[16] *St. Paul Daily Globe,* February 19, 1890.
[17] *Minneapolis Tribune,* February 20, 1890.
[18] *Minneapolis Tribune,* February 20, 1890.

*Blouet's impression of
American newspaper reporters
as caricatured in his
book,* A Frenchman in America

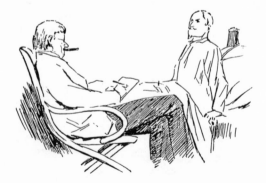

of February 21, 1890: "Blouet has all the wit and grace that one expects in a Frenchman, and is a clever critic of manners. He has learned one trait of the American people by heart, and that is their good nature. He has found out that an American audience will pay money to hear themselves talked about, even though they are made ridiculous." The reviewer observed further that the lecturer had seen America only superficially — that his comments were limited to the railroads and streetcars and to the travelers met en route, but that whatever Blouet had perceived he reported with singular vivacity. Thus, "The American was the only man under the sun in his estimation who can play poker and swear a blue streak one hour, and sing gospel hymns with just as much gusto the next hour. Foreigners were adepts in one or the other, but never in both."

Blouet also praised the gallantry toward women which had made the American world famous and declared that although the United States was as yet a youthful nation and its typical citizen probably not yet born, the time would come when it would exercise an influence unparalleled by that of any other nation.[19] Apparently whatever umbrage might have been taken at Blouet's censure of American manners was dispelled by his practised compliments and invariable amiability.

In England

PAUL BLOUET was the only professional humorist imported by Major Pond in his long career of catering to American audiences, and Pond remarked astutely that the Frenchman lost some of his favor by writing several rather acidulous books on the sights and persons he had observed.[20] Despite Blouet's inveterate good nature and jocularity when on the lecture platform, he was unable or unwilling to expunge completely from his writing his Gallic barbs. His wit flashed with a rapier's speed amid the peccadilloes of Anglo-Saxon humanity and flicked the quiddities of Briton, Scot, Gaul, and Yankee. It was, as a consequence, not surprising that a raw spot should be exposed now and then by the swordsman's skill. The American public, perhaps remembering the savage indictment administered by Frances Trollope a half

[19] *Minneapolis Journal,* February 21, 1890.
[20] J[ames] B. Pond, *Eccentricities of Genius: Memories of Famous Men and Women of the Platform and Stage,* 235 (New York, 1900).

century earlier, was not always ready to accept such treatment with complacency.[21]

The lyceum phenomenon represented by Blouet is today obsolete. Certainly the partial reporting of speeches by newspaper, radio, and television has made it inadvisable for any platform celebrity to tour the country and deliver the identical lecture from every rostrum. But in 1890 the lecturer found it needless to vary his remarks other than topically, with the result that the press reports of his lectures include the same anecdotes and the same inferences. The reader of Blouet's books, too, will find that he was not averse to dwelling on similar ideas in successive volumes. Such matters as the insolence of American reporters, the liveliness and inaccuracy of American journalism, the annoying curiosity of strangers whom one encountered while traveling, the phenomenal rapidity of city growth in the United States, the Yankee's consummate contempt for distance — these subjects constantly arrested Blouet's attention and formed the nucleus for a string of illustrative stories.

These stories did not lack point, for, as Pond well said, Blouet was the "heroic mirth provoker of his time." To realize the peculiar flavor of his humor, one has only to examine the illustrations in his volume, *A Frenchman in America.*[22] One series depicts the typical English, French, and American married couple: the English lord and master stalks into a room with force and emphasis, his mate almost hidden behind his ample figure; the French couple glide along together with perfect mutual sympathy and understanding, each holding the other's hand; but the American wife brushes vigorously forward with a swish of her Victorian skirts while her husband trudges meekly in train.

Blouet's remarks were obviously based on swift, often incomplete observation of men and manners as the traveler was catapulted about America in the Pullman cars which he so much admired; and too often, as the *Minneapolis Times* noted, they were bounded by the streetcar and the cuspidor.[23] Blouet had the flair of

In France

In America

---

[21] See Frances Trollope, *Domestic Manners of the Americans* (1832). The writer of the sketch of Max O'Rell's life in the *Dictionary of National Biography* remarked that the Frenchman followed in the path of Voltaire and Taine, that he was a tolerant and shrewd observer, mixing flattery with his criticism.

[22] Pond, *Eccentricities of Genius*, 235. The illustrations were the work of the American commercial artist, E. W. Kemble.

[23] *Minneapolis Times*, February 21, 1890.

The Pullman car

the trained journalist for the picturesque, for the eccentric, for the high lights, regardless of whether they were representative. Indeed, he himself was often the best example of the false practices of which he accused American reporters.

Twin City audiences seem to have appreciated Blouet's sallies even if they did not value his social criticism too highly. The articulate, witty Frenchman, renowned equally as raconteur, soldier, and journalist, was a pleasant contrast to the usual midwestern platform fare, and as an entertainer he occupied a niche only a few steps below that of the already immortal Mark Twain. Blouet received no more significant compliment than that which classified him as *almost* a native humorist.

ALL CARTOONS used with this article are from Blouet's book, *A Frenchman in America,* which is cited elsewhere. The pictures on pages 14 and 15 are from the *Northwest Magazine* of March, 1885, April, 1887, and February, 1888.

The MINNESOTA Backgrounds
of SINCLAIR LEWIS' Fiction

SINCLAIR LEWIS was once questioned about the autobiographical elements in *Main Street* by a friend whose apartment he was temporarily sharing. The novelist remarked to Charles Breasted that Dr. Will Kennicott, the appealing country physician in his first best seller, was a portrait of his father; and he admitted that Carol, the doctor's wife, was in many respects indistinguishable from himself. Both "Red" Lewis and Carol Kennicott were always groping for something beyond attainment, always dissatisfied, always restless, and although both were frequently scornful of their immediate surroundings they nevertheless lacked any clear vision of what could or should be done. And then Lewis revealingly added this comment about *Main Street:* "I shall never shed the little, indelible 'Sauk-Centricities' that enabled me to write it." [1]

One is tempted to remark that Lewis not only preserved these "Sauk-Centricities" in his later fiction, but that because of them

his picture of Gopher Prairie and Minnesota and the entire Middle West became both durable and to a large extent accurate. A satirist is of course prone to exaggeration. Over-emphasis and distortion are his stock in trade. But despite this tilting of the balance, his understanding of places and events and people must be reliable, otherwise he risks losing touch with reality completely. Lewis was born in Minnesota, he spent the first seventeen years of his life in the state, and he returned on frequent visits, which sometimes involved extensive stays in Minneapolis, St. Paul, or Duluth. A number of his early short stories and six of his twenty-two novels are localized wholly or in part in Minnesota. Claims in this connection might even be made for *Babbitt* and *Elmer Gantry*, although Lewis places the action for each in the fictional town of Zenith in the equally fictional state of Winnemac. [2] In other words, Minnesota was the birthplace, for a considerable time the residence, and by his own request the burial spot of Sinclair Lewis. [3] It was also in actuality or by imaginative projection the physical habitat of much of his fiction. Lewis' "Sauk-Centricities" were real, and even in any aesthetic evaluation of his work they are important.

---

[1] Charles Breasted, "The 'Sauk-Centricities' of Sinclair Lewis," in *Saturday Review*, August 14, 1954, p. 33.

[2] See *Elmer Gantry*, 81 (New York, 1927).

[3] Lewis died in Rome. His ashes were buried in Greenwood Cemetery, Sauk Centre, January 20, 1951.

SINCLAIR *Lewis in 1933*

In a reminiscent article which he contributed to *The O-sa-ge*, the annual of the Sauk Centre Senior High School, Lewis spoke nostalgically of his Sauk Centre days, of the friendliness of the people, and of the indelible memories of boyhood.[4] He still remembered vividly fishing and rafting on Sauk Lake, tramping the fields and woods on October afternoons, sliding down Hoboken Hill which, to the young son of Dr. E. J. Lewis, symbolized the West. Yet twenty-nine years had elapsed since his departure for an Eastern college, and for most of that period he had been out of touch with the town. There were visits, of course, prompted partly by filial devotion.

In the spring of 1916 Lewis took his wife (born Grace Hegger) to Sauk Centre to meet his family. One can infer from Mrs. Lewis' later account of the visit that both she and her husband felt that the experience was somewhat trying.[5] They found the rigid mealtime routine irksome, the bridal dinner party with its formal decorations rather ludicrous, and both relatives and friends impressed by Lewis' money-making ability through writing but hardly

sympathetic with his vocation. Mrs. Lewis' portrait of Lewis' stepmother sounds like an adumbration of Carol Kennicott who, in 1916 of course, had not yet been conceived. The doctor's second wife was prominent in civic affairs, had launched an antifly campaign in the effort to improve sanitation in the local stores, and was president of the Gradatim Club, a local organization dedicated to current events. Moreover, she had been a pioneer in establishing rest rooms for farm women when they came to Sauk Centre to shop, an activity which not only anticipates one of Carol Kennicott's great reforms, but recalls a familiar Hamlin Garland short story.[6]

During this first extensive visit to Sauk Centre, Lewis tried hard to re-establish his working habits and engaged an empty room over Rowe's Hardware Store where he could type his three to five thousand words daily.[7] At the moment he was working on *The Job*, an early novel about a career woman which had nothing to do with the Middle West. But it is not hard to imagine that he was storing away material he would eventually use in the novel he first thought of as "The Village Virus" but which appeared in 1920 as *Main Street*. Lewis as always was restless. After a short time in Sauk Centre, he and his wife visited Dr. Claude Lewis in St. Cloud and then began a four-months hegira from Duluth to San Francisco in a newly purchased Ford. Part of this journey, incidentally, was to be reflected in the novel *Free Air*.[8]

---

[4] "The Long Arm of the Small Town," in *The O-sa-ge*, 1:83 (Sauk Centre, 1931).

[5] Grace Hegger Lewis, *With Love from Gracie: Sinclair Lewis, 1912–1925*, 88–108 (New York, 1955).

[6] "A Day's Pleasure," in *Main Traveled Roads* (New York, 1903), is supposedly based on a visit to Worthington.

[7] Grace H. Lewis, *With Love from Gracie*, 95.

[8] The copy of *Free Air* (New York, 1919) in the special Lewis collection in the University of Minnesota Library is inscribed by the author as follows: "Written in a bare room behind a photographer's studio in Mankato, Minn. to make it possible to write 'Main Street.'" Mankato, incidentally, figures in *It Can't Happen Here*, 449 (New York, 1935).

In the next dozen years Lewis was frequently in Minnesota and lived for short periods in different places. The year 1917 saw him residing in St. Paul, in a lemon-colored brick house on Summit Avenue, and in Minneapolis. During this Minnesota sojourn, Lewis also visited the Cass Lake lumber camps and slept in a bunkhouse.[9] Two years later he was back in Minneapolis again hard at work on *Main Street;* the novel was continued during a summer spent in Mankato and was finished in Washington, where Lewis' stay was financed in part by a loan from his father. In 1926 Charles Breasted met Lewis at a house party on an island in Rainy Lake, where the novelist was somewhat gloomy because of the imminent death of his father and because he felt that Dr. Lewis had always resented *Main Street.* Lewis commented: "He can't comprehend the book, much less grasp that it's the greatest tribute I knew how to pay him." [10]

The decade of the 1940s saw Lewis spending part of his time in Minnesota and on one occasion deciding to make Duluth his permanent residence. Lewis' Minnesota diary is clear testimony that he felt a very strong pull toward the state, but that his innate restlessness would never permit him to sink deep roots.[11] While feverishly working on a particular project he could adjust himself to almost any locale and could enjoy the immediate environment; the novel completed, he sought other stimulation and the horizon beckoned.

In the fall quarter of 1942 he taught a

writing class at the University of Minnesota and apparently liked his contact with students and the university atmosphere. The preceding spring he had rented a house at Lake Minnetonka and in the fall of that year he lived in a house on Mount Curve Avenue in Minneapolis. But if he relished the society of the city, his impression of the downtown area was hardly favorable. He wrote on April 8, 1942: "Minneapolis is so ugly. Parking lots like scabs. Most buildings are narrow, drab, dirty, flimsy, irregular—in relationship to one another—a set of bad teeth." [12] The city actually impressed him as an overgrown Gopher Prairie, without either planning or style. On the contrary, Lewis found the Minnesota rural landscape highly attractive and was particularly pleased by the rocky, hilly farms and the wooded banks of the St. Croix Valley near Marine. At this time the novelist was working on *Gideon Planish,* which one writer termed Lewis' "Made in Minneapolis" novel, despite the curious fact that it has few references to Minnesota.[13] The heroine, however, Peony Planish, hails appropriately enough from Faribault.

It was in 1945 that Lewis decided he had had enough of roaming the world and determined finally to settle down in Minnesota; the city he chose for his residence was Duluth. He bought the enormous house of Dr. E. E. Webber at 2601 East Second Street and there installed his personal possessions and his library of some thirty-five hundred volumes. Apparently he also plunged immediately into the composition of *Cass Timberlane.* But the Duluth winter irritated him, and on March 11, 1946, he observed that the ice was too sullen to melt. "Superior Street now seems meager, ill-constructed and -assorted; a small town —the First National Bank's proud building just a huddle of assorted brick boxes." The novel completed and the long winter over, Lewis' customary nomadism reasserted itself; he sold his house "because it is time to wander again" and left by car for New York on March 21, 1946.[14] This decision

[9] Grace H. Lewis, *With Love from Gracie,* 115.

[10] Breasted, in *Saturday Review,* August 14, 1954, p. 33.

[11] Mark Schorer, ed., Sinclair Lewis, "A Minnesota Diary," in *Esquire,* 50:160–162 (October, 1958).

[12] *Esquire,* 50:161.

[13] William J. McNally, in *Minneapolis Tribune,* April 20, 1943.

[14] *Minneapolis Tribune,* January 30, 1945; *Esquire,* 50:162. In January, 1946, Frederick Manfred, his wife, and the young novelist Ann Chidester visited Lewis by invitation at his Duluth home. See Manfred's "Sinclair Lewis: A Portrait," in *American Scholar,* 23:162–184 (Spring, 1954).

spelled the end to any close connection with Minnesota. He returned to the state for short visits and worked in the collections of the Minnesota Historical Society in 1947 doing research for *The God-Seeker*. But there was no further idea of permanence.

Geographically Minnesota is a big state, and even so indefatigable a traveler as Lewis did not see all of it. Indeed certain areas, such as the Red River Valley, the Pipestone region, and even the Arrowhead country seemed never to strike his fancy. On the other hand, he became rapturous about sections which were strongly photogenic, and if he discovered some of them too late to utilize them in his fiction he did not hesitate to recommend them to the public. On one occasion he listed seven areas which he had found scenically memorable.[15] First came the St. Croix Valley, notably the view which the automobile traveler has as he begins to descend the hill on Highway No. 8 leading into Taylors Falls. Second was the Leaf Mountains section of Otter Tail County, with the spectacular view of surrounding waters and woods from the top of Inspiration Peak. Third he cited most of Fillmore and Houston counties, chiefly the region adjacent to Chatfield, Lanesboro, and Preston. Next Lewis was impressed by the Mississippi River bluffs extending from Red Wing to La Crescent, a sight which evoked the familiar comparison to the Hudson Valley. Finally he mentioned two lakes for their special charms, Minnetonka and Minnewaska, and he added the area around New London in Kandiyohi County. When Lewis made this list in 1942 he had not yet seen the North Shore of Lake Superior. Presumably his sojourn in Duluth familiarized him at least in part with the littoral of the largest American lake.

BY BIRTH, by occasional residence, and by intermittent travel, then, Sinclair Lewis

---

[15] " 'Red' Lewis Discovers Minnesota," in *Minneapolis Tribune*, June 2, 1942. A reprint appears in the *Conservation Volunteer*, 4:21 (August, 1942).

AMONG *scenes favored by Lewis was this view of the St. Croix Valley near Taylors Falls*

knew Minnesota. The interesting question is how freely and fully did he convert this knowledge into his fiction. Are specific people and places recognizable, are trends of settlement and economic and industrial development reflected, are specific historical events introduced? Lewis of course was a writer of fiction with the novelist's mandate to disguise and alter his material. Moreover, he wrote only one historical novel, *The God-Seeker*, and was thus little inclined to preserve the facts of history for their own sake. Yet there is ample evidence that his Minnesota heritage played a large part in his literary work.

It would be difficult and probably futile to attempt to establish personal models for many of Lewis' characters. The identity of Dr. E. J. Lewis and Dr. Will Kennicott is probably most complete. There is a good deal of Lewis in Carol Kennicott and probably much also in Carl Ericson, the barnstorming aviator of the early *Trail of the Hawk*. Undoubtedly Lewis knew radicals and liberals like Bone Stillman, Miles Bjornstam, and Seneca Doane;[16] scientists like Max Gottlieb of *Arrowsmith;* sincere editors like Doremus Jessup of *It Can't Happen Here*. It has been contended that certain lineaments of Grace Hegger Lewis appear in Fran Dodsworth. Undoubtedly the Sharon Falconer of *Elmer Gantry* owes something to Aimee Semple McPherson, at that time notorious, and the radio priest and demagogic politician of *It Can't Happen Here* to Father Coughlin and Huey Long. But George F. Babbitt is certainly a composite character (even his patronymic was established only after Lewis had rejected

such names as Jefferson Fitch, Hornby, and G. T. Pumphrey) in whom many details and aspects were fused. To his great gifts of observation and mimicry, Lewis also added enormous inventive powers and an almost interminable ability to reproduce conversation.[17] Under these circumstances it is unlikely that he would have been content merely to photograph individuals. When he does introduce historical characters like Father Augustin Ravoux, Chaplain Ezekiel G. Gear, William D. Phillips, and Joseph R. Brown in *The God-Seeker*, they are stiff and puppet-like, and are meant to give a sense of milieu which unfortunately proves specious.

With the physical background, the situation is somewhat different. It is true that Minnesota's larger cities—Minneapolis, St. Paul, Duluth—are mentioned occasionally. The smaller towns, however, rarely appear under their own names. Instead Lewis invented place names liberally and used them in several stories—hamlets like Schoenstrom, New Kotka, Curlew, Plato, and the famous village of Gopher Prairie, somewhat larger communities like Vernon and Wakamin and St. Sebastian, the town of Northernapolis, and finally Grand Republic, the scene of both *Cass Timberlane* and *Kingsblood Royal*. Indeed, Sinclair Lewis might well have drawn a map comparable to William Faulkner's chart of Yoknapatawpha County on which he indicated the interconnecting actions of his stories and identified the communities.

In the second chapter of *Free Air* the reader is mired in gumbo with the heroine on "this oceanically moist edge of a cornfield, between Schoenstrom and Gopher Prairie, Minnesota," some sixty miles north of Minneapolis. Fortunately Milt Daggett, a garage mechanic from Schoenstrom, comes along to extricate both heroine and car. In subsequent chapters Daggett becomes the romantic squire who follows Claire Boltwood from Minnesota to Seattle and is duly rewarded for his fidelity. In the first fifty pages of the novel, however, Lewis refers

---

[16] Bone Stillman is the eccentric atheist of *The Trail of the Hawk* (New York, 1915); Miles Bjornstam is the village radical and indispensable town handyman of *Main Street* (New York, 1920); and Seneca Doane is the liberal lawyer of *Babbitt* (New York, 1922).

[17] As a young writer, Lewis actually sold some twenty-three plots to Jack London. See Franklin Walker, "Jack London's Use of Sinclair Lewis Plots," in *Huntington Library Quarterly,* 17:59–74 (November, 1953).

not only to Schoenstrom and Gopher Prairie, but also to Joralemon and Wakamin, towns which were to become familiar to readers of his later stories. Moreover, he sketches two of these communities in the acid manner of *Main Street*.

Schoenstrom, for example, consisted of a brick general store, a frame hotel, a farm machinery agency, "the Old Home Poolroom and Restaurant, which is of old logs concealed by a frame sheathing," and Daggett's Red Trail Garage, the agency for tires, Teal cars, sewing machines, and binders, as well as the weekly office of the veterinarian. Daggett, incidentally, was the son of a New England-born doctor. Gopher Prairie, on the other hand, as Lewis conceived it in the fourth chapter of *Free Air*, had five thousand people, a commercial club, and an infinitely better band than Joralemon, its neighbor. The lobby of the hotel to which Claire Boltwood and her father went was notable for its poison-green walls, brass cuspidors, and insurance calendars; drummers lounged in the ragged chairs; and of the two baths available to hotel guests one was reserved and the other out of order. Another local color touch in this novel of 1919 was the slangy, talkative waitress who was more interested in learning about her customers than in serving them food. This same dismal hotel was probably referred to by Lewis in an earlier short story, "A Woman by Candlelight," in which the protagonist, a wholesale groceries salesman, proceeded from St. Sebastian via Joralemon to Gopher Prairie in a blizzard. "The rows of two-story brick stores running off into straggling frame houses, which made up Gopher Prairie, were covered with snow like a counter of goods with a linen cover smoothly drawn across them." [18]

Gopher Prairie, of course, receives its fullest exposition in *Main Street*, where it assumes some of the dimensions and color of the actual Sauk Centre but, more importantly, is universalized into the typical small town of the second decade of the twentieth century—shabby, dull, provincial, and strangely complacent. The portrait is too familiar to repeat here. One should remember only that even on the physical level there are two Gopher Prairies, the tawdry, provincial community that was revealed to the disgusted eyes of Carol Kennicott fresh from college and the Twin Cities, and the glittering, inviting city that impressed Bea Sorenson, newly arrived from Scandia Crossing, population sixty-seven.

In 1924, at the request of the editor of *The Nation*, Lewis paid a return visit to Gopher Prairie and "interviewed" Dr. Will Kennicott. He found the Thanatopsis Club still operating and the materialism of the community focused in the general discussion of automobiles and golf. But he emphasized that in the ten-year interval since he had last observed the prairie community vast changes had occurred; the streets had been paved, the lawns seemed prettier and neater, old houses had been rejuvenated, and there was some new construction. When the two men stopped to talk "on the edge of Gopher Prairie—this prairie village lost in immensities of wheat and naïvetés, this place of Swede farmers and Seventh Day Adventists and sleeve-garters," Dr. Kennicott rebuked his creator for his radicalism and his scorn of material success. The physician also announced his intention to support Calvin Coolidge for the presidency in the coming election. [19]

Lewis' town of Joralemon receives passing reference in several stories. In "The Kidnaped Memorial," a Civil War veteran goes from Wakamin to recruit enough ex-soldiers to stage a Memorial Day parade. And it is from Joralemon that Young Man Axelbrod, whose name gives the title to one of Lewis' best short stories, goes to Yale at the age of sixty-four to get an education. Axelbrod learns soon enough that

---

[18] *Saturday Evening Post*, July 28, 1917, p. 12.

[19] "Main Street's Been Paved," in *The Nation*, 119:255–260 (September 10, 1924). The article is reprinted in Harry E. Maule and Melville H. Cane, eds., *The Man from Main Street*, 310–327 (New York, 1953).

MAIN *Street*
of Sauk Centre
in the 1920s

age and youth do not mix well; indeed he is somewhat pathetic as a serious college student. But he conducts himself with dignity, has one or two stimulating experiences, and is content to return to his prairie community without a degree.[20]

Joralemon is also the home of Carl Ericson, a young boy who after leaving high school attends near-by Plato College. Carl is interested in machinery more than in academic subjects, but his devotion to a certain liberal instructor permits Lewis to picture a fresh-water college with corrosive scorn. In due time Carl grows interested in aviation and, nicknamed "Hawk" Ericson, becomes famous as a stunt and exhibition flier in the novel called *The Trail of the Hawk*. The protagonist's subsequent travels take him far from Minnesota, but Lewis devotes the whole of Part 1—twelve chapters —to the Joralemon-Plato scenes.

In 1935 Lewis to a large extent retold the story of *Main Street* in a magazine tale entitled "Harri."[21] The setting is New Kotka, "a clean town, with birch trees and a few Norway pines and an unusually large water tower, in Otter Tail County, Minnesota, half an hour's drive from Fergus Falls." New Kotka, a dairy center, has seventeen hundred people. Harri, really Mrs. Harriet Bra-

ham, arrives with her two children to operate the Old Barne Souvenir and Booke Shoppe; lacking both experience and capital, she nevertheless has unlimited assurance. Indeed, although she resembles Carol Kennicott in her energy, her projects, and her reforming instincts, she is really a sinister opportunist who preys on both her suitors and her benefactors. Her base of operations eventually shifts to the Twin Cities, but not before Lewis has had ample opportunity to sketch the regional landscape and to praise the Leaf Mountains and Inspiration Peak. Of his later tales this is perhaps the richest in its details of the Minnesota locale.

THE TOWN of Vernon, the exact location of which is uncertain, is the scene of several Lewis narratives. Most of the action of "The Willow Walk," a curious mystery story in which a bank teller, Jasper Holt, plays a Dr. Jekyll and Mr. Hyde role, takes place there. Holt is so successful in his self-disguise that he is never apprehended as a defaulter; on the other hand, he loses the money he steals and has to resort to day labor to support himself. Palmer McGee, in "The Cat of the Stars," lives in the University Club of Vernon and is an assistant to the president of the M. & D. R. R., which Lewis elsewhere identifies as the Minneapolis and Dakota Railroad. The action of the story, however, has little to do with Vernon.[22] In "Habeas Corpus" the protagonist is

[20] *Selected Short Stories of Sinclair Lewis*, 281–298, 321–337 (New York, 1935).
[21] *Good Housekeeping*, August, 1935, p. 19, 64–75; September, 1935, p. 44, 166–181.
[22] *Selected Short Stories*, 99–140, 143–158.

Leo Gurazov, a Bulgarian radical who owns a tobacco store in Vernon. The plot concerns his strained efforts to get himself deported so that he can join a homeland revolution, but they result only in landing him at Ellis Island for an indeterminate stay.[23]

A more impressive story is "Things," a satiric account of social climbing and its perils. Lyman Duke is a Vernon real-estate operator who has had extensive interests in the woodland north of Grand Marais and who makes a comfortable fortune. His wife and daughter insist that he lead a social life commensurate to his financial standing. With misgivings, Duke builds an elaborate house in Vernon, fills it with expensive and fragile treasures, including Japanese ceramics, engages an army of servants, and puts himself at the complete mercy of the "things" that he has worked so hard to acquire. When he sees that the artificial life he is forced to lead has begun to warp his personality and bring unhappiness to his daughter, he deliberately sets fire to the house and—a later Silas Lapham by conviction, not by accident—reverts to a simpler existence.[24]

"A Matter of Business" and "The Shadowy Glass" also have Vernon as their locale.[25] In the first tale James Candee, proprietor of the Novelty Stationery Shop, is torn between his normal desire to make money and his ambition to raise the aesthetic tastes of his community. He sells writing paper, cards, book ends, and gifts, but when he finds in the outskirts of Vernon a truly creative craftsman who has a flair for making original dolls, he invests in the Papa Jumas dolls. They are angular and gauche, but authentically different; despite the offer of a large manufacturer to make him sole agent of a conventional line of fluffy, commercial products, Candee continues to back the Papa Jumas line. "The Shadowy Glass" has somewhat more local color, and here Vernon is identified, inconsistently with other references, as being in the state of North Iosota. This is the story of Lelia Cor-

valan, who, after being reared in a convent, falls in love with Otis Corvalan and sees only too late that he is both deceitful and irresponsible. Life with Otis proves less romantic than she had envisaged it at first. Eventually, when he has been dismissed from several positions, Lelia decides to take up nursing and, abetted by her mother-in-law, she leaves to go into training in Chicago.

Details in several of these stories suggest that Lewis had a kind of fusion of Minneapolis and St. Paul in mind as a model for his fictional Vernon. It is neither the state capital nor a flour-milling center, but it is the hub of a railroad network, it has steel mills and glass industries, and it is the site of a university. Once the terminus of the Red River carts, it was settled about 1840 by emigrants from the East. "Nothing is very old in the Middle-Western city of Vernon," Lewis writes in "Habeas Corpus," but "in Mississippi Street remain the gloomy stone buildings erected by the early fur traders and a mysterious ancientness clings to the dark irregular way."[26] Vernon boasts of an Iosota Club and a Garrick Stock Company, and fashionable people live along its Boulevard of the Lakes. "Vernon society goes to Palm Beach and New York; it is in wholesaling, the professions, or the railroad; it attends either Saint Simeon's P.E. Church or Pilgrim Congregational; and it frowns upon vulgarity, labor unions, and all art except polite portrait painting."[27] To the north of Vernon, incidentally, an iron range richer than what Lewis calls the Mesaba has been discovered.

[23] *Saturday Evening Post*, January 24, 1920, p. 10, 112, 114, 118, 121.

[24] *Selected Short Stories*, 235–277.

[25] *Harper's Magazine*, 142:419–431 (March, 1921); *Saturday Evening Post*, June 22, 1918, p. 5–7, 81. "A Matter of Business" appears also in a recent treasury of material from *Harper's*, edited by Horace Knowles and published under the title *Gentlemen, Scholars and Scoundrels*, 460–477 (New York, 1959). It supposedly represents the best contributions to *Harper's* from 1850 to the present.

[26] *Saturday Evening Post*, January 24, 1920, p. 10.

[27] *Saturday Evening Post*, June 22, 1918, p. 5.

Finally, there are Northernapolis and Grand Republic. Though details are vague, it is possible that Duluth was Lewis' archetype here. Northernapolis is the scene of "The Ghost Patrol," the rather unconvincing story of an old policeman who refused to stay in retirement but would walk his nocturnal beat, trying doors and watching for pranks, until the authorities finally persuaded him to remain in a county home.[28] Northernapolis is the locale also of "Hobohemia" and "Joy-Joy," companion stories published in 1917 which deal with the courtship of Elizabeth Robinson by Dennis Brown.[29] Elizabeth, who prefers to be called Ysetta, has artistic ambitions; she wishes to write, to dance, or at least to lead a Bohemian existence. She leaves Northernapolis for the greater opportunities of New York. Dennis Brown, a Northernapolis lumber magnate, follows her and by a succession of remarkable exploits convinces her of his own artistic ability and persuades her to return to Northernapolis as his wife. As the mistress of a luxurious house in the fashionable suburb of Hydrangea Park, Elizabeth is about to sink into suburban opulence when the neighborhood is disrupted by the arrival of Mrs. Henrietta Flint. Mrs. Flint is writing a novel, to be called "Joy-Joy," in which she will preach her doctrine of the need for sunshine, happiness, and gaiety in life and for their symbolic realization in dancing. Elizabeth's original ambitions are dangerously reawakened by Mrs. Flint, but again her husband is more than equal to the emergency and soon brings his wife back to an even keel. Mrs. Flint, it might be remarked, has some of the reform impulses and the aesthetic insistence that were later to characterize Carol Kennicott and Harri.

With the exception of Gopher Prairie,

Grand Republic is the most fully pictured of Lewis' fictional communities presumably located in Minnesota. In Cass Timberlane it is described as a city of eighty-five thousand people. In Kingsblood Royal, the action of which postdates World War II, the population has grown to ninety thousand. Grand Republic is situated eighty miles north of Minneapolis and seventy-odd from Duluth, though the exact direction is not stated. "It is large enough to have a Renoir, a school-system scandal, several millionaires, and a slum." The city lies in Radisson County at the confluence of the Big Eagle and Sorshay rivers; the combined stream then flows west to the Mississippi. Lewis is careful to keep Grand Republic out of proximity to Lake Superior so that there can be no easy confusion with Duluth. But his account of its growth has a familiar ring: "Grand Republic grew rich two generations ago through the uncouth robbery of forests, iron mines, and soil for wheat."[30]

Grand Republic has preferred residential districts, such as Ottawa Heights and Sylvan Park, the latter being somewhat less pretentious than the former.[31] Streets bear the names of Flandrau, Beltrami, Schoolcraft, and there is even a Joseph Renshaw Brown Way. The Radisson County Courthouse, comic in its hideous melange of architectural styles, might well serve as Lewis' final comment on the ugliness of many of the older public buildings in Minnesota. Built in 1885, "It was of a rich red raspberry brick trimmed with limestone, and it displayed a round tower, an octagonal tower, a minaret, a massive entrance with a portcullis, two lofty flying balconies of iron, colored-glass windows with tablets or stone petals in the niches above them, a green and yellow mosaic roof with scarlet edging, and the breathless ornamental stairway from the street up to the main entrance without which no American public building would be altogether legal." Downtown Grand Republic has other large buildings too, notably the twelve-story Blue Ox National Bank and "the Pantheon of the Duluth & Twin

[28] Selected Short Stories, 215–231.
[29] Saturday Evening Post, April 7, 1917, p. 3–6, 121, 125, 129, 133; October 20, 1917, p. 63, 67, 70, 73, 76.
[30] Cass Timberlane, 10 (New York, 1945).
[31] Kingsblood Royal, 9 (New York, 1947).

JOE *Brown, a character in* The God-Seeker

temporary and the diurnal. Historical fiction in general did not appeal to him (he obviously preferred Dickens to Scott) because it seemed to lack immediacy; he could project through his eye rather than through his imagination. But in the centennial year of Minnesota Territory he published his one historical novel, *The God-Seeker,* the action of which takes place in 1849 in the area around the fictional Bois des Morts, two hundred miles west of Fort Snelling on the Minnesota River.[33]

It takes Lewis fourteen chapters to transport his hero, Massachusetts-born Aaron Gadd, to the West. Aaron is motivated in his decision by missionary zeal, ambition, and a craving for romance. He travels mostly by river steamboat via St. Louis, Dubuque, and Galena; the final stretch of the river he sees from the deck of the "Dr. Franklin," with Russell Blakeley as first officer and clerk. Minutes after his arrival at the muddy St. Paul landing, Aaron meets Father Ravoux, Vital Guerin, and Joe Brown; and Brown in particular is given a full characterization.[34] At Fort Snelling, prior to his departure for his missionary post where he would act as a carpenter, Gadd is introduced to Thomas S. Williamson, to Stephen Riggs, and to the Pond brothers, although none of these figures largely in Gadd's future adventures. Transportation to Traverse des Sioux is later arranged by a trader on Gray Cloud Island, and eventually, by canoe and horseback, Aaron reaches his destination.

Gadd, a shrewd, industrious young Yankee, rises quickly amid his unusual surroundings. In relatively short time he meets Selene Lanark, daughter of the frontier trader and impresario Caesar Lanark, and

Cities Railroad Station."[32] But across the tracks and along the Sorshay River are decrepit shacks and incipient slums which remind the observer of the frontier village that was to be seen on the same site seventy-five years earlier.

In *Cass Timberlane* the reader is kept constantly aware of the Grand Republic background; buildings and streets continually impinge upon the consciousness, and the social stratification is tied in with the economic development. In *Kingsblood Royal,* on the other hand, the real themes of the novel—race prejudice and the ostracism of Negroes—acquire inflated importance, and interest in the physical scene is supplanted by Lewis' strident exposition of the dangers of bigotry.

BOTH THESE NOVELS are tributes to Lewis' social observation, to his amazing ability to accumulate details that are at once amusing, relevant, and suggestive. They also confirm Lewis' interest in the con-

[32] *Cass Timberlane,* 11, 12. See also Lewis' equally scornful picture of the Zenith Athletic Club in *Babbitt,* 54–60.
[33] *The God-Seeker,* 53 (New York, 1949). In an appendix Lewis carefully distinguishes between the historical and the fictional characters. See p. 419–422.
[34] *The God-Seeker,* 113. In his appendix Lewis pays tribute to the ability and virtuosity of Brown. See p. 421.

the two are married, first in a civil ceremony by Joe Brown, later by a Unitarian clergyman using an Episcopalian ritual. When Gadd joins the trading firm of Buckbee, Lanark and Gadd, his subsequent fortunes are assured. Most of the rest of the novel can be quickly forgotten by the discriminating reader. Lewis' gift for caricature is always apparent, and his ridicule of certain evangelists and self-seekers is amusing if superficial. The characters, however, never come alive. He is perhaps least successful in delineating Indians. Certainly his hypocritical Black Wolf, a pure-blood Dakota who has attended Oberlin, is the least convincing of all. Black Wolf can discuss existentialism in perfect English; he also participates in the tribal feast of the raw fish and readapts himself to the blanket. As Caesar Lanark says cynically: "The typical Dakota is Isaac Weeps-by-Night, who is merely a little ahead of his fellows in giving up hunting for plowing, building a wretched shack and getting drunk on forty-rod whisky. That's what the children of Black Wolf will do . . . if they get born and survive." [35]

In *Elmer Gantry* Lewis attacked the hypocrisy and excesses of irresponsible evangelism with all the virulence of which he was capable. In *The God-Seeker* he shifted his perspective from the contemporary to the historical and he also modified his satire. If Aaron Gadd's missionary associates are naïve, ill-informed, and even on occasion unscrupulous, Gadd himself is honest and moral. Lewis' picture of frontier evangelism is unflattering rather than vicious. He could not understand, for example, the consecration to a cause which led Edward Eggleston on the Minnesota frontier to adopt the peripatetic life himself until his health broke down, and then to choose a Methodist circuit rider as the hero for his fiction. Nor could Lewis sympathize with

the proselytizing activities of a Bishop Whipple. On the other hand, Lewis also resented the rapacity and cynicism of the Indian traders who exchanged shoddy merchandise and gaudy trinkets for valuable furs. His Caesar Lanark, to whom he ascribes a certain amount of intellectual sophistication, represents the more predatory frontier merchant. But even Lanark is a one-dimensional figure. Indeed most of the characters in Lewis' later novels remind one of a remark of Mark Twain when he was disparaging photography as a source of fictional portraiture. "Observation? Of what real value is it? One learns peoples through the heart, not the eyes or the intellect." [36] Lewis never ventured further from human reality than in his one historical novel.

IN A SENSE, however, Lewis was most faithful to his Minnesota background when he was least deliberately photographic or representational. As a native of a prairie community in Stearns County he was intimately aware not only of the rural area around him but also of the settlers. The German and Scandinavian farmers of the region figure prominently in most of his early stories and provide the often anonymous but always evident background of *Main Street*. Moreover, Lewis practiced his mimicry of speech by rendering the dialect of Teuton and Swede, and prided himself on his fidelity of transcription. His protagonists, to be sure, seldom represent these national strains, but his minor figures are frequently of immigrant stock. Lewis was also conscious of other ingredients in the Minnesota melting pot; the Yankees, who came early and quickly controlled lumbering and mercantile activities; the French, more nomadic and less socially important; the Central Europeans, who provided much of the manpower for the iron mining industry. In *Cass Timberlane* Lewis was especially careful to emphasize the fusion of races and tongues in his fictional northern town, though he made less use of them than

[35] *The God-Seeker*, 299.
[36] Mark Twain, "What Paul Bourget Thinks of Us," in *Literary Essays*, 148–170 (New York, 1899).

did Phil Stong in his novel, *The Iron Mountain*. In an essay which Lewis contributed
to *The Nation* he labeled Minnesota the
Norse State and emphasized the prominence
of the Scandinavians in state politics, but
he also tried to dispel the notion that Minnesota's population was made up only of emigrants from northern Europe. This was as
much of a misconception, he argued, as the
beliefs that Minnesota's topography is uni-
form or that a commonwealth which con-
tributes dairy products and corn and lumber
and iron ore to the nation is a region of
one crop — namely, wheat.[37]

History impinges frequently on Lewis'
descriptions. The only Minnesota aborigines
who appear *in propria persona* are the unconvincing Sioux of *The God-Seeker*, but
Lewis was fond of impressing the recent
development of Minnesota on his readers
by stating that less than a century ago a
particular town was a Chippewa-haunted
wilderness. Indian legends are alluded to
sparingly, the voyageurs are cited, and particular patronymics like Radisson are preserved as place names. The Sioux-Chippewa
feuds are referred to occasionally, and

Lewis' ear was historically attuned to the
creaking axles that characterized the Red
River carts.

The varied economic history of Minnesota also is reflected in his fiction, although
he wrote neither a novel of industry nor
one of labor. No Lewis novel is set in the
area of the iron ranges or in the northern
forests; when he did tell a story about the
wilderness he went across the border into
Saskatchewan for a locale, as in *Mantrap*.
But lumbering in general has a place in
his novels—the streams which floated the
logs, the lakes which held the booms, even
the banks which pyramided the industry's
money. Certainly the Blue Ox National
Bank of Grand Republic is Lewis' bow to
the Paul Bunyan stories. In the same way
the milling industry is alluded to and is said
to be one of the mainstays of such a city
as Vernon. Agriculture, of course, is the
occupation of most of the people who go
to market in Gopher Prairie or the adjacent
hamlets. Lewis' references to the cornland,
the interminable fields in which the tiny

---

[37] "Minnesota: The Norse State," in *The Nation*,
116:624–627 (May 30, 1923).

A *Main Street
view in
Sauk Centre, 1957*

communities stand like oases, are usually satiric, but he could grow enthusiastic about the pleasures of field sports and the lure of lake and forest. Not even Mark Twain, recalling idyllic days on his uncle's plantation near Florida, Missouri, was more nostalgic than Lewis writing about fishing and hunting as a boy in Stearns County. Lewis never developed a projected novel about education, but one may presume that if this had materialized it might have dealt with the University of Minnesota, as some of the faculty members of that institution once feared.

AFTER the great decade of the 1920s, during which Lewis' best novels appeared, his work became repetitious, clamorous, imitative. Reviewer after reviewer complained that each new Lewis novel covered familiar ground and used familiar methods. Locale and names might be different, hotelkeeping or the penitentiary system or the dangers of Fascism in the United States might be substituted for small-town provincialism and Zenith real estate, but the technique was unchanged. Lewis' gifts of mimicry and selection of details remained as remarkable as ever, yet the stridency was more pronounced, the humor more labored. Unwilling or unable to change his approach, he wrote in the same way until the end, and his later fiction became attenuated and unconvincing.

It is always interesting to speculate why a writer reaches a point, either midway in his career or later, beyond which there is no development. Some writers say essentially what they have to say in their first book and do nothing but parrot themselves thereafter. Others are delayed in finding their real theme or their happiest medium until several books have come off the

presses. Only the rare few progress consistently and reveal increased stature and maturity as one published work follows another.

It seems quite apparent that in Lewis' case his fiction began to decline as soon as he got away from the Minnesota or at least the Middle Western background. Always a diligent researcher, he filled notebooks with details, names, phrases pertaining to whatever theme he had decided to develop, so that his picture of a location or a career is superficially authentic whatever it may lack in vitality. But "getting up" a subject in this fashion is not quite the same thing as writing from a reservoir overflowing with impressions and experiences. Lewis' youth in Minnesota and his early years as student and companion to his doctor-father were the reservoir out of which flowed six or more novels and many stories. When he tapped this source in his early maturity he produced his best work—*Main Street, Babbitt, Elmer Gantry, Arrowsmith, Dodsworth*. Upon returning to the source toward the end of his career he could still write with some authority, despite the familiarity of his technique. But much of the intervening fiction is stiff and self-conscious, and even the famous mimicry often palls. Lewis never lacked gusto even when not at his best as a storyteller, yet one can tire of excessive exuberance.

In later years Lewis was too restless, too nomadic ever to settle down anywhere. During his creative throes he was not especially conscious of surroundings—chair, table, typewriter, and isolation from society were almost his only necessities. But the book finished and out of the way, he needed change, and his peregrinations were endless and hectic. Nevertheless, he remained conscious of his formative years, and the impressions he gained from them served to solidify his fiction. He once paid sincere tribute to his Sauk Centre boyhood "It was a good time, a good place, and a good preparation for life." [38] His fiction justifies the tribute.

---

[38] *The O-sa-ge*, 1:83.

THE PICTURE on page 12 is from a photograph taken by Lee Hanley. It is reproduced here through the courtesy of Father Colman Barry of St. John's University, Collegeville. The view on page 4 comes from the Minnesota department of conservation.

MINNESOTA'S COMMUNITY OF THE BOOK

Moira F. Harris

Each of the literary visitors who came to Minnesota in the nineteenth century went to see the Falls of St. Anthony, Minnehaha Falls, and Fort Snelling. Had they come a century or more later, where might they have gone? Would Captain Marryat have explored our skyways or would Knut Hamsun have watched another sort of Vikings battle in the din of the Metrodome? Would Hamlin Garland have done his walking on the Nicollet Mall and would Fredrika Bremer have marvelled at the Mall of America — perhaps even shopped at Swedish-named Nordstrom's? And what would Oscar Wilde have thought of our museums and their striking buildings?

Their destinations and subjects for literary commentary would certainly have changed as they explored the seven-county metropolitan area, where the tiny beginnings of St. Paul, Minneapolis and St. Anthony were originally located. These literary visitors would note, as most tourists and reporters still do, the beauty of Minneapolis' lakes and the elegance of St. Paul's Summit Avenue. As authors they would certainly be impressed by Minnesota's literary activity, as evidenced by the number of local writers, publishers, periodicals and bookstores.

Theodore Blegen noted in 1963 that "Minnesota has been described as "a writing state" (Blegen 1963: 508). It is also a state with a long tradition of support for literature, a tradition surely brought about in part by the visits of the author lecturers. What follows are some notes on that tradition, focusing on the infrastructure of literary activity rather than attempting to be a critique of writers or the art of writing. It is an overview of what is often called "The Community of the Book," written from the perspective of a constant reader. The overview has been divided into sections, but it will be obvious that within the Community there is a great deal of synergism as people and institutions do overlap.

Lyceums and Lectures

In 1893 Mrs. Isaac Atwater recalled early days in the settlement of St. Anthony. The books, magazines and newspapers which arrived here in the 1850's were shared almost to destruction. A copy of Dickens' *David Copperfield* was passed eagerly from reader to reader. By spring when the ice went out and people were less housebound, the book was worn to rags (Atwater 1893: 2). Bringing more information to local readers was clearly needed.

Early settlers shared knowledge as well as books by establishing lyceums, which were courses of lectures on various subjects. They were offered at first by local residents. As such programs became better established, local sponsors were able to invite speakers from national lyceum lists. Emerson, Garland, Thoreau, Twain, Taylor, Julia Ward Howe and Max O'Rell were all listed as lyceum speakers during their careers. In his 1906 book, *Who's Who in the Lyceum,* A. Augustus Wright listed as lyceum presenters writers, politicians, musicians, dramatic readers, chalk talkers, travelers with stereopticon slides, and even a whistler (Wright 1906: 25). By the 1980's, any important literary visitor who gave a talk or reading would be interviewed on local radio talk shows and on commercial or cable television programs in addition to autographing his or her latest works at local bookstores. These aspects of the contemporary book tour would certainly have amazed the lyceum lecturers who often expected only F.A.M.E. or "fifty dollars and my expenses" for their appearances (Wright 1906: 25).

Talks by authors given on the lyceum circuit began in the 1850's in Minnesota. Carl Bode noted that lyceum programs were active in Austin, Cannon Falls, Hastings, Mankato, St.

Anthony, Stillwater, Taylors Falls, Winona, St. Paul and Minneapolis (Bode 1956: 179). Arrangements for speakers could be made through national agencies such as the American Literary Bureau, Redpath's or Major J. B. Pond's. Writing in 1900 Major Pond felt that, although newspapers carried a great deal of commentary on "progress, genius, education, reform, and entertainment," there was still a demand for good lecturers (Pond 1900: 548, 550).

The literary lecturer, and the politician and the reformer who are often authors as well, have continued to find audiences in Minnesota as conference, commencement and convocation speakers. A list of all such speakers in the state would be lengthy, perhaps not too valuable and probably hard to discover, but there have been several distinguished lecture programs involving literary figures of importance which should be mentioned.

Following the death in 1954 of Gideon Seymour, the executive editor of the *Minneapolis Star-Tribune,* the newspaper sponsored a series of lectures in his memory at the University of Minnesota. The first lecture was delivered by James Reston on February 22, 1955. The lecture committee hoped to present "world leaders in widely varied fields of public interest" (*Minneapolis Star-Tribune,* September 26, 1954). In succeeding years, students, faculty and the community heard Arnold Toynbee, T. S. Eliot, Walter Lippman, Lester B. Pearson, James B. Conant, the Maharajah of Mysore, Harrison Brown, and Archibald MacLeish. The series ended in 1960 with Detlev Bronk. Many of these lectures were published by the University of Minnesota Press in small pamphlets.

The University of Minnesota English department sponsors the Joseph Warren Beach Lectures in memory of the critic and scholar who headed that department from 1940 until 1948. The annual lecture, begun in 1959 with Lionel Trilling, brings writers, critics and professors to the campus each spring. Robert Penn Warren and Allen Tate, both members of the department at one time, were early lecturers. Alfred Kazin,

Leon Edel, Edward Said, N. Scott Momaday, and George Steiner are among the thirty-four lecturers to date.

Another important lecture series at the University of Minnesota has been funded by Curtis Carlson, founder of the Carlson Companies, and sponsored by the Hubert H. Humphrey Institute. The Carlson lecturers tend to be political figures (such as Presidents Bush and Carter) or those who have had an impact on public policy (Anita Hill, Philip Habib, Jehan Sadat, George Will, and Beverly Sills). John Gardner delivered the first Carlson lecture at Northrop Auditorium on October 29, 1980. Tickets for the Carlson lectures are free and often highly in demand. For Professor Anita Hill's lecture during October of 1992, radio speakers and television monitors were available at various campus locations for those who could not obtain a seat in the auditorium. Two or three Carlson lectures are presented during each academic year.

A town hall seems a likely place for a lecture so when members of Westminster Presbyterian church and their pastor, Rev. Donald Meisel, decided on a noon-time lecture series, Town Hall Forum was its name. The underlying theme was ethics with lawyers, journalists, critics, advocates of the arts and children's rights and writers each viewing problems in their own fields. The first lecturer, in October of 1980, was Archibald Cox. The Westminster series is free, broadcast over public radio stations, and is co-sponsored by local corporations and foundations. Author lecturers have been Isaac Bashevis Singer, Garrison Keillor, Michael Dorris, Robert Coles, Studs Terkel, Maya Angelou, and Georgie Ann Geyer. From three to seven lectures are given each year.

A fourth program, perhaps closer in nature to the lyceum offerings, was offered by the St. Paul's Women's Institute between 1939 and 1971. The Institute was the brainchild of B. H. Ridder, publisher of the *St. Paul Pioneer Press Dispatch*. Ridder's idea was to organize a series of programs which would attract women to downtown St. Paul where they might then shop and patronize the city's hotels and restaurants. For every season ticket purchased by a St. Paul woman, a free ticket would be offered to a woman from another Minnesota town or city. Economic stimulus was one goal of the Institute's programs, the other was civic beautification. During World War II the Institute and its many committees were involved in war work, such as collecting scrap materials, clothing and soap for various relief efforts. While the Institute's programs were eagerly attended and its projects successful, the inexpensive tickets ($2.40 paid for a season of twelve events) never covered the total costs incurred. The St. Paul newspaper covered deficits running between $25,000 to $50,000 each year.

In 1971 the program of the Institute came to a halt, the victim of television. According to Mrs. Bernard Ridder it had become virtually impossible to book artists and speakers as they all wanted an escape clause in their contracts, allowing them to cancel if a television appearance were offered. Ticket prices would have had to be raised for future seasons, but it was the competition of television which ended the Institute programs (Grossman 1971). During the thirty-two years of Institute programs the ladies saw fashion shows and heard many concerts. Among the writers and critics who spoke were Dorothy Thompson, Margaret Culkin Banning, Will Durant, Bennett Cerf, Clifton Fadiman, Emily Kimbrough, Fannie Hurst, Randolph Churchill, Franklin P. Adams and John Mason Brown. For two dollars and forty cents a year, it was quite a bargain.

Women's Clubs and Library Friends

Minnesota's first women's club was the Ladies Floral Club of Austin (founded in 1869), whose aims included city beautification. At the second meeting of this Club, one hundred dollars was collected to purchase books and "Library Association" became a part of the Club's name. The growing book collection moved from one member's home to another until space was found in the basement of the newly built county courthouse. In 1904 the 3,425 volume collection was moved to the Austin city library in its new Carnegie building. A similar link between women's clubs and the development of libraries was forged throughout the state. And often, if the founding organization faltered in its support, a women's club would take over the declining library and restore it to life (Carlstedt 1934: 24).

Women established three types of organizations in Minnesota: the Woman's Christian Temperance Unions, women's rights groups, and women's clubs (Bingham 1989: 438). Women's clubs mixed the self improvement aspects of the lyceum movement with their community betterment programs. The women's clubs, founded from the 1870's on, were frequently known as study or literary clubs or reading circles. Members would choose a country or historical period and then organize a year's programs around that theme. Members would present talks on that subject, often being encouraged to do so without relying on papers or notes. As the motto of the Merriam Park Woman's Club of St. Paul (1895) read:

"To sew, to bake, to mend, a woman's task 'tis true,
But to these homely tasks to tend we fain would add a few.
To read, to think, to learn is women's work the same;
What matter if she sometimes turn to reach the higher plane?"
(Foster 1924: 206).

By 1895 when the Minnesota State Federation of Women's Clubs was founded, most of the member clubs had literary programs. The Federation, whose first president was Margaret Evans of Carleton College, encouraged local clubs to work in five areas:

(1) Establishment of town and country clubs where rural and urban members could meet.
(2) Support for libraries and travelling libraries.
(3) Town and village beautification.
(4) Assistance for the public schools.

(5) Support for the Minnesota Art Interchange, which
    provided clubs with stereopticon slides, photographs
    and books for the study of art (Croly 1898: 726).

In addition to their literary programs, many early clubs
sponsored writing groups and book review programs. Books
were reviewed by members, professional critics, faculty
members from local colleges, and booksellers. While not all
women's clubs still have book review groups, the concept
continues to be popular. In 1990 there were a number of active
book clubs in the Twin Cities organized by college alumni, a
branch library, and the Chicago-based Great Books Foundation (Meier 1990). Other book clubs are sponsored by book
stores or begun by friends who like to read. *The Minnesota
Women's Press,* a twice monthly newspaper, has sponsored
groups since 1985 studying books written by women.

Library support continued in another important way,
through groups called "Friends." As members of women's
clubs completed the drive to obtain the bricks and mortar and
the donation of money from Andrew Carnegie which would
build their local library, they realized that support for library
staff and collections needed to be ongoing. There needed to be
more "concerts, basket socials, suppers and oyster stews" to
support the libraries (Carlstedt 1934: 25–26). While many of
the women's clubs continued in this manner to assist their local libraries over the years, organized "Friends" or "Associates
of the Library" groups were not formed in Minnesota until after World War II. The Friends of the St. Paul Library (1945)
may well be the state's oldest Friends' group. A statewide
organization was organized in 1969 and, by 1979, was placed
on a firm footing as the Minnesota Association of Library
Friends. Today Minnesota has about 330 public libraries and
about 100 Friends' groups affiliated with public, private, or
academic libraries. Membership is open to both men and
women.

The goal for the Friends' groups is to support the library

through fundraising projects, programs and trained volunteer assistance. Lunchtime brown bag talks and readings, tours to local sites famous in literature (such as a recent visit by the Minneapolis Friends to Mankato to view locales described by Maud Hart Lovelace in her Betsy-Tacy books), and involvement in bookfairs and used book sales are frequent activities. The Friends of the Minneapolis Public Library (1949) operate a used book store as well as the city's planetarium. Two Minnesota bookfairs called A Book Affair, were organized and partially funded by the St. Paul Friends in 1988 and 1989. The festivals occupied Landmark Center across Rice Park from the central library.

Most Friends' groups are affiliated with public library systems, but two of the University of Minnesota's special book collections have their own organized support groups. The nucleus of both of these "libraries within the library" were given to the University by collectors. James Ford Bell, the grain merchant, was interested in history, travel, the Mississippi river, exploration and maps. His collection, which was given to the University in 1953, and is housed in Wilson Library, includes many unique editions and volumes. John Parker served as the curator of the Bell Collection from its beginning, retiring in 1991. The Associates of the Bell Collection include other collectors, scholars, and dealers in rare books throughout the world. The Associates have sponsored bookfairs featuring dealers in antiquarian books, as well as their own regular programs. Those who share an interest in the history of books and fine printing are often members of clubs such as The Ampersand, begun in 1931, the Manuscript Club, the Library Council of the Minneapolis Institute of Arts, and the Minnesota Center for Book Arts.

Children's books were what interested Dr. Irvin Kerlan (1912–1963), a St. Cloud native who received his medical training at the University of Minnesota. Dr. Kerlan began collecting books and, following the suggestion of J. Harold Kittleson, branched out into the manuscripts and drawings

Children's Literature Research Collection
109 Walter Library

The Arthur Upson Room, Walter Library.

which preceded the final product. He began giving his collection, which by then included Caldecott and Newbery award winning books, to the University of Minnesota in 1949. The final donation came after his death in 1963. The Kerlan Collection can be consulted in the Arthur Upson room of the university's Walter Library. The Kerlan books and original materials are now a part of the 55,000 volume Children's Literature Research Collections curated by Dr. Karen Nelson Hoyle since 1967.

Members of the Kerlan Friends organization include teachers, booksellers, librarians, writers and illustrators active in the field of children's literature. Kerlan summertime forums feature discussions by scholars. Exhibitions in this country and at the Children's Bookfair in Bologna, Italy in 1985, have made the collection available to a wider public. The annual Kerlan Award is given to a writer or artist of significance whose work is well represented in the collection. Some awards, like those to Margaret Wise Brown and New Ulm native Wanda Gág, have been posthumous, but most of the Kerlan award winners have spoken at the annual banquet. Among them have been Tomie dePaola, Charles Mikolaycak, Madeleine L'Engle, Katherine Paterson, Marguerite Henry and Roger Duvoisin.

Booksellers from Small to Super

The copy of *David Copperfield* so eagerly read by Mrs. Atwater and her friends was probably ordered through the mail, since at that time there were no local booksellers. Frank O'Brien, who came to Minnesota in 1855, wrote that the first Minneapolis bookseller was L. W. Stratton who opened a business called the Farmers' Exchange at Main Street and Third Avenue Northeast in 1850. The Farmers' Exchange sold newspapers, magazines, and books in addition to groceries. The hours were long, from six in the morning until ten at night during the week. Books could be purchased or borrowed, as Stratton also had a lending library "with all the popular novels of the day" (O'Brien 1904: 193–5).

The Farmers' Exchange was probably typical of the early variety store. M. D. Merrill's store, listed in E. E. Barton's guide to St. Paul businesses in 1888, stocked books, magazines and newspapers, and, just as proudly, sold 75 to 80 gallons of milk every week (Barton 1888: 156).

Another early Minneapolis bookseller, Thomas Hale Williams, maintained a lending library in his Bridge Square shop. In 1859 these books became the basis for the subscription library known as the Minneapolis Athenaeum and Williams was named as its first librarian. Rare books belonging to the Athenaeum and books purchased with funds bequeathed to it are now grouped with collections on the third floor of the Minneapolis Public Library's Central library building. Invaluable for anyone doing research on the city is the Minneapolis Collection which was begun in 1940. Two other library special collections, one devoted to World War II and the other to nineteenth century American authors, were formed by J. Harold Kittleson. These collections include books, manuscripts, periodicals and ephemera. Curator of the Special Collections department is Edward Kukla.

Mr. Kittleson, often regarded as one of the most important book persons in the area, began his career in Dayton's book department. He managed Mabel Ulrich's Minneapolis store briefly before moving on to Powers' in 1930. Following World War II he became a sales representative for Random House. Mr. Kittleson has served as president of the Friends of the Minneapolis Public Library, as a book buyer for their store, and as a trustee of the Library itself.

In 1954 John K. Sherman wrote in the *Minneapolis Tribune* about bookstores which he remembered from the 1920's: the Doorway, Mabel Ulrich's, Oudal's, the Century, and St. Paul Book & Stationery. Several readers wrote to that newspaper to mention booksellers they recalled from even earlier times. Melbin Erickson wrote that he had worked for Charles M. Cushman who opened his Minneapolis bookstore in 1858 and M. Swedenborg recalled buying school books at the store of "a likable chap named Raymer" (*Minneapolis Tribune*, Letters to the Editor, January 9, 1955). Charles Raymer's shop at 243 Fourth Avenue South advertised "old, rare, curious and reference books." A drawing used by Raymer as his trademark showed a gentleman in 18th century dress standing on a library stool to inspect shelves of books. For several years in the nineties Raymer also published a combination catalogue and literary periodical called *The Literary Light*. Each month's issue carried essays on books and bookselling, reviews, notices and listings of books for sale or sought by other dealers. Raymer charged one dollar per year for his magazine which he said had a circulation of five thousand copies.

Raymer printed lists of other Minnesota booksellers and announced in the fall of 1891 the formation of what may be the first trade group in the community, the Northwestern Booksellers and Newsdealers Association. Raymer was the first assistant secretary of the group. C. E. Musser of Mankato was president, Alex. McNie of Winona was treasurer, and C. S. Crabtree of Minneapolis served as secretary.

Just as Mr. Stratton sold groceries in addition to books, so later booksellers displayed prints, artifacts and paintings on their walls and shelves. The biographer of Edmund Brooks considered him to be the "greatest bookseller in Minnesota" (Grove 1945: vii). Brooks (1866–1919) opened his Minneapolis shop at 605 Marquette Avenue South in 1900. An announcement from 1909 shows one of his book rooms with antique furniture, a fireplace and a chandelier hanging over a refectory table where customers could examine his "books, painter-etchings, original drawings and manuscripts." An obituary noted that Brooks was a frequent visitor to Europe and "knew intimately all the leading literary men of England" (*Minneapolis Journal,* February 12, 1919). Brooks was also a publisher with sixteen volumes given his imprint (Grove 1945). One of these books contained the poems of Arthur Upson edited by Dr. Richard Burton. Upson had worked for Brooks as a cataloguer and was part of a circle of book people who gathered at the shop.

By the 1920's more bookstores had opened their doors in the Twin Cities. Oudal's opened in 1901 and Perine's, known to generations of University of Minnesota students, lasted from 1914 to 1978. John K. Sherman remembered, rather wistfully, that "there was a thrill in buying a book in those days that I have since nearly lost, for being now a book reviewer I receive for free practically all the books I need or can digest. The worth of an article is mysteriously enhanced when you lay out your cold and hard earned coin for it" (*Minneapolis Tribune,* December 26, 1954). One of the bookstores he often visited in the twenties was Mabel Ulrich's, at 12th and Nicollet Avenue South. He termed it "one of the town's

Invitation to book shop of Edmond Brooks, 1909.

intellectual centers" run by a "formidably intelligent and witty woman."

Mrs. Ulrich (1876–1945) and her husband were both medical doctors. She graduated from Cornell University and the medical school of Johns Hopkins University. After coming to Minnesota she served on the state Board of Health, the Minneapolis Board of Public Welfare, and was regional director for the American Red Cross. When she decided to open a bookstore in 1921 it sold more than books marked with her distinctive Pegasus label. Eventually there was a print shop and a gallery with exhibits of J. M. Whistler lithographs, etchings by Childe Hassam and Peggy Bacon, Georg Jensen silver, and baskets from the Niger river. A flyer called *Bookshop Trivia,* which was sent to Mrs. Ulrich's customers, mentioned the treasures she had found on European trips, listed new books with her frank assessments, and spoke about upcoming events.

Through her contacts in the book world Mrs. Ulrich organized lectures by distinguished authors. Among those who came to Minneapolis in the mid-twenties were Vachel Lindsay, Carl Sandburg, Sherwood Anderson, Hugh Walpole, Edna St. Vincent Millay and William Beebe. Some authors appeared not only at her Minneapolis shop, but also at the branch stores in St. Paul, Duluth, and Rochester. After Sandburg's appearance, as Mrs. Ulrich noted in one issue of her *Bookshop Trivia,* she gave up the idea of originating the lectures. Being an impresario was a lot of work.

Mrs. Ulrich closed her stores in 1933 and soon undertook a new challenge, the editing of Minnesota's volume in the WPA Writers' American Guide series and directing the large corps of WPA researchers. The closing of her Minneapolis store ended what one writer described as the nearest thing Minneapolis had seen to a literary salon (Bigelow 1936: 50). Her store, like that of Edmund Brooks, was often described as a very attractive series of rooms where people interested in art and books could gather, perhaps over tea.

Minnesota Booksellers' Marks.

Most of the early bookstores established in Minnesota were independently owned and many still are. One which was not, yet was known as one of the best sources for books for many decades, was the book department of Powers' Dry Goods Store. The Powers store traced its beginning to the M. D. Ingram Company (1881) which became the S. E. Olson Company in 1887. Olson sold his store to the Associated Dry Goods Company of New York in 1916, whose president had been Alonzo J. Powers. The Powers chain eventually expanded to include stores in St. Paul and the suburbs, but it was the Minneapolis store at Nicollet Avenue and 5th Street which became noted for its book department. Guided by Leonard Wells, J. Harold Kittleson, and later Alice Carlson, Powers sold new books, rare books, and even musical scores on occasion. The Powers chain was sold to Allied Stores, the corporate owner of Donaldson's, in 1985.

The training of a bookseller can follow many paths, but the apprenticeship of Leonard Wells (1868-1933) was probably more varied than most. Before he left his Iowa home at the age of fourteen to seek his fortune, he had already clerked in a drug store. From Kansas to Oklahoma, and then Oregon, Utah, Colorado and Washington state, Wells earned his living as a pharmacist and, for a time, as a travelling beauty cream salesman. During a visit to his mother in St. Paul in 1893 he decided to take a job at the Schuneman-Evans department store and not long after left that store for a better opportunity as manager of eight departments at Powers.

In the 1890's books were a minor sideline in a department store. Wells soon changed that. The four shelves, two counters, and twenty-five feet of shelving he was given for the book section soon needed to be expanded as Wells acquired more stock. Within ten years he began making trips to Europe where he purchased Shakespearean folios, a King James Bible of 1611, first editions, and "enough books to pave Nicollet Avenue" (*Minneapolis Journal,* February 16, 1930).

In an interview completed just before his death Wells was

described as elegantly dressed (by Sulka), his pince-nez suggesting "a gentle unworldly scholar" with a devotion to literature. Yet, as the writer concluded, Wells did not seem to be a great student of literature. He was more interested in books as books. The financial success of the Powers book section, unusual in any department store, was due to Wells' ability as "one part scholar, two parts collector, and three parts merchandiser" (MacGaheran 1933: 62).

For bookbuyers in St. Paul, the main place to shop for many years was the St. Paul Book & Stationery Company, the city's second oldest continuing business. Founded as Yankee Notions in 1851 "when the ice went out in the spring," the "book" in its name originally indicated "ledger book" as the company was more a purveyor of office supplies and textbooks than literature. A furor over prices charged by publishers of textbooks led to the company's entry into that aspect of bookselling. In 1877 the owner, Daniel D. Merrill, proposed to the state legislature that his firm would supply textbooks to the public schools at one-half the regular price for fifteen years. Despite much argument legislation supporting Merrill's proposal, strongly advocated by Ignatius Donnelly, was passed. After 1892 other publishers were permitted to sell textbooks to the school boards (Folwell 1930: IV, 153–162).

By the 1880's the store began sending its own monthly magazine, *The Literary News,* subtitled "An Eclectic Review of Current Literature" to customers and subscribers. Merrill, listed as editor, reprinted reviews, poems, excerpts from novels and literary gossip from *Publishers' Weekly.* There were lists of new books and of articles appearing in each month's national magazines. By 1889 drawings and engravings were sprinkled throughout the text. The following year a 250-page store catalogue listed books, maps, globes and blackboards. Available through the catalogue were books by Thoreau, Marryat, Taylor, O'Rell and Eggleston, usually at eighty cents to one dollar each; Twain's novels were a pricey $2.40 apiece.

Most booksellers have welcomed the opportunity to talk to

groups about new books. For St. Paul Book, the speaker in the 1950's and later was Jeanne Fischer. Ever since somebody called the store and asked Kirker Bixby, manager of the book department, if there was anyone who could give "a little talk," she has shared her love of books with talks to groups and through reviews published in the *St. Paul Pioneer Press.*

When St. Paul Book moved its downtown store to Town Square, its owners decided to stop selling books since a B. Dalton store was only 400 feet away. Thus, one of St. Paul's oldest bookstores and businesses has now returned to its roots: a line of office and school supplies.

The 1960's and 1970's witnessed the openings of a variety of new bookstores in the Twin Cities and the birth of the B. Dalton Bookseller chain. Among the independent bookstores were Savran's, Gringolet, the Amazon Bookstore, the Hungry Mind and the Bookcase. Savran's, on Cedar Avenue, was located in the West Bank area of the University of Minnesota from 1965 to 1987. Its logo of a bearded man holding a book can still be seen on the wall of the building which it occupied. Gringolet, named after a horse in a medieval romance, was operated by Michael Leimer in Riverplace from 1979 to 1991. Like a Rizzoli branch in that same upscale mall, Gringolet closed its doors when the development lost its attraction for customers.

The Bookcase has had two locations (downtown Minneapolis and Wayzata) since it was opened by Benton Case and his wife in 1963. Gail See and Jane White purchased the store in 1974 and sold it to Peggy Burnett in 1991. Mrs. See, a strong advocate of independent bookstores, served as president of the American Booksellers Association in 1984.

The Amazon Bookstore opened in Julie Morse's home in 1970. Volunteers helped run this bookstore (and women's center) whose focus was on books written by women. It is now owned by a six-woman cooperative, is located on Harmon Place in Minneapolis, and is considered to be the oldest women's bookstore in the country.

The Hungry Mind, also a child of the 1970's, was opened by David Unowsky on Grand Avenue in St. Paul near the Macalester College campus. When the college decided to close its own bookstore, Hungry Mind was able to pick up that business and to move into larger quarters next to a yarn shop and an oriental restaurant. The store began scheduling readings by local authors in 1976 and introduced *The Hungry Mind Review,* edited by Bart Schneider, in 1985. Unowsky had felt the need for a midwestern publication which would focus upon small press and midlist books. *The Review* appears quarterly and is distributed free through independent bookstores.

At the eastern end of Grand Avenue several strips of old commercial buildings were developed into malls. In 1978 Michele and Dan Odegard opened their first store in the Victoria Crossing mall. Business flourished so they were able to move across the street, creating a new bookstore to the east. The older location was then called Encore and was reserved for publishers' overstocks. After their divorce, Dan Odegard opened Odegard Books Minneapolis in 1984 in Calhoun Square in the heart of a bustling retail area at Hennepin and Lake Streets. An attempt at chain-building brought both the Calhoun Square and Centennial Lakes Odegard stores into bankruptcy eight years later. Odegard's former wife, now Michele Cromer-Poiré, continues to operate the two St. Paul Odegard stores. She has added a Books for Travel shop and a bookshop for children called Red Balloon, in which she shares the ownership with Carol Erdahl. Only one independent bookstore remains in downtown Minneapolis, Baxter's, opened by Brian Baxter in 1988.

In 1972 Roy Close wrote an article criticising the Twin Cities for their lack of a "complete" bookstore where students, scholars and professionals in any field could find what they needed (*Minneapolis Star,* April 20, 1972). At that time he estimated there were 25 general bookstores in the area, with Perine's, Powers' and the St. Paul Book & Stationery considered the best. Twenty years later Perine's and Powers' had closed while office and school supplies fill the shelves at St. Paul Book & Stationery. The *1992 Booksellers Catalogue* of the Upper Midwest Booksellers Assocation lists 52 member stores in the Twin Cities. There are thirty-four chain bookstores and, in addition, two dozen dealers in used books. One source suggests that the Twin Cities have 1.19 bookstores per 10,000 inhabitants, slightly below the national average. While there still may not be a complete bookstore in the sense Close described, offering a large stock of both new and older titles, those interested in books have many more sources to visit than was possible in 1972. Virtually all museums have shops selling their own and related publications. Those colleges with bookstores sell both required textbooks and general titles.

Probably the greatest growth has been in the field of children's books, however. Most general bookstores have a children's section, but there are a number of specialized children's shops, such as Red Balloon, Bookhouse, Wild Rumpus, and the state's oldest children's bookstore, The Tree House in St. Cloud, founded by Charles and Gertie Geck in 1980. Given the number of children's books published each year no shop would dare suggest to parents as a Minneapolis store called The Doorway did in 1925:

> "The children want some Christmas books,
> Can't you give 'em one?
> We have almost all of them
> Underneath the sun."
> (Advertisement, *Minneapolis Journal,* December 13, 1925.)

The two newest children's bookstores opened in 1992, one in the Minnesota Historical Society's History Center in St. Paul, and the other, P. B. Pages (B. Dalton's new chainstore for children's books) in the Mall of America in Bloomington.

When the Dayton Company opened its first B. Dalton store in the Southdale Shopping Center in 1966, probably few people imagined how successful it would be—or that in less than thirty years, booksellers and reporters would talk about the "war between the independents and the chains."

The first B. Dalton store in the country's first covered shopping mall was not an immediate success. The early stores were supposed to resemble an English country manor with wooden desks, leather chairs and brass lamps. Even the name was supposed to suggest an English image and not a misspelled version of the name of Dayton's then CEO — Bruce Dayton (*Minneapolis Tribune,* February 19, 1984). Two factors soon changed the B. Dalton store concept. One was the acquisition of the Pickwick Bookstores, and the other was the hiring of Kay Sexton.

Sexton's background was in merchandising. She had worked for Donaldson's, Dayton's, and the Emporium until that St. Paul store had closed. According to one interview, "She messed up things" by banishing "the unnecessary aura of elitism surrounding books" (Papa 1980: 113). Inspired, too, by the layouts of the Pickwick stores, the B. Dalton stores soon became more crowded with more books and more shelves and tables piled high so buyers were inclined to shop faster and not browse. Sexton served as B. Dalton's director of merchandising, communications and publications, until her retirement in 1987. An in-house news bulletin intended for wholesale buyers, her "little green rag," became a sought-after indicator of which books Sexton thought would sell best. Literary agents, publishers and authors eagerly subscribed to this weekly pea-green bulletin.

B. Dalton stores were opened in all of the large suburban shopping centers, the "Dales," which Garrison Keillor used to lovingly enumerate, "Mondale, Hillandale, and Chippendale." There they competed directly with stores of the other national bookselling chain, Waldenbooks, owned by Kmart.

After twenty years the Dayton Hudson Company sold its B. Dalton chain to a consortium consisting of Barnes & Noble, Leonard Riggio, the Barnes & Noble president, and a Dutch firm. Under the same management are other established bookstore names including Scribner's and Doubleday (two stores with the Doubleday name have opened and closed on the Nicollet Mall).

The sale of B. Dalton's to Barnes & Noble was the opening salvo in the war of the superstores. While the B. Dalton stores were tenants in the Dales, the Barnes & Noble superstores were located in 13,000 to 15,000 square feet spaces in strip malls. The first Barnes & Noble superstore opened in 1989 in Roseville. Despite a stock of 100,000 titles the space for customers there is ample. Browsers can sit while they consider their purchases and signs boast the discounts available on best sellers. Rather than presenting a larger B. Dalton format, the Barnes & Noble superstores seem to have borrowed ideas from the independent bookstores in their layout and approach. After the Roseville store, Barnes & Noble opened others, in Ridgehaven, Calhoun Village, Burnsville, The Galleria, and Woodbury Village, effectively surrounding the Twin Cities.

Waldenbooks, the nation's largest chain, is part of the specialty retailing division of Kmart. None of the Basset superstores in that division have as yet been promised for the Twin Cities, but with a recent corporate acquisition, Kmart now owns two Borders' bookstores in Minnesota; one in the Calhoun Square space formerly occupied by Odegard's, and the other at the Bonaventure Mall in Minnetonka.

While some worry that the superstores will drive the independent bookstores out of business, that hasn't happened as yet. Independent bookstore owners argue that the loss of their stores will mean fewer outlets where small publishers can sell their books. This, they suggest, will reduce or limit the publishing of new authors and unfamiliar viewpoints since the chainstores are not interested in selling such books. For the customer there is now an incredible amount of choice. For the bookstore manager, marketing and promotional activities become even more important in building customer recognition and loyalty. To a degree that would have surprised Mabel Ulrich, authors still visit the Twin Cities for promotional pur-

poses. They read, recite, sign and appear at independent bookshops, chain bookstores, and museum shops. Each Sunday the
literary events columns of local newspapers list a week's
worth of ten to a dozen of such events, and there may well be
more than that. Whether such events build repeat business or
whether customers select a bookstore based on such intangi-
ble qualities as service, distance, parking, and price is not
known. It may be, as one letter writer to *The New York Times*
saw it, "since we are a land bereft of public places," that the
superstores are our new public spaces. According to that writer, the superstores are safe, pleasant, have benches, serve
coffee, and even offer entertainment in the readings (November 22, 1992, B11). A bookstore thus becomes a destination,
a place to spend time, not just a place to shop.

The shelf life of a new book is short, perhaps a few months
on a chain bookstore shelf, or up to a year in an independent
store. As a used book it will have a far longer existence, going
from homes to dealers and back again. The Twin Cities have
about two dozen dealers in used books, with a variety of
specialized holdings. Several are located in the Dinkytown
area north of the University of Minnesota campus. Dinkytown has always had bookstores, including Oudal's, Perine's
and the unforgettable jumble of the Melvin McCosh store.
Larry Dingman of the Dinkytown Antiquarian Bookstore
compiled a guide to all of the used and antiquarian dealers in
1992. Dingman is also very active in the Midwestern Book-
hunters which has sponsored used bookfairs at the State
Fairgrounds during the summer. Other well-known used or
antiquarian booksellers are Leland Lien (downtown Minneapolis), James and Mary Laurie, Robert Rulon-Miller, and
Harold's (at Seven Corners), all in St. Paul, James Cummings
in Stillwater, and Melvin McCosh in Excelsior.

Literary Journals, Magazines, and Small Presses

*Loonfeather, Milkweed Chronicle, Lake Street Review, The Busy
West, North Country Anvil, Globe, Dacotah Territory* and *The*

Bellman are names of some of Minnesota's journals of literature and the arts. Launched with great hopes, some lasted only
for a few issues before succumbing due to a loss of energy,
time or money.

Before 1900 *The Frontier Monthly* (Hastings, 1859), *The
Minnesota Monthly* (St. Paul, 1869–1870), *The Busy West* (St.
Paul, 1872–1873), *Northwestern Monthly Magazine* (St. Paul,
1878) and *The Literary Northwest* (St. Paul, 1892–1893) had all
appeared and just as quickly vanished. Two magazines, one
launched in St. Paul and the other in Minneapolis, lasted
longer and offered more varied fare. These were *De Lestry's
Western Magazine,* published by Edmond L. De Lestry (St.
Paul, 1897–1901) and William C. Edgar's *The Bellman* (Minneapolis, 1906–1919). As John T. Flanagan pointed out *The
Bellman* was, and still is, unique among Minnesota's literary
journals in its focus, its contributors, its duration as a weekly
magazine for thirteen years, and finally, for its success (Flanagan 1945: 304).

The list of Minnesota literary periodicals is a long and
growing one. Julia Morrison discovered 87 publications in
existence between 1850 and 1961. Her compilation included
student magazines produced at the various colleges, bookstore publications (like those issued by Charles Raymer and
St. Paul Book & Stationery) as well as ventures such as *The
Bellman.* Ms. Morrison's list ends well before 1965 when federal funds and state grants became available to support not-
for-profit literary journals and publishing houses. A listing
compiled by Mary Bround Smith in *Minnesota Literature Newsletter* in 1990 discloses forty-eight other periodicals not found
in the Morrison study. Ms. Smith plans to publish a new list
in early 1993 which will certainly show many additional
names.

Locating copies of literary journals is often a problem because of their limited and erratic distribution. While an editor
might promise in the first issue that subscribers could expect
to receive a copy every month, such a target was often not

realistic. The journal promised monthly was later published on a bi-monthly or semiannual schedule or, even as *North Country Anvil* eventually admitted, "as it can be." Most of the current literary journals publish poetry, essays and short fiction with few illustrations. Explanatory notes by the editor and biographical information on the contributors complete the basic contents. Thus the achievements of *The Bellman* and the short-lived *Globe* seem even more remarkable in retrospect.

The Bellman's William C. Edgar (1856–1932) was born in La Crosse, Wisconsin, the original home of *The Northwestern Miller*. When that magazine moved to Minneapolis in 1882 Edgar joined it as business manager. A few years later he began writing editorials for the magazine, and he continued in this capacity until his retirement in January, 1924. At that time Edgar was president of the Miller Publishing Company and *The Northwestern Miller* had celebrated its fiftieth anniversary.

In 1906 Edgar introduced *The Bellman,* a weekly illustrated review, for which he served as both editor and publisher. The cover always featured the Bellman, a town crier figure in eighteenth century dress. Smaller Bellman figures were used as column heads for the various departments within the magazine. For the last three years of his life Edgar wrote a column titled *The Bellman,* which appeared every Monday in the *Minneapolis Tribune.* His last column, published posthumously on December 5, 1932, began "Men often show an almost pathetic desire to be remembered after death." Even if he had not published *The Bellman* for thirteen years Edgar would be remembered for his work with *The Northwestern Miller* and with European relief activities, as he arranged for shipment of flour during the famine days of 1891 and after World War I.

Early issues of *The Bellman* carried reviews, essays, commentary and even a social column. (Edgar was twice president of the Minneapolis Club and wrote a history of that club which was published in 1920.) Contributing writers included local literary figures such as Arthur Upson, Mabel Ulrich, and

Cover, *The Bellman.*

Professors Richard Burton and Oscar Firkins from the University of Minnesota. As *The Bellman* became better known, Edgar was able to commission works from writers of national significance, including Booth Tarkington, Carl Van Vechten, Louis Untermeyer, Christopher Morley and Sara Teasdale (Flanagan 1945: 308). When Edgar determined to close *The Bellman* he was able to reimburse the original investors in full. Neither the name nor the subscription list was sold as Edgar did not intend to see his magazine in other hands. His Bellman would never hunt anybody else's snark. Edgar later published one book of verse and one of prose extracted from thirteen years of his magazine.

John Warner Griggs Dunn (1903–1975) of Marine-on-St. Croix had a different concept for a literary magazine. Dunn, a Stanford graduate, had spent two years in the merchant marine and another two years travelling in Europe and North Africa. What his magazine, called *Globe,* would offer was the reality of travel. Not the world of luxury hotels and expensive restaurants, but more unusual and picaresque tales of exotic and familiar places written by well travelled writers.

Had adventure travel and ecotourism been mentioned in Dunn's day, he would have sought writers on the subject. As it was, his research methodology was quite unusual. In an interview written by J. H. Leinhard for the *St. Paul Pioneer Press* a week before *Globe*'s debut in 1937, Dunn described his eighteen months of preparation. He returned to Europe and in the forty cities he visited would choose a cafe and there set up his office. He bought local newspapers and magazines, and visited tourist offices, clubs for artists and photographers, museums and universities. By the end of his second week in a town, there would usually be an interview with Dunn about *Globe* in a local newspaper. That publicity introduced Dunn to other potential writers, who then came to his hotel or his cafe office. Waiters, Dunn said, were his best guides to a city, serving inside information along with coffee, liqueurs and writing materials. The first issue of *Globe,* the international magazine, appeared in February, 1937. James Gray praised its first 130 page issue highly. It was, he said, the size of *Reader's Digest,* based on a very original idea, and very well produced (*St. Paul Dispatch,* February 19, 1937).

From the beginning Dunn sought travel pieces from established writers and from beginners who had something unusual to say. *Globe* printed essays by Ludwig Bemelmans, Langston Hughes, William Saroyan, Ruth Suckow, Jesse Stuart, Caskie Stinnett and Henry Miller. Ezra Pound was engaged to write a letter from Europe for each issue. *Globe* was illustrated with photographs or drawings (often by Dunn's brother, Montfort). One issue offered a portfolio of sketches by Cameron Booth and another had lithographs by Adolf Dehn. But despite its high aims, *Globe* changed from a monthly to a bimonthly by the second year. The November-December, 1938 issue was the last, as both expenses and the impending war made a travel magazine impossible to continue. Dunn went on to serve for a year as travel editor of the *St. Paul Pioneer Press* and later to write travel articles about Mexico for Texas newspapers and a night club column in Spanish for *El Comercio* of Quito, Ecuador.

Edgar and Dunn probably had an image of the reader whom they hoped would buy their magazines: someone who was educated, literate, well-travelled, and perhaps affluent. Wilfort H. Fawcett's readers had done their travelling with the military (in the Spanish-American War and World War I) and then returned to a farm or small town afterwards. What Fawcett (1885–1940) thought they would purchase was a different sort of magazine; small, pocket sized, crammed with jokes, short poems, stories, and later, cartoons. The motto for his *Capt. Billy's Whiz Bang* (1919–c.1942) was "to make it snappy" and that it most certainly was.

Fawcett mimeographed the first issues of his monthly magazine, but after a few months the printing run had risen to 350,000 copies. It was the first magazine to be launched by what later became a very successful magazine publishing company.

The heyday for *Capt. Billy's Whiz Bang,* named for the sound made by an artillery shell in flight, was in the 1920's. Its novelty, the racy quality of its jokes, and its "explosion of pedigreed bunk," as its cover caption read, found a wide audience. Fawcett and his brothers soon began other magazines which were sold, like *Capt. Billy's Whiz Bang,* on the newsstand rather than by subscription. Among the sixty-three titles originated by Fawcett Publications before World War II were *Romantic Stories, True Confessions, Mechanix Illustrated,* and *Amateur Golfer and Sportsman.* The latter magazine eventually was published by Virginia Safford.

As Gary Fine pointed out in an unpublished paper (Fine 1983), *Capt. Billy's Whiz Bang* was the most prominent comic magazine in America during the twenties, occupying a niche similar to that held by *Playboy* several decades later. Meredith Willson referred to the magazine in his song "Ya Got Trouble" from *The Music Man,* a Broadway musical comedy. Citing dangers that will harm young boys, the comedy character (Professor Harold Hill) tells the mothers of River City that if they see their sons hide dime novels in the corncrib or memorize jokes from *Capt. Billy's Whiz Bang,* these are "tell-tale signs of corruption."

By the mid-twenties Fawcett had become a millionaire, able to indulge his interests in travel, big game hunting, and rifle shooting (he served as captain of the United States Olympic shooting team in 1924). To entertain the many celebrities he had met through the years, Fawcett built a resort on Big Pelican Lake east of Pequot Lakes, calling it Breezy Point Lodge.

When Fawcett died in 1940 Cedric Adams devoted his "In This Corner" column to the man who had given him his first job as a writer. As Adams noted, Fawcett's successful career as editor, publisher and resort owner had been a colorful one and it had all begun with *Capt. Billy's Whiz Bang* (*Minneapolis Star Journal*, February 8, 1940).

Globe was edited in St. Paul, *The Bellman* in Minneapolis, and *Capt. Billy's Whiz Bang* in Robbinsdale. Later literary journals have appeared throughout the state, sometimes because founder-editors are faculty members at college and state universities. The format, size, paper stock, and even focus vary, but all of the journals have published fiction and brief essays, contain occasional illustrations and a lot of poetry. Some of these outstate publications have been *North Country Anvil* (1972–1989), edited by Jack Miller in Millville; Bemidji's *Loonfeather* (1986–date) begun by William Elliott at Bemidji State University and continued by Betty Rossi and Jeane Sliney through the Bemidji Arts Center; and *Great River Review* (1977–date) at Winona State University, founded by Emilio de Grazia and Orval Lund.

Names of literary journals, like names of independent bookstores, may suggest place or evoke literature. *North Country Anvil* intended to be a peoples' magazine of general, not literary interest. On its title page were lines quoted from Carl Sandburg's "The People, Yes": "This old anvil laughs at many broken hammers. There are men who can't be bought." Over its lifetime *North Country Anvil* contained poetry, book reviews, short stories and commentary about causes and concerns. In the earliest issues, Syd Fossum wrote about art of the thirties while later correspondents discussed everything from spear fishing to how to heat a house with wood. *North Country Anvil* was published in Millville, a small town between Lake City and Rochester.

Dacotah Territory (1971–1980) was one of several literary ventures launched by Mark Vinz in the Fargo-Moorhead area. The magazine published poetry, reviews, some interviews and aimed for three issues each year. Special numbers were devoted to Native American poetry and the poems of several of the Poets-in-the-schools. Vinz helped start the Plains Distribution Service, Inc., which distributed literary journals,

chapbooks (published by Dacotah Territory), and other publications by the literary presses. There was even the Plains
Bookbus which trekked around the Midwest filled with
writers destined for workships and readings. Dacotah Territory Press continues as a publisher of Minnesota writing.

The James White Review (1983–date), a quarterly published
in Minneapolis, specializes in gay fiction and poetry. In its
opening issue the editors hoped readers would comment, but
for those who had no opinion they said "may Oscar Wilde
have mercy upon you." *Sing Heavenly Muse!* (1978–date),
founded by Sue Ann Martinson and *Hurricane Alice* (1983–
date), edited by Martha Roth, are feminist journals. *Milkweed
Chronicle* (1980–1987) was published by Emilie Buchwald and
Randy Scholes until they decided to devote all of their time
and energy to their Milkweed Editions Press. *Milkweed
Chronicle* was considered unusual among literary magazines
for its attention to graphic design. Buchwald and Scholes
were successful in tapping not only national donors of funding for small presses, but in finding Minnesota foundations interested in supporting the literary arts.

Other literary journals include Kevin Fitzpatrick's *Lake
Street Review* (1985–1991), Tom Heie's *Sidewalks* (1991–date)
in Champlin, Bev Voldseth's *Rag Mag* (1982–date) in Good-
hue, and Patrick Mackinnon's new *North Coast Review*
(1992–date) in Duluth. David Unowsky's *The Hungry Mind
Review* (1985–date), a quarterly, probably has the widest distribution of any literary journal through its network of independent bookstores.

All of the literary journals publish poetry and fiction which
suits their missions and themes. A reader looking for the work
of Minnesota writers like Bill Holm, Thomas McGrath,
Robert Bly, Mark Vinz, Carol Bly, Meridel Le Sueur, Keith
Harrison or Patricia Hampl, may well find examples in their
pages.

Many of the literary journals as well as a few of the small
presses have not-for-profit status. Although some have

managed to finance their operations through loans, advertising and subscriptions, for most funding has been sought through gifts and grants. In 1984 an officer of COSMEP (a national organization for small presses and magazines) spoke about his group during a visit to St. Paul. Half of COSMEP's 700 members were publishers of literary journals, poetry and fiction. Most, he said, had a dozen titles in their catalogues and grossed $25,000 per year. C. W. Truesdale of New Rivers Press had broken ground, he said, for all small presses who wanted to be classed as not-for-profit organizations (*St. Paul Pioneer Press,* June 23, 1984).

Truesdale moved his New Rivers Press from New York to Minnesota in 1978. He had realized that many of the writers submitting work to him were from the state and that there seemed to be an interest in supporting literature in Minnesota. Two years later Emilie Buchwald, who had moved to Minnesota to study for a doctorate in English literature, co-founded *Milkweed Chronicle* with Randy Scholes. Scott Walker moved his Graywolf Press to Minnesota from Port Townsend, Washington in 1984, Allen Kornblum brought his Coffee House Press north from Iowa in 1985, and Jim Perlman moved Holy Cow! Press to Duluth from Wisconsin in 1988.

Although each of these literary presses publishes fiction and poetry, their manner of selection and content is different. Truesdale conducts an annual Minnesota Voices contest for new writers from the Upper Midwest. The winner's book is published in that series. Milkweed Editions books are notable for their attention to art and design. Buchwald and Scholes' first book under the new imprint was a book of short stories by Carol Bly which sold out and needed to be reprinted. Graywolf assembles an annual short story collection and has had great success with some once familiar books. Brenda Ueland's *If You Want to Write,* originally issued in 1938, has sold 140,000 copies since it was reissued as a Graywolf paperback edition in 1987.

In Minnesota small independent presses can be found almost everywhere. The membership of the Midwest Independent Publishers Association stretches from Duluth to Fargo and from Owatonna to Mankato. This 150 member group was founded in 1982 by Loris Bree and Monica O'Kane. MIPA publishers exhibit their books at library and bookseller trade shows and regional library conferences. The group publishes an annual catalogue, a periodic book review newsletter, and sponsors an annual book awards contest for excellence in publishing. MIPA publishers concentrate on non-fiction, with travel guides, self-help advice, canoe and fishing guides, and art and popular culture among other special niches in publishing.

The Critics

What impulse or urge leads a person to buy a book? This is one of the hardest questions to answer successfully. Is the buyer "cover-driven" so he or she eagerly snatches up the new book because of its appearance? Or, did he or she read a review in *The New York Times* and set off in search for that title? Many of the 40,000 to 50,000 books published annually in the United States will never be widely reviewed, but for those that are mentioned in local newspapers, who are the reviewers?

Small, one-paragraph capsule reviews often appeared in early Minnesota newspapers. They were not the work of Minnesota journalists, but carried the credit lines of Boston or New York newspapers. In the 1890's, when St. Paul and Minneapolis newspapers began to expand, there was more space for news about books. Theater and music were usually given full pages, and books shared a page with art.

Reflecting that emphasis, writers interested in either drama or music criticism were given bylines and regular columns earlier than those who wanted to focus on books. One early music critic was Victor Nilsson (1867–1942) who wrote for the *Minneapolis Journal* from 1908 to 1938. Nilsson earned the first doctorate in Scandinavian literature granted by the University of Minnesota. He lectured and translated the works of Hamsun, Strindberg, and Lagerlof, in addition to his writings on music.

A second linguist and academician was James Davies (1870–1940). Davies wrote about music for the *Minneapolis Daily News* in addition to teaching German at the University of Minnesota. Another well-travelled writer was Frances Boardman (1879–1953), who began as a general news reporter on the *St. Paul Pioneer Press* in 1910. She wrote for the Denver and Winnipeg papers and the *Minneapolis Daily News* before returning to the *Pioneer Press*. From 1922 until 1947 she served as the music critic for that newspaper. When she retired she was saluted as the "first lady of Minnesota journalism" (*St. Paul Pioneer Press,* January 12, 1947).

Books and theater seemed a logical paired assignment. By the mid-1920's there was a writer in each city assigned to handle these arts: James Gray in St. Paul and John K. Sherman in Minneapolis.

Gray (born in 1899) joined the *St. Paul Dispatch* in 1920 after he graduated from the University of Minnesota. He spent five years as drama critic before taking over the book beat as well. His column, first called "The World of Books, Drama and Art" and later given his byline, ran on the editorial page. At first it appeared as the far right column, but later was moved to the center, immediately below the cartoon. Gray wrote about books five days each week for the *Dispatch* and later did a book column for the Sunday magazine of the *Pioneer Press.* In 1946, when he took leave from the paper for a three month stint in Hollywood as a dialogue coach, the newspaper calculated that Gray had reviewed 7,200 books over the previous twenty-one years. Writing with a daily deadline has always presented its difficulties. As Gray commented in his book, *On Second Thought,* "There is no time to roll judgment under the tongue, to test its flavor for either cloying sweetness or tart imprudence" (1946: 5).

Gray's reviews were often quoted and reprinted. In *On Second Thought* (1946), he grouped his opinions of contemporary writers in essays which attempted to analyze trends. Gray wrote several plays, novels, a history of the University of Minnesota, and other essays for national magazines. In one commentary on regionalist writing Gray offered his description of a potential Minnesota Muse. Wearing a decent though shabby Mother Hubbard "she sings exclusively of ruined wheat harvests and she sings of them with a strong Swedish accent" (*Saturday Review of Literature,* June 12, 1937). Gray pointed out in this article that all Minnesota writers did not focus narrowly on Minnesota or confine themselves to lugubrious celebrations of "the sorrows of the soil and of the soul." He discussed Minnesota authors Sinclair Lewis, F. Scott Fitzgerald, Margaret Culkin Banning, Grace H. Flandrau and Meridel Le Sueur, observing that all of them were inspired to write about regional topics yet also looked farther afield for material. He called Charles Macomb Flandrau unique and a literary tradition in himself whose writings made other Minnesotans proud of their heritage. Flandrau's *Viva Mexico,* Gray wrote, seemed to be revived and appreciated anew every five years. After leaving the St. Paul newspapers Gray served as book editor of the *Chicago Daily News* and then taught in the English department of the University of Minnesota from 1948 to 1957.

Following the departure of James Gray news about books and reviews were handled by Kathryn Boardman (1907–1986). Mrs. Boardman joined the St. Paul newspaper in 1933 and wrote about films under the name of Kathryn Gorman. With her marriage to Larry Boardman, also a member of that newspaper's staff, she became part of a family of critics. His sister was Frances Boardman, the music critic, and her sister Irene married John Harvey, who reported on drama and music. Kathryn Boardman retired in 1982 and at that time Gareth

Hiebert wrote in his Oliver Towne column, "As a movie critic in the 1930s and in recent years as book reviewer and editor, her writing has been pungent, yet perceptive, descriptive and colorful . . . You could send her anywhere, anytime, and know that the job would be done with skill. Yet she was always a lady. When she leaves, a fabled era of people in the story of these newspapers ends. She is the last of them" (*St. Paul Dispatch,* March 29, 1982). Mrs. Boardman's column "About Books" appeared in Saturday and Sunday editions of the newspaper.

Music, drama and books were John K. Sherman's assignment for forty-four years with the *Minneapolis Tribune* and *Star.* Following Sherman's death Peter Altman wrote that Sherman (1898–1969) had done more than anyone else to stimulate the development of the arts in Minnesota. He had written about the performing and visual arts, served as editor of the *Tribune*'s Sunday arts section, and in 1967 oversaw the establishment of daily books and arts pages in the paper. Altman wrote that he hoped he had learned from Sherman "the paramount importance of fairness in criticism, the critic's obligation never to be more interested in the brilliance of his review than in its subject . . . " (*Minneapolis Star,* April 21, 1969, B30).

When John Harvey (1912–1992) retired after three decades as music critic of the *St. Paul Pioneer Press Dispatch* in 1978, he echoed Altman's thoughts with the comment that "I don't think it serves any useful purpose to be particularly harsh unless a person obviously is a phony" (*St. Paul Pioneer Press Dispatch,* August 12, 1978).

Being fair and supportive continue to be good qualifications for a critic. Elegance of style and wit are other characteristics which would seem to be appropriate. In a delightful column called "How to Cook an Author," Sherman wrote about a new book compiled by a colleague, Virginia Safford. She was a sportswoman, magazine owner and editor (*Golfer and Sportsman*) and columnist for both the *Minneapolis Star Jour-*

nal and *Tribune.* Her columns dealt with travel, people and food. In 1944 Mrs. Safford (1893–1974) published a celebrity cookbook called *Food of My Friends.* When the book arrived in the newsroom, chaos erupted. There was such bedlam, Sherman wrote tongue in cheek, that linotype operators in the second floor made "147 typographical errors." He was sure that if he ever published a book he would need to take to his bed for two weeks and bar all visitors. But, he predicted, that given Mrs. Safford's energy level, the first edition would be exhausted long before she was (*Minneapolis Star Journal,* December 16, 1944).

Sherman did publish a selection of his columns and reviews in *Sunday Best; Collected Essays* (1963) and wrote an important essay titled "Music and Theater in Minnesota History" for William van O'Connor's *A History of the Arts in Minnesota* (1958).

Robert Sorensen (1931–1984) followed Sherman as book editor of the *Minneapolis Star Tribune,* holding that post for seventeen years. Increasingly the subject of "books" came to cover not just standard reviews, but feature articles on publishing, conferences and seminars, interviews and discussions of issues affecting libraries, and booksellers. Many feature writers wrote these articles and reviewed books in their special areas of expertise. Columnist Barbara Flanagan wrote about Minneapolis history for the paper and in her own books about the city. Reviews of books on cooking, gardening, sports and business are regularly found in those sections of the newspaper.

Jane Resh Thomas, who began writing reviews on children's books for the *Star Tribune* in the 1970's, credits Sorensen with recognizing the importance of children's literature since few newspapers in cities the size of Minneapolis have regular columns reviewing children's books. Most papers devote space only to a roundup of best books for holiday giving. Ms. Thomas points out that interest in children's literature is strong in Minnesota due to the Kerlan Collection, specialized children's bookstores, courses in children's literature taught by Norine Odland at the University of Minnesota, and the strength of writers' groups. She feels writers of children's books are helpful to beginners and show a remarkable generosity of spirit. Beginning with Wanda Gág, Carol Ryrie Brink, Maud Hart Lovelace and Laura Ingalls Wilder, Minnesota writers and illustrators have continued to earn awards and praise for their work. Ms. Thomas notes that at least twenty-five nationally known writers and illustrators in the children's field call Minnesota home. Among them are Stephen Gammell, Steve Johnson, Marion Dane Bauer, Debra Frasier, Judy Delton and Gary Paulsen.

In 1984 Dave Wood became book editor of the *Minneapolis Star Tribune*. Wood, a specialist in eighteenth century English literature, had been teaching at Augsburg College. He was asked to begin a new journalism course and with that as inspiration began writing for his hometown paper in Whitehall, Wisconsin. That foray into the newspaper field led to a rural nostalgia column for *Grit* magazine and to a post at the *Tribune* writing feature articles for the Neighbors' section. Some of his longer articles for the Neighbors' section were later published in *The Pie Lady of Winthrop* (1985), co-written with another *Tribune* staff writer, Peg Meier.

Wood commented once that, as book editor, he often received 500 new books each week. Even after paperback books and children's books were sent to other reviewers there were still too many for the newspaper to even consider reviewing. If fifteen books are reviewed in each Sunday's book pages, Wood tries to ensure that at least one of these books will have a Minnesota connection in author, subject, or perhaps publisher.

Like Wood, Mary Ann Grossman, his counterpart on the *St. Paul Pioneer Press,* writes a column of book news, often with a local slant. Miss Grossman joined her paper's staff in 1961. After serving as a fashion writer and editing both the women's and trends section, she was named assistant features editor in March of 1984. She became books and publications critic in May of that year. In her first "Readers and Writers" column she noted, "It's been many years (nobody here remembers exactly how long) since anyone has written a column about books. Yet, Minnesota is among the most literate states in the nation, local bookstores have national reputations for excellence, and there is a thriving (and sometimes not so thriving) community of writers, poets, and publishers of small journals" (*St. Paul Pioneer Press Dispatch,* May 12, 1984, B8).

One of the criticisms which Ms. Grossman has to face, given the growth in the local book publishing world, is how to handle the "Minnesota book." In a 1987 column she responded by denying (as performing arts editors have long needed to do) that she and the paper had any policy of printing only "good" reviews of local works. According to Ms. Grossman's guidelines for freelance reviewers she will not permit anybody with a financial or personal relationship to a book's author or publisher to review a book. That problem, she wrote, was easier to solve than that of the reviewers who felt too "Minnesota nice" and could not criticise a book (*St. Paul Pioneer Press Dispatch,* April 18, 1987, B3, 4).

Reviews of Minnesota books (and others) are carried in the Twin Cities' monthly magazines, *Mpls-St.Paul* and *Minnesota Monthly. Twin Cities Reader* and *City Pages,* the metropolitan area's alternative weeklies, carry occasional book reviews written by their arts editors and freelance reviewers. *The Minnesota Daily,* the student newspaper at the University of Minnesota, also has an occasional book review section.

Book editors provide their readers with what they hope will be an interesting review mix of national and local books. For the librarian who wants to order Minnesota books and journals from the many small presses, locating both the organizations and their publications is a continuing problem. A group of librarians decided to attempt to remedy this situation in 1983. *Minnesota Reviews,* a four-page newsletter, was first published in September of that year and distributed at the Minnesota State Fair. The aim was to review books, chapbooks, broadside series, pamphlets and reports, magazines, films and video tapes produced in Minnesota. Signed reviews were written by librarians, teachers or experts in various fields. At the beginning, *Minnesota Reviews* appeared ten times each year and was distributed free through library channels. Joanne Hart of Grand Portage and Emmett Davis of the Hennepin County Library were the first editors. Gail Nordstrom handled editing responsibilities from 1985 until 1988, when Roger Sween, multitype library specialist in the office of library development, took on the job. Minnesota Reviews, Inc., as an organization has been one of the sponsors of the annual Minnesota Book Awards, initiated in 1988. The Minnesota Book Awards are given to writers and illustrators resident in the state.

Another newsletter, produced by Chris Dodge and Jan DeSirey for members of the Minnesota Library Association's Social Responsibilities Round Table, focuses on the alternative press. The *MSRRT Newsletter* (1988–date), begun as an in-house information circular "with lots of white space," now represents a wide spectrum of opinion and constituencies.

While the *MSRRT Newsletter,* which is sent to subscribers ten times each year, both lists and reviews publications, the *Utne Reader,* subtitled "the best of the alternative presses," (circulation: 284,000) excerpts articles from the out-of-the-mainstream world. Founded by Eric Utne in 1984 and edited by Jay Walljasper and others, the *Utne Reader* has managed to find a large audience for its eclectic mix of opinion pieces. Its readers, editors of the bi-monthly feel, tend to be liberal, curious, and wish to read writers from uncommon journals. Reviews of books, periodicals, videos and recordings appear in its "Mixed Media" department.

For the reader with an interest in nonfiction books about Minnesota, the major source of information since 1915 has been *Minnesota History,* the quarterly journal of the Minnesota

Historical Society. The articles on Minnesota's literary visitors, reprinted as the first eleven chapters of this book, first appeared in that journal. Among the editors of *Minnesota History* have been Solon J. Buck, Theodore Blegen, Bertha Heilbron, Kenneth Carley, Mary Cannon and Anne Kaplan.

Writers' Groups and Writers' Sources

Writing by its nature is a solitary pursuit, but once the words are committed to the page, the author's voice needs to be heard. Writers' groups provide an initial forum for peer criticism and appreciation. Such groups exist throughout the state. Some offer public readings and publish journals. The Marshall Festival, for example, held at Southwest State University, brings writers, critics and readers together for four days of talks and readings celebrating rural Minnesota. With both private and non-profit support, the Marshall Festival has been able to draw on the active community of poets and writers in the southwestern part of the state.

The mother of all writing groups in Minnesota, though not the oldest, is the Loft. Located now in the Pratt Community Center in Minneapolis, the Loft began in a space above Marly Rusoff's Dinkytown bookstore in 1973. Writers Jim Moore, Patricia Hampl, Michael Dennis Browne, David Luhn, Monty Clevenger, Elizabeth Sanford, Jim Perlman, David Wojahn and Sue Ann Martinson thought that it was time to have a place for writers to gather and read. Their vision has been realized in a number of ways. The Loft has offered classes taught by writers, lectures by writers, open readings, a story hour for children, performances involving music and art, and an important series of fellowships.

Sue Ann Martinson served as the Loft's first part-time coordinator. As its programs grew, the staff responsibilities increased. Susan Broadhead, a poet with a doctorate in English renaissance poetry, began as financial officer for the Loft in 1980. She was named executive director in 1981. Commenting on her leadership, Loft founding member Jim Moore said, "I think she really invented the Loft" (*St. Paul Pioneer Press,* April 29, 1990). By 1992 the Loft had over 2,000 members, a staff of thirteen part or full time employees, and a projected budget of almost one million dollars. The Loft is now the largest literary center in the nation (*Star Tribune,* October 14, 1992). The first national conference of literary centers was held at the Loft in 1985.

Working with the Minnesota State Arts Board, the Lila Wallace-Reader's Digest Fund, and local foundations such as Dayton-Hudson, McKnight, Bush and Jerome, the Loft has earned support for a variety of innovative programs. The Loft- McKnight Mentor Series, begun in 1982, brings five established writers each year to the Twin Cities to work with local poets and prose writers. The mentor writer typically spends a weekend residency in Minneapolis, giving an open reading one evening and then participating in a master class, an open workshop, and finally, in a tutorial with each of the fellowship winners. Eight Loft-McKnight fellowship winners are selected annually through a submission process involving outside judges. The mentors have included Derek Walcott, Tess Gallagher, Denise Levertov, Rudolfo Anaya, Toni Cade Bambara, Audre Lorde, Michael Ondaatje, Francine du Plessix Gray, Leslie Marmon Silko, Louise Erdrich, Bobbie Ann Mason, Helen Yglesias, Maxine Hong Kingston and Stanley Elkin. As with the Women's Institute, Beach, Seymour and Carlson lectures mentioned earlier, the Loft-McKnight Mentor Series has brought nationally known writers to the Twin Cities to give public lectures. Established Minnesota writers are eligible for other Loft-McKnight Awards of Distinction.

While literary centers in other cities were linked either directly to colleges or begun in direct opposition to them, the non-academic Loft has attempted to reach out to a broader literary community. Not only does it try to provide a forum for those interested in different types of poetry, creative nonfiction and prose, but offers opportunities for those coming from a variety of racial and ethnic backgrounds. The Inroads program, funded by the Dayton-Hudson Foundation, began in 1990. It was developed so that writers of color could learn from mentors of their own heritage.

Loft programs are often co-sponsored with other organizations such as the small literary presses, the Walker Art Center and Minnesota Public Radio. The Loft publishes a monthly newsletter and literary journal called *A View from the Loft* for its members. Other publications derived from Loft programs include a series of chapbooks and broadsides published in cooperation with the Minnesota Center for Book Arts.

Writers were the first organizers of a series of quite successful bookfairs held in the Twin Cities in the 1970's and 1980's. Held at the College of St. Catherine in St. Paul between 1976 and 1980, these bookfairs offered an opportunity for writers to give readings and the small presses to display their books. Each time the venue changed, sponsors and events were added, and what came to be called the Great Midwestern Bookshow (between 1981 and 1985) was regarded as one of the largest such affairs in the country. Held at the University of Minnesota, and then at indoor shopping malls such as Butler Square and Calhoun Square in Minneapolis, the bookfairs attracted exhibitors and presses from other midwestern states. In 1988 and 1989 the bookfair was held in St. Paul, co-sponsored by the Friends of the St. Paul Library and the *Star Tribune,* and was organized by the Loft. The opening day, called A Book Affair, featured a display of books with programs held in both Landmark Center and Rice Park. During the following week other organizations, including libraries and bookstores, scheduled events. The finale of the Festival of the Book was the book awards ceremony. Judy Geck of the Hungry Mind bookstore chaired the Book Affair committee, while Scott Walker of Graywolf Press served as Festival of the Book chairperson. Although both A Book Affair and the Festival of the Book were considered highly successful (the 1989 attendance for A Book Affair was estimated at 15,000 persons), no group wanted to continue with necessary fund raising and management, so the bookfairs came to an end.

Bringing teachers to poets and then poets to the schools was the job undertaken by Molly LaBerge in 1968. The fledgling National Endowment for the Arts wanted to fund a literature project so it turned to the Academy of American Poets with an offer of $40,000 to create four projects. One project was to be in the Middle West. Molly LaBerge, then head of the Center Arts Council at Walker Art Center, was asked to administer and essentially invent what was called the "Art of Poetry."

For the first year visiting poets offered Saturday seminars for Minneapolis high school English teachers. These poets gave public readings, while other local poets were hired to read and talk to students in the Minneapolis high schools. Interest and knowledge of the program quickly spread to other school districts. From 1970 to 1974 what was known as Poets-in-the-Schools was operated by the St. Paul Ramsey Arts and Science Council. Then COMPAS (Community Programs in the Arts and Sciences) was formed as a statewide arts agency and Molly LaBerge became its executive director.

Although Poets-in-the-Schools operates through residencies in public schools throughout Minnesota, not all projects are identical. St. Paul, Stillwater and Olivia have had year or longer residences by poets while Stanley Kiesel spent twelve years as Minneapolis' poet-in-residence.

During the seven year existence of "Time of the Indian" (another COMPAS program) poets Jim White, Gerald Vizenor and Roberta Hill Whiteman took the poets-in-the-schools concept to Indian reservations as well as to Twin Cities Indian schools such as Red School House and Heart of the Earth.

As writers and artists in different disciplines were added to the roster, the COMPAS program became known as WAITS (Writers-and-Artists-in-the-Schools). The current COMPAS manual lists 22 names of writers available for one week or longer residencies. What has also changed is the thrust of the residency. Writers are expected to teach students at the elementary and high school level, conduct workshops and give readings in the community. The students are expected to write. At the close of the residency each writer in residence selects what he or she feels are the best poems for the annual COMPAS student anthology. Fifteen student anthologies have been published by COMPAS since 1977. In *Particular Gifts* (1988) Norita Dittberner-Jax traced the first twenty years of the poets-in-the-schools program.

Poets and writers in the schools work with students, but for those whose schooling ended many years ago, another COMPAS program exists. Called the *Literary Post*, it grew out of workshops conducted by Carol Bly for older Minnesotans. Two hundred eager writers responded when the pilot program was announced. In 1985, when COMPAS sent news releases promoting the program, an avalanche of 700 responses overwhelmed the post office at Sturgeon Lake where Ms. Bly lived.

Through the *Literary Post*, writers sixty years or older sent their poems, memoirs, or even novels to Ms. Bly for her comments and suggestions. Often the writers were encouraged by their adult children to record family stories. For some of the seniors, isolated or even shy in revealing this interest in writing, mailing their writing was far easier than attending a class. It proved a welcome outlet for their creative needs. What might have seemed an impersonal correspondence with an unseen editor became, for some, an exchange of letters with a friend who realized, as Ms. Bly once wrote, "that all of us feel we have a book inside us."

The *Literary Post* began in 1982. By 1987 it became necessary to charge a small fee for participants although scholarships are available. Several editors now handle the correspondence and the program is administered by Margaret Swanson of COMPAS' Accessible Arts. Selections of the poems, short fiction and essays of *Literary Post* writers have been published in four anthologies by COMPAS, the latest being *With A Voice of Singing* (1992). Interest in the *Literary Post* by Minnesota's seniors continues to grow, and there is now a waiting list for participants. COMPAS administrators have found, however, that despite such enthusiasm it has sometimes been difficult to find funding for programs which center on the creative rather than the health needs of seniors.

Had the Minnesota Center for Book Arts been open when Mark Twain came to town he, as a former printer, would have felt right at home. The MCBA, opened in 1985, focuses on the creation of a book. Students can learn papermaking, bookbinding, and how to select type. They can also print broadsides and chapbooks in its work spaces. The MCBA was the inspiration of Jim Sitter who spent four years as its director before moving to New York and a new job as director of the Council of Literary Magazines and Presses. The MCBA schedules classes taught by local professionals and visiting artists in residence, holds exhibitions, and since 1988 has published an annual winter book. These books, written by Minnesota writers Will Weaver, Meridel Le Sueur, Carol Bly, Jon Hassler and J. F. Powers, are illustrated by artists selected by an MCBA panel of judges.

The MCBA, as school, gallery, and publisher, is not to be confused with another important institution, the Minnesota Center for the Book. In 1977 the Library of Congress inaugurated a plan to establish a Center for the Book in each state as a way to stimulate public interest in books, libraries and reading. The Minnesota Center for the Book shares office space with Metronet, the library organization for the seven-county metropolitan area, and the Minnesota Association of Library Friends. Information about the Center for the Book programs as well as almost every other matter involving books, libraries and literacy, can be obtained by contacting Metronet director, Mary Birmingham.

Some Final Thoughts

Despite many pages, this overview of the Community of the Book remains a glimpse, not an in-depth study. Many institutions warrant a deeper analysis and, as they reach celebratory milestones, perhaps someone will trace their effect on the state's literary history. To write such accounts, future historians will have much to study.

Lists of contemporary Minnesota authors have been compiled by Doris Pagel (in the field of children's literature), Ron Barron (for adult fiction and poetry) and Darlene Joyce. Author and literary community interviews have been shown weekly on television (cable channel 6) since 1988. Organized by Eileen Cavanagh of the Hennepin County libraries, the interviewees include local writers, publishers, librarians and critics ("Northern Lights and Insights"). Other programs focus on children's literature ("All About Kids") and feature national writers on tour. Several hundred interviews exist on video cassettes which may be borrowed for home viewing.

Mary Bround Smith's monthly *Minnesota Literature Newsletter* was started in 1975 as a publication of the Minnesota State Arts Council. It was edited by Mary Ellen Shaw until 1983 when the newsletter gained independent non-profit status. The *Newsletter* plays an important role in disseminating information about the literary community.

The Corresponder, a newsletter edited and published by members of Mankato State University's English department, was subtitled "a fan letter on Minnesota writers." Edited by Robert C. Wright from 1978 until his death in 1981 and after 1983 by Ron Gower, its focus has been the achievements of the state's poets and prose writers, as well as authors of science fiction and romance (such as Gordon Dickson, Kathleen Woodiwiss and LaVyrle Spencer).

The willingness of major local foundations (including McKnight, Northwest Area, Jerome, Bush, and Dayton-Hudson) to support literary programs and writers is significant. Various literary organizations would not have grown or even survived without such foundation or corporate support. National donors offering matching gifts (the NEA, Mellon, and Lila Wallace-Reader's Digest) have also been generous in their support of Minnesota groups. For both the not-for-profit organizations (like the Loft, the Center for Arts Criticism, and the Minnesota Center for Book Arts) and the individual artists, learning how to write the grant becomes a skill as important as computer literacy. The development director, whose job it is to obtain the grants, also becomes a necessary staff member of any not-for-profit group.

The world of grants and grantsmanship would have seemed especially strange to Minnesota's literary visitors, two of whom (Thoreau and Twain) even published their own works. The necessary change in attitude is also revealed in the story told of a matching grant offered in 1977 to the Loft by the Dayton-Hudson Foundation. Although the money was ultimately accepted, several members of the Loft's board of directors wanted to reject it, feeling that it was tainted by proximity to B. Dalton, the chain which they thought was killing independent bookstores like Marly Rusoff's (*Star Tribune,* March 19, 1989).

With all of these literary activities is there a consistent voice for the Minnesota Muse? There are clearly more people writing about rural Minnesota, its farms and small towns. There are also writers who specialize in the sensitive description of the "Outdoor Beautiful," as Garrison Keillor described what he called the most boring sort of writing, without drama, humor, dialogue or conflict. "It is man standing there and drawing deep breaths. It is all inhaling" (*St. Paul Pioneer Press,* October 5, 1992). There are also more women writers and writers of color sharing their experiences and insights. But probably for many readers elsewhere it is not the Minnesota Muse which fascinates, but what has been called the "Minnesota model": the success of its not-for-profit organizations with the fundgiving agencies. Others wish to emulate this record and no longer consider Minnesota, in the words of a Boston novelist quoted by James Gray, as some "weird state in the middling west." For the literary visitors of a century ago that would be thanks a plenty for their visits and inspiration.

COMMUNITY OF THE BOOK BIBLIOGRAPHY AND ACKNOWLEDGEMENTS

In addition to the valuable sources located in the Minneapolis Collection of the Minneapolis Public Library and the archives of the Minnesota Historical Society, important materials upon which this chapter is based were supplied by many individuals. My thanks are due to Molly LaBerge, Margaret Swanson, Jane Resh Thomas, Mary Ann Grossman, Dave Wood, Marlin and Loris Bree, Mary Birmingham, Roger Sween, Mary Ida Thompson, Larry Dingman, Edward Kukla, Karen Hoyle, Susan Broadhead and Tom O'Sullivan.

*   *   *

Mrs. W. J. Arnold. *The Poets and Poetry of Minnesota.* Chicago: S. P. Rounds, 1864.

Annette Atkins. "Minnesota, Left of Center and Out of Place," in *Heartland. Comparative History of the Midwestern States,* edited by James H. Madison. Bloomington: Indiana University Press, 1988, 9–31.

Mrs. Isaac Atwater. "Pioneer Life in Minneapolis from a Woman's Standpoint," *in* Isaac Atwater, ed. *History of the City of Minneapolis, Minnesota.* New York: Munsell, 1893.

Ron Barron. *A Guide to Minnesota Writers.* Mankato: Minnesota Council of Teachers of English, 1987.

Helen Bigelow. "Portrait in Oils and Ink," *Golfer and Sportsman,* June 1936 [Mabel Ulrich].

Marjorie Bingham. "Keeping at It: Minnesota Women," in *Minnesota in a Century of Change,* edited by Clifford E. Clark, Jr. St. Paul: Minnesota Historical Society Press, 1989, 433–471.

Theodore C. Blegen. *Minnesota. A History of the State.* Minneapolis: University of Minnesota Press, 1963.

Carol Bly, editor. *Everybody's Story. Writings by Older Minnesotans.* St. Paul: COMPAS, 1987.

Carl Bode. *The American Lyceum. Town Meeting of the Mind.* New York: Oxford University Press, 1956.

Ellsworth Carlstedt. "The Public Library Movement in Minnesota, 1849–1900," 1934. Typescript. Minnesota Historical Society Library.

Deirdre Carmody. "From Some 2,000 Alternative Magazines, A Digest," *The New York Times,* January 4, 1993. [*Utne Reader*].

Roy Close. "Cities' cultural lack: a complete bookstore," *Minneapolis Star,* April 20, 1972.

Rev. John Conway. "Literary St. Paul," *Midland Monthly,* 11: 3 (September 1894), 163–172.

Jennie June Croly. *The History of the Woman's Club Movement in America.* New York: Henry G. Allen, 1898. [Minnesota: 718–751].

Barbara H. Davis and Timothy C. Glines. *From Generation to Generation: Exploring a Community's Regard for Its Arts and Culture.* St. Paul: The St. Paul Foundation, 1990.

Dorothy Day. "Mabel Ulrich Sparked City's Cultural Growth," *Minneapolis Sunday Tribune,* August 26, 1945.

Larry Dingman. *Booksellers Marks.* Minneapolis: Dinkytown Antiquarian Bookstore, 1986.

Norita Dittberner-Jax. *Particular Gifts.* St. Paul: COMPAS, 1988.

Lee Egerstrom. "Rural Minnesota nurtures poets," *St. Paul Pioneer Press and Dispatch,* December 1, 1985.

Jane Engh. *Minnesota Authors.* Mankato: Traverse des Sioux Library System, 1988.

Jean Ervin. *The Minnesota Experience. An Anthology.* Minneapolis: The Adams Press, 1979.

Gary Alan Fine. "Captain Billy's Whiz Bang," 1983. Unpublished manuscript. Archives, Minnesota Historical Society.

John T. Flanagan. "A Specialist Before My Time," *Minnesota History,* Spring 1978, 17–23. [University of Minnesota English department].

John T. Flanagan. "Early Literary Periodicals in Minnesota," *Minnesota History,* 26:4 (December, 1945), 293–311.

William Watts Folwell. *A History of Minnesota.* 4 vols. St. Paul: Minnesota Historical Society Press, 1921–1930.

Mary Dillon Foster. *Who's Who Among Minnesota Women.* St. Paul: 1924.

Amy Gage. "Graywolf Brings Business Sense to Literary Publishing," *City Business,* June 19, 1985.

James Gray. "New Publication Commended for its Originality," *St. Paul Dispatch,* February 19, 1937.

Susan Greiger. "The Loft. Perpetrating a cultural renaissance in South Minneapolis," *Minnesota Monthly,* May 1979, 12–16.

Mary Ann Grossman. "Women's Institute Ends Programs" and "Women's Institute—32 Years of Quality," *St. Paul Pioneer Press,* May 25, 1971.

Mary Ann Grossman. "The State of Writing," *St. Paul Pioneer Press,* September 9, 1988.

Mary Ann Grossman. "The Quiet Force Behind the Loft," *St. Paul Pioneer Press,* April 29, 1990.

Mary Ann Grossman. "The Battle of the Books," *St. Paul Pioneer Press,* June 14, 1992.

Mary Ann Grossman. "Minnesota moxie puts the press on funding," *St. Paul Pioneer Press,* April 14, 1991.

Mary Ann Grossman. "Book Fans Honor Great Patron," *St. Paul Pioneer Press Dispatch,* July 19, 1986. [J. Harold Kittleson].

Lee Edmonds Grove. *Of Brooks and Books.* Minneapolis: University of Minnesota Press, 1945.

Laura B. Hurlbut. "Seventy-Fifth Anniversary of the Austin Ladies' Floral Club," Typescript, 1944. Minnesota Historical Society Library.

Darlene Cruikshank Joyce. *Naming a Writing Community: Contemporary Authors in Minnesota.* Master's thesis, Hamline University, St. Paul, 1992.

J. H. Lienhard. "St. Paulite's World Magazine to Debut Soon," *St. Paul Pioneer Press,* February 7, 1937.

Bob Lundegaard. "Late-blooming writers flood mail-order mentor," *Minneapolis Star and Tribune,* January 30, 1986. [Carol Bly and *Literary Post*].

Joe MacGaheran. "Among Those We Know," *Golfer and Sportsman,* November, 1933, 19, 56–62. [Leonard Wells].

Frederick Manfred. *Dinkytown.* Minneapolis: Dinkytown Antiquarian Bookstore, 1984.

Peg Meier. "Books are magnets pulling people together," *Star Tribune,* June 25, 1990.

Julia Maria Morrison. *Literary Journals in Minnesota. November 1850—April 1961.* Master's thesis, University of Minnesota, 1961.

Grace Lee Nute. "A History of Minnesota Books and Authors" in William Van O'Connor, ed. *A History of the Arts in Minnesota.* Minneapolis: University of Minnesota Press, 1958.

Margaret Lansing Oakey. "Woman's Club Movement in Minnesota." Typescript, 1931. Minnesota Historical Society Library.

Frank G. O'Brien. *Minnesota Pioneer Sketches.* Minneapolis: H. H. S. Rowell, 1904.

Doris Pagel. *Minnesota Authors and Illustrators.* Mankato: 1991.

Mary Bader Papa. "The Best Bookseller of Them All," *Twin Cities,* September, 1980, 48–52, 109–114. [Kay Sexton].

Theodore Peterson. *Magazines in the Twentieth Century.* Urbana: University of Illinois Press, 1956. [Fawcett Publications, 284–290].

Major James B. Pond. *Eccentricities of Genius: Memories of Famous Men and Women on the Platform and Stage.* New York: 1900.

P. J. Rader. "Pressing the Point," *Mpls-St.Paul,* December, 1986. [Literary presses].

Carmen Nelson Richards, ed. *Minnesota Writers.* Minneapolis: T. S. Denison & Co., 1961.

Maude C. Schilpin. *Minnesota Verse. An Anthology.* St. Cloud: The Times Publishing Company, 1934.

John K. Sherman. "A Trip Down Memory Lane to City's Old Bookshops," *Minneapolis Sunday Tribune,* December 26, 1954.

Staff Writer. "Many new bookstores, only so many customers," *Star Tribune,* January 14, 1991.

Mabel Ulrich. "Salvaging Culture for the WPA," *Harper's,* May, 1939, 636–664.

Wendy Webb. "War of the Words," *Skyway News,* February 25–March 2, 1992.

Dave Wood. "Lofty Vision," *Star Tribune,* October 14, 1992.

Dave Wood. "New Rivers a giant in small press publishing," *Star Tribune,* February 29, 1992.

A. Augustus Wright. *Who's Who in the Lyceum.* Philadelphia: Pearson Brothers, 1906.

Seymour Yesner, ed. *25 Minnesota Poets.* Minneapolis: Nodin Press, 1974. [Minneapolis Poets-in-the-Schools poets].

Dick Youngblood. "B. Dalton is attacking illiteracy," *Minneapolis Tribune,* February 19, 1984.

——. "Women's Institute Wins National Acclaim," *St. Paul Pioneer Press,* December 31, 1939.

——. "Critic goes to Hollywood," *St. Paul Pioneer Press,* March 26, 1946. [James Gray].

——. *Resources of Minnesota series. City of St. Paul.* St. Paul: E. E. Barton, 1888.

INDEX